Praise for *Loving the Enemy:*

Loving the Enemy is a moving memoir. But it is far more than a journal of significant personal experience. Read it, and you will encounter an invitation to reimagine your life journey through the eyes of compassion. With poetic passion, humility, and wisdom, Catherine Fransson describes the transformation of relationships that can only emerge when love is stronger than fear. This is a groundbreaking book—a spiritual compass for adult children caring for their aging parents.

-Fran Ferder, FSPA, PhD, and John Heagle, MA, JCL, LMHC. Co-Directors, Therapy & Renewal Associates (TARA). Co-Authors, *Tender Fires: The Spiritual Promise of Sexuality.*

I wanted to read this memoir because I, too, have an elderly parent who needs my attention. But *Loving the Enemy* swept me into its path and kept me up late, reading hungrily. I expected a simple chronicle of the author, her parents, and their last years together, but instead found a mix of personal and spiritual, past and present. It's a tapestry woven of a lifetime of memories, rich though often painful; wisdom from poets and spiritual thinkers; and heartfelt guidance for how to find the words beyond the words. In chapter one, Cathy as a child escapes from a rainstorm into a church sanctuary where she plays the organ (breathing "remnants of candle wax, floor polish, and old hymnals"), a small scene that is a metaphor for the way Loving the Enemy offers a respite from the deluge of family losses--for both the author and the reader--into the solace and healing power of art.

-Bethany Reid, author of *Sparrow* and *Body My House.*

Catherine Fransson has approached and passed over the threshold leading to that vast, uncharted territory called unconditional love, what Christian people all too glibly called grace. Imagine the work, the joy and the fulfillment of loving someone without conditions. It is one of the key journeys of life. This beautifully written book provides many insights and much guidance for that journey.

-Pastor Don Mackenzie, PhD, now living in Minneapolis, is devoting himself to interfaith work after retiring as Minister and Head of Staff at Seattle's University Congregational United Church of Christ.

LOVING THE ENEMY

When the favorite parent dies first

A memoir

by

Catherine Fransson

STILWELL PRESS

Cover and Book design: Vladimir Verano, Vertvolta Design

Published in the United States
by Stilwell Press. Edmonds, Washington

stilwellpress@gmail.com

Print ISBN: 978-1-7326690-0-0
ebook ISBN: 978-1-73266-901-7

Dedication

To my parents Carl Ramstad and June McGhee,
who gave me life, faith, and music, gifts that buoyed
me through innocence and understanding, loss and blessing,
green pasture and peaceful sea. I am grateful.

... nature is never spent;

There lives the dearest freshness deep down things;

And though the last lights off the black West went

Oh, morning, at the brown brink eastward, springs—

Because the Holy Ghost over the bent

World broods with warm breast and with ah! bright wings.

Excerpt from "God's Grandeur" Gerard Manley Hopkins

Table of Contents

FOREWORD

I am a fortunate woman who grew up with a remote and critical father—
not a formula for building confidence. When in her 80s, my mother
died, leaving my brother and me to deal with my father. I faced one of
the toughest assignments of my life—caring for Dad in ways he had not
cared for me.

Most of us live inside our families with little perspective on how different we might be in a different context. I accepted my parents' rules and
knew few kids my age who didn't. Our social arena was a Baptist church
that, although moderate (in favor of civil rights, for example, but against
dancing), was limiting. Both parents believed my musical gifts obligated
me to perform. They saw to it that I played the piano and organ and
sang on demand. I was at church several times a week either practicing
or performing.

As I grew up in the forties and fifties, I tried to understand why I was
so miserable in a family that looked like, Dad said, an example to others.
I was going to church three times a week and following a well-worn path
of "normalcy." The dissonance compelled me to write. In a five-year diary
my Aunt Evelyn gave me in fifth grade, I wrote with great devotion about
what I noticed, every event I thought worthy and many that weren't.

Diaries turned into journals in my twenties as my first real romance
morphed into a difficult marriage. I graduated from college certified to
teach English and was rewarded with my own classroom, where I came
of age. But coming of age is never a single triumph. All of us surmount
obstacles and then meet others. No life is "finished" until we are.

After years of teaching and counseling students, Dad and I attempted to weave a new beginning while I followed my call into ministry, one

that empowered me to write words to the music in my heart. This is the story of the relationships I struggled with and how they developed over time. I may have failed sainthood, but I found self.

My Faith

My faith is an ever-expanding arena of *what I know today* as I study, worship, pray, work and learn. I am a Christian, a follower of Jesus, an admirer of the Holy Spirit, awed by God. I love that an old opera house in Germany has these words on the wall: BACH GAVE US GOD'S WORD. MOZART GAVE US GOD'S LAUGHTER. BEETHOVEN GAVE US GOD'S FIRE. GOD GAVE US MUSIC THAT WE MIGHT PRAY WITHOUT WORDS. Music speaks volumes to me. Although I write openly here, and share in spiritual direction with others, my beliefs are never a *prescription* for others. I believe in soul freedom. And I respect the faith others develop and live. All of us journey spiritually; we learn as we grow. Naturally, how we explain our faith (if we can at all) will change over time and through circumstances both fortunate and unfortunate. I have worshipped happily, and with great blessing, in the free church as well as the liturgical church. Enriched by the gifts of both, I find choosing only one or the other can be limiting.

You may be Protestant as I am, or evangelical, Catholic, Muslim, or Jew. Hindu, Buddhist ... one of a multitude of religions in this world—or None (the term for many who no longer claim affiliation with any religion). Each of the religious categories we have inherited, adopted, or rejected as we've come of age, is ours to choose. I would not try to direct your beliefs nor would I allow you to direct mine. But I would value honesty, openness and sharing along this journey. I am a person of faith, period. Please accept the faith herein as an expression of one woman's search for meaning. Interpret it according to your own beliefs.

Chapter 1

Prelude 1957

❧❧❧

A gray midwinter sky greeted me as I left North Junior High located near Broadway Avenue in Everett, Washington. As I tightened my grip on my textbooks, I could see some friends lingering to talk before heading home. Others rushed to club meetings. But committed to learning the organ, I walked alone hurrying along wet streets toward First Baptist Church, trying to outrun the deluge that was surely coming. My mother was a singer, and it was she I sought to please as I attempted to become a more accomplished pianist and organist.

Arriving at our family church, I walked under the entrance arch toward large, carved, wooden doors. I pushed to swing them open, pausing before putting some weight behind the next set of doors leading into the sanctuary.

As I expected, it was as cold inside as it was outside—and very dark. In the darkness, I felt my way down the side aisle by groping for pew after pew.

Arriving at the front, I felt for the seat and put my books down. While placing my music on the organ rack, I breathed in the remnant scents of candle wax, floor polish, and old hymnals. After I snapped on the light under the keyboards to illumine the pedals, I slid up the heavy, dusty tambour cover to reveal the black, yellow, red, and white stops above three keyboards. I centered myself in the middle of the seat so I could reach every stop. I pushed the switch in the stillness, and there was a familiar *thunk* beneath me, then came the whoosh of air as the organ blower filled the chest with pressurized air.

I turned to the well-worn hymnal (the best for music stands) and thumbed to page 8, "All Hail the Power of Jesus' Name," set the piston for congregational singing, and launched into the hymn with my cold fingers on the Swell organ.

> *All hail the power of Jesus' name, let angels prostrate fall.*
>
> *Bring forth the royal diadem and crown him Lord of all;*
>
> *Bring forth the royal diadem and crown him Lord of all!*

~Tune *Coronation* Oliver Holden. Lyrics: Edward Perronet 1793

At first, I played as if for a prelude, and then the first stanza as I warmed up. I changed the registration to something bolder, and finally, on the fourth verse, coupled the Great to the Swell organ, shoved in the crescendo pedal, and slowing to a majestic pace, closed grandly with "and crown Him Lord of all!"

Lifting my hands from the keys, I listened to the reverberations echo throughout the large church, with the sounds from the pipes themselves traveling into the far corners of the balcony and back again from ceiling to wall to choir loft, until finally absorbed once again into the vibrating pipes themselves. Over my left shoulder was my silhouette—projected by the light on the pedals beneath me—giant sized against the far wall. I stared a while at my shadow. Silence enveloped me.

Slowly I came to hear the sibilance of tires on wet streets, turned to see rainwater streaming down outside the yellow-gold stained glass in the large window to my right. Rain. Darkness. Sound and silence.

In these solitary moments, I grew from a lonesome teenager into a witness: to the sacred, to being itself, to the power of sound, and the power of silence. Although my parents expected me to practice faithfully like this, in the midst of this duty I was swept into the beauty and power of music.

For me, the silence was not empty but fulsome. Not bleak, but promising. It took me out of the barrenness of walking alone in the rain and sitting in an empty church, to the community of saints singing together, reminding us that we are not alone, just as I was not alone. My mood changed from solitude to community, from emptiness to a spirit of fullness.

And so, I was ready to get serious—about pedals, fingering—linking notes from key to key, from notes to lines, and from lines to phrases, and to music. Music was more than sound to me. And silence was more than emptiness. Music with silence, and silence itself, were Spirit.

It took me years to appreciate this rhythm of sound and silence, silence and sound. A signal to me to listen well, for God might well speak. God, the *still, small voice*, the hush of angels' wings, the presence of the Holy. I had yet to give silence its full due. If faith is a relationship with the Mysteries of God, I had to learn to hear God's voice. God's many voices. One of God's voices is music. And one is the *still small voice*. Silence itself. Whispering,

> *Do not be afraid, for I have redeemed you;*
> *I have called you by name; you are mine.*
> *When you pass through the seas, I will be with you;*
> *when you pass over the rivers, you will not drown.*
> *Walk through fire, and you will not be singed;*
> *walk through flames, and you will not be burned.*
> *I am Yhwh, your God,*
> *You are more precious to me than Assyria;*
> *you are honored, and I love you.*
>
> *~Isaiah 43: 1b-3, 4a*

CHAPTER 2

Life as I Knew It

✦

My father was an enigma to me even as I grew to adulthood. We hadn't seen eye to eye for years, but as adults, conversations remained safely within known parameters. I avoided disagreeing with him. I had only a vague idea what he really thought and was so involved in my own life that there was no time—or we made no time—to explore unfamiliar ground. What I eventually discovered, however, was that unfamiliar ground was a place neither of us wanted to go.

My partner Ardene and I saw both my parents occasionally and helped with family gatherings. I was originally "mother's little helper." With Ardene's help now, I continued with occasional assistance. But there were clues that my folks' routines were becoming a challenge even to them. It was time for a family conference that should wisely precede major transitions from their home to assisted living; for example, helping or getting help to provide meals a couple of times a week and seeing that they had freshly laundered clothes, and a changed bed. We did not have this kind of conference and we weren't having it now.

My family included Carl and June (Dad and Mom), my older brother Dave, our brother Lew's widow, and my partner and I all living in or near Everett, Washington. Our younger brother Lew had died at age 48 from the complications of Diabetes I. He left his wife and two adult daughters. My older brother Dave's son and daughter lived out of town. Each brother's family included two grandchildren.

Ardene and I kept in touch with my parents by phone and took meals to share for the holidays. Privately, we wondered aloud how their lives would proceed in their last years.

As I reached fifty, I had already survived a painful break-up with a beloved companion. It broke my heart to discover my then-partner not as keen as I about claiming my voice—our own distinct voices—in our marriage. But it grew more and more clear that God wanted me to be wholly *myself*, not someone else's minion. I found that in many relationships the more I gave, that much more was expected. My attempts to have more of my own life and time apart met with anger and restraint. Yet I was growing more aware of parts of me that were different from being simply a compliant partner. I was in my late forties then and realized I could no longer sustain a commitment without giving myself a chance to explore what I had been patiently setting aside.

Our traumatic break-up challenged my faith, but as I outgrew my formative faith, I found a new calling in ministry. The collapse had shaken me and sent me on a search for a deeper and more livable understanding of what is called the theology of the cross. How could it be that giving up my life to someone—anyone—"as the good shepherd lays his life down for the sheep," would bring life abundant? To whom was I giving it up? Would my death, as Jesus' death promised, give others life? How?

In these years I entered the School of Theology and Ministry at Seattle University, quite unsure where a Divinity degree would lead, but ready to take the risk. Graduate school beckoned as it always had; this would be my third master's degree. Although I felt my faith was deep, I had picked up bad habits as I loved "my neighbors as myself." Now I sought "truer" meanings of theology—more realistic, more livable. In the late nineties deeply studying Scripture became my passion. Would I, a lesbian, find ministry a new call? Almost before I trusted that was possible, I was ordained to the ministry by my own church on Pentecost, June 11, 2000, the turn of the third millennium. I was writing a whole new book of my life.

I was surprised how the satisfaction of attaining a goal I had sought for years, a teaching degree, for example, and then a counseling degree, faded as I discovered ever newer calls to further growth. It was as if I took off the layers of "fitting" behavior to discover more of my real self, such as being gay, and being deeply spiritual. Each time, coming to myself was a profound spiritual awakening. No less was this decision to enter ministry.

Thomas Merton is said to have pointed out that some of us spend much of our lives climbing a ladder to success, eventually discovering that we arrived at the wrong spot after all. My ladder had been set in several different positions and luckily, successive climbs led me to several successes and worthy callings. There had been nothing wrong with my first professions, as teacher, counselor, or partner, but rarely did my early relationships with others grow into anything I'd read about; that is, sharing love, interests, and interdependence. Years passed as I struggled to learn that God wanted me to be committed to others while also devoted to myself, so I could be a full and equal partner. I needed to walk out from under the shadow of other egos and claim *myself*. I was an effective high school counselor, but I could no longer hide, or assume I was "doing everything right." Too many new dimensions of myself were emerging. As a result, I needed the courage to be who I was becoming. This I realized in the last years of my vocation as an educator, confirmed it in seminary, and embraced it in a new relationship to my faith, my calling, and my God.

CHAPTER 3

The Routine
Fall 1999

❧❧⟊⟊

When Mother was 81 and my father 95, I frequently drove from our Edmonds home to Everett for lunch. They'd lived independently all their married lives, but my concerns for them were increasing. My 25-minute drive seemed a wise investment of time to stay abreast of their lives, but I wasn't there often enough to notice some increasingly worrisome changes. Regular, expected visits found them both clean, well dressed, and competent. I failed to note that their clothes were often the same visit after visit. They could not explain small abrasions or dismissed them and they rarely commented on the cryptic, yellow sticky notes attached to doors, refrigerator, and stove. I seldom asked enough questions. I remained the "dutiful daughter." Mother called me her "Darling." Dad rarely volunteered anything, although he asked keen questions with an element of skepticism about what I was studying at the School of Theology and Ministry and what my church was doing. Dad and I had never been close.

At lunch Mom arranged bread, cheddar cheese, peanut butter, sandwich spread, cottage cheese, fresh pineapple or grapes, and handed Dad the English muffin bread, a slice of which he put in the toaster behind him. We sat at the chrome and beige kitchen table looking east into their mature and well-pruned back yard. We admired the red, yellow, and peach rhododendrons they prized. From an Almaden wine bottle fitted with a handle her arthritic hand could grasp, Mom poured a nondescript white wine into each of two repurposed Kraft cheese glasses. Dad drank milk. We took the same places at table and shared a silent prayer, after which I habitually spread a slice of white bread with peanut butter and honey—something I rarely ate. I felt as if I were reliving the fifties. In many ways I was.

Our conversations weren't revelatory. Their news, unchanging. Dad ran errands to the hardware store (yes, he was driving at 95), checked the gutters (he was on both the ladder and roof), replaced ceiling light bulbs, and kept his red Chevy station wagon and Mom's blue Dodge clean and serviced, full of gas and oil. They bought groceries together. They split one Lean Cuisine serving for supper explaining that, "We don't need all that much food." They watched *The MacNeil/Lehrer Report* on public television, then Rick Steves' *Travels in Europe*, and finally listened to Classic KING FM* the rest of the evening. I had grown to love this station in the late fifties on the Heathkit FM tuner Dad built. Dad had fashioned the cabinet, too, on his shopsmith in the basement.

This cabinet now held new components, a system with twenty-four inch speakers—whose fidelity Dad boasted of—the cords running mostly unseen behind the couch and one recliner. Too loud for me and conversation. My parents were ensconced in their customary recliners in the far living room corners on either side of a large front window looking onto Fowler Street and across it, two large yards. They turned the blinds to dim the bright sun as it approached the western horizon beyond. As far as I could tell they read different books without sharing and listened to music, the table between them adorned with an enthusiastic dark green vine that I had never seen in bloom. Years later, after it had been in my own home draped around a lampshade for a year, it did bloom; I was astonished to find that it was a delicately beautiful *Hoya carnosa*.

Their solidly built home, the third they had shared in their lives together, had radiant heat that had cracked the plaster. With the windows kept tightly shut except in summer, the house was always too warm for me. Heating frozen dinners meant there were few cooking odors, but I began to miss Mom's practice of placing cut gladioli, roses, and pinks from her gardens on Dad's handmade clear-cedar mantel.

I brought flowers to place beside the German 300-day clock sent from Europe by Dad's brother and sister-in-law, Art and Effie. On the mantel, it marked time, whirling its gold orbs under a glass dome. My uncle and aunt were teachers who traveled in their summers off to Eu-

---

* Seattle 98.1

rope and to Norway where we had Ramstad relatives. Uncle Art kept up with the relatives and read their Norwegian letters, but Dad had shut the door on his past and paid scant attention to any Norwegian relatives, holidays, or food. His curiosity was otherwise boundless. Beneath the clock were several shelves of books on art, religion, and ancient history. He built furniture with a Shopsmith in the basement, listened to classic music on FM, and loved his gardens.

Signs of trouble begin to appear. Dad left yellow sticky notes on the freezer door, "Microwave not oven," and the sliding glass door noted, "At the barber's." Mom said, "I can't remember a thing!" but apparently she learned little of what to do about it, or perhaps, forgot what she heard. I should have asked her doctor what I should be looking for or asked them directly what was wrong, but I didn't have their permission. I'd have had to ask for it since we lived at such emotional distance. I didn't hear of any crisis, if I heard about it at all, until after it had been addressed by their doctors or the Emergency Medical Technicians. I was never consulted about their health.

My well-dressed, outwardly confident and courtly father continued to have coffee with his cronies at English's Cafe on Hewitt Avenue in historic Everett, a classic gathering spot dating from the town's boom time. My older brother Dave alleged that none of Dad's peers could hear a thing, but they told stories, laughed, and carried on as if they did, feigning Norwegian accents mocking their own fathers. At 95 my Norwegian Dad still had silky light brown hair with blond highlights, the silver barely detectable. Mom had rich dark hair that had turned pearl gray, waving softly across her forehead and curling at her ears. Her Mediterranean complexion was striking and she was admired as a local soloist. While Dad had coffee and ran errands, Mother liked the house to herself, enjoying lunch with friends and several hobbies.

At lunch while Mom and I chatted, Dad ate, excused himself, put his plate and silver in the sink, and went to the spare room for a nap. This was a habit he'd kept since they first met in the late thirties. Mom and I walked arm-in-arm back to the living room.

I heard of a few accidents. Dad fell at least twice, hitting his head on the glass-topped coffee table in the center of the living room and bleeding on the gold shag carpet. EMTs came. But once assured that my folks had things in hand, they left. I wondered whether that was the whole truth. In the smaller of two kitchen ovens a black plastic food container was permanently melded to the rack. "We didn't need it anyway," Mom rationalized. Dad looked pained. He was more than a little impatient with Mom's forgetfulness. He volunteered nothing. But then challenging him resulted in endless argument.

Dad's graciousness outside our family hid his long history of depression and self-criticism, judgments of others and his kids, commonly his eldest son. He was always eager to put someone straight. Yet, beneath this armor I'd find a wounded child who couldn't express his tender emotions.

I once shared ownership of a classic 1939 Chris Craft sedan cruiser. One afternoon my parents and brother came to see it at moorage, and Dave got down on his knees in the salon with me to survey the Hercules engine. "A workhorse, " he said, as he proceeded to show me the parts as I enjoyed a rare personal moment with him. When I glanced up at my parents, I was shocked by the distant and disapproving look Dad gave us. It seemed the wrong expression for the situation. Unexpectedly I asked myself, What's wrong? Is it Dave? Why is Dad so critical of what Dave does, of his interests in cars and engines? He's also a bright, gentle, creative soul with many loves and talents. After years of paying little attention to each other, Dave and I began to compare notes. I grew much closer to him as the result of these conversations, which revealed how, unknowingly, we had common experiences growing up.

Dad's sad childhood story was family knowledge, but we took it with a grain of salt. I wasn't in touch with my own deep feelings, nor was I able to empathize with what he felt as he was growing up. He held himself together and protected our mother as long as he could. That was his promise to her. But in these next years, I began to realize that it was his devastating childhood that denied both Dave and me the presence of a warm, caring father, and continued to limit his emotional responses.

Now, no longer in the Seattle Schools, and having accepted only a part time position as a new pastor in my church, I am able to visit my folks more often. On one of my drives north to Everett I am filled with a nostalgia that spurs me to surprise them with a pumpkin for Halloween. I stop at a corner Safeway, choose a small one and carry it into the house. When I enter the living room from the cold, the warmth is a relief.

"You are a can-do person!" Dad exclaims with a big smile when I step in the door—he surprises me. I've never heard him say he's glad to see me. I notice his shirt is fresh from the laundry as he leans over for a kiss. Mom unfolds out of her recliner for a hug and, pleased, I take the pumpkin to the kitchen, looking for a knife.

Mom settles into a kitchen chair to watch while Dad resumes his reading. He usually leaves the two of us alone, believing mothers and daughters should be together in their roles, as fathers should be with their sons. As youngsters, my two brothers helped Dad clean the basement, yard, and garage, and I helped Mom cook and clean. Typical 50s roles. Mom is eager to talk but Dad, reserved, prefers logical "discussion" that verges on argument. He's never demonstrated much enthusiasm for my life, though he held sway over it until I left home at 21 and even after, never too shy to offer his opinion, to correct word usage in articles I wrote for the local Seattle *Times*, and for work. Occasionally he—the knowing Lutheran—asks skeptical questions about American Baptists. I avoid him.

On this day, when I see the two of them, I feel more like *their* parent. They evoke my compassion. Holding a paring knife, I contemplate the pumpkin, then slice around the stem to create a lid.

"Look at all that!" Mom remarks, as I pull the stringy innards out and slop them on the newspapers covering the table. She is charmed, seeing the orange pulp as if for the first time. With a large spoon I scoop out handfuls of strings and seeds. Once it's clean, I ask, "Now, where's a candle we can put inside?" I make holes for eyes and carve a large mouth in a smile while she goes to the hall closet. A small votive candle fits perfectly, and I put the pumpkin on their mantel.

When I drive away I am pleased; I've done something tangible. Should I be doing this more often? Should I be caring for them as if *I* were the parent? Is it time? Will they permit it, I wonder? Mom's marveling at the pumpkin worries me. Why, for her, is this so fresh? Has she forgotten she'd led this exercise for me and my brothers and her grandchildren for years?

I am still learning to take risks. My father provided my first unyielding male relationship. As a result, I didn't learn to be comfortable with him or men in general. The authority in our home, Dad relied on other authorities—a pastor, sometimes teachers, always male—for his opinions. He lived by the book and tolerated little questioning of his take on issues of the day. He simply wouldn't acknowledge a point any of us made. When I read Milton's *Areopagitica* in my junior history class with Mr. Zalesky, I decided to debate the principle of freedom of the press with him. I thought I had a fighting chance. At the dinner table, our forum for family debate, I paraphrased the following,

> *I cannot praise a fugitive and cloistered virtue, unexercised*
> *and unbreathed, that never sallies out and sees her adversary,*
> *but slinks out of the race where that immortal garland is to be run for,*
> *not without dust and heat....That which purifies us is trial,*
> *and trial is by what is contrary.*

> ~John Milton, *Aereopagitica* 1664

It seemed perfectly logical. We needed to engage in everything in our lives, rather than insulating ourselves and not gaining experience enough to judge. But not Dad. There was no moving this man whose pastor once said: "Carl, I've never known such a Lutheran conscience." He knew strict "right from wrong" and took responsibility for everything and everyone as if others had no minds of their own. Dad also buttressed his heavy-handed control with Scripture. One of his favorites was, "Jesus said to his disciples, 'Stumbling blocks will inevitably arise, but woe to those through whom stumbling blocks come. Those people would be better off thrown into the sea with millstones around their necks, than to make one of these little ones stumble.'" (*Luke* 17. 1-2). Obviously, there were no immortal garlands to be won by sallying out toward adversaries. We must be examples to others, keeping ourselves uncorrupted. Purity was not only the ideal; it was the only way. And purity must never result from trial. The brand of Christianity we followed was moderate religion, comparable to many other midcentury Protestants.

Everything in our family life was tied to what others might think. We went to church twice on Sundays because we "were an example to the neighbors." Any of our mistakes was followed by his horrified question, "What if someone had seen you?!" I ponder whether Dad ever did anything in his life for himself. Well, yes: he went to the hardware store whenever he liked.

To punctuate that he was right, not to mention being in charge, he came home from choir practice not many weeks after my failed Milton argument and abruptly snapped off the black-and-white television set in the midst of my watching *The Turn of the Screw* with Ingrid Bergman.[‡] He believed she was a flagrant sinner because of her relationship with Roberto Rossellini, obviously nullifying her talent and probably sullying Henry James as well. (He was not alone: Colorado Senator Edwin C. Johnson condemned Bergman publicly as "A powerful influence for evil.")[*]

I was not only incensed, I felt violated. I loved drama and was acquainted with Henry James. I intuitively appreciated art apart from "sin" and hesitated to use the word. I was sure Dad's heavy-handed criticism cured me of inheriting the trait. (I wish I could say that was true, but the apple still falls near the tree.) That I could make absolutely no inroads, even with logical argument relying on an icon such as Milton, was maddening. I resorted to my comfortable myth: I had been brought home from the hospital to the wrong family, a clan to which I was invisible. And me with at least some intelligence, I thought. I read the *Saturday Review of Literature* in our home, and was part of an honors class of 25 peers at Everett High School. I was learning how to read closely, how to make wise judgments, and to lead my youth group from time to time at church. But my father's control over me and our branch of the Ramstad family was enough to make me doubt that I could aspire to anything beyond what he foreordained. I was afraid to aim for anything unique to me lest he dash my hopes.

When my brothers and I were kids, Dad was softer. There were gifts, too. He took us tent camping as a family of five, building crackling hot, long-lasting bonfires. He had an orderly routine for setting up and taking down the tent. Eager to help him, I swept the canvas as he folded it section by section to put on top of our car. I was ever looking for ways to gain approval from this man who was able to identify every tree in the

---

‡ Startime, television episode 1959

* Senator Edwin C. Johnson (D-CO), a rank moralist who opposed FDR's New Dea; policies, slut-shamed the actress on the Senate floor. www.thedailybeast. com/when-congress-slut-shamed-ingrid-bergman March 14, 1950

forest. After I was married he built a pigeon coop with Lew and the two of them fancied pigeons for years. He saw that an old black Ford was placed on piling in the back yard so David could learn its parts.

One summer he enlisted us in a project to make root beer, each of us with a task, including adding the yeast and capping the bottle. After a whole afternoon of working together, we stored it neatly in a cupboard and then took off on our week-long camping trip, leaving the newly filled and capped bottles shut in. It was unusually warm that week, and when we returned the root beer had exploded. We walked in the back door to see sticky brown syrup running down under the cupboard doors and onto the floor. Silence settled on us as we proceeded to help Mom clean it all up. I suspect Dad was chagrinned.

Now with Halloween past and Thanksgiving approaching, I am feeling grateful for my own riches. There is much to be thankful for, although I am more often moved by a fear of scarcity. I see what's missing, not what's there. Not only did my parents discourage us from taking risks, they seemed to think there were only so many new experiences to go around. When I was dating, Mother warned me not to do too many things on a weekend with friends, lest I do it *all* and there be *nothing* left for me to enjoy in my twenties. As far as their expectations of me, they were pleased, but said little so it wouldn't go to my head, and of course, more was always required. One of the influential writers I read in seminary, Susan Nelson, wrote that those of us "refused by life" learn "dances of alienation" that prevent us from taking further risks. I recognized that inclination in myself. She named this avoidance of risk the "sin of hiding."*

The concept struck me as a perfect description of myself. Naming hiding as a fault led me to investigate where and how I had learned to be so self-effacing. But I didn't have to look far. I didn't risk incurring Dad's censure. Or that of any authority, Scripture included? And those old "blood" hymns? Of course.

For her part, Mom was not only a singer of note but a gifted seamstress and tailor. She made all my clothes, including a wool plaid sewn-down pleated skirt and jacket in the Pendleton style, skirts for school and organdy and silk dresses for dances. When Lew began first grade, she had

---

* Susan Nelson. "The Sin of Hiding: A Feminist Critique of Reinhold Niebuhr's Sin of Pride."

gone to work and had much less time but persisted with her sewing and singing.

By the time I was eleven or twelve, I began to accompany her singing and was often drafted when I had a load of homework to do. I was proud of Mom, loved hearing her warm, mezzo-soprano voice, and pleased to play. But I also grew weary of being obligated to help her prepare for her solo work.

On one of my trips to Everett I find Dad at home alone. I turn to walk away, but instead, I take a deep breath and sit down across from him in the living room. We rarely make small talk. How to start a conversation? But after he asks me how things are going, I am honest: I am apprehensive about finding a new position, and particularly a part-time, rather hastily thought-out "Minister of Spirituality" at my own church. In spite of my new degree, I don't know whether this calling will last or a further calling will materialize. The family anxiety strikes me as well as it did Dad. He sits forward in his recliner to say,

"It must be frustrating." I look up, catching my breath, surprised he heard me, audibly as well as the feelings beneath the words. Now I am at a loss for words. After a pause, he says, "Sometimes, in times like that, I remember this Scripture." He offers these words from memory:

> *The fig tree has no buds,*
> *the vines bear no harvest,*
> *the olive oil yield fail,*
> *the fields produce no yield,*
> *the sheep vanish from the fold,*
> *and there are no cattle in the stalls.*
> *But I will rejoice in Yhwh,*
> *I will exult in God my Savior.*
>
> ~Habakkuk 3.17-18

I was speechless. This man, so spare in his emotion, so severe in his judgment, recites comforting words from an ancient prophet I don't even recall. How could such compassionate words have come from such a cipher?

Struggling to place this unique moment with Dad in some safe place as I traveled home, I breathe deeply, slowly, realizing that as we lament our pain we must also acknowledge and welcome the surprises of grace. Sharing the visit with my disbelieving partner Ardene, I ask, could it be that Dad and I might forge a way to share our lives, even our faith? Perhaps such a verse helps him give thanks in the midst of his own losses. And at the end of his life?

This suits my personal commitment to keep trying to be authentic in everything—positive, honest, and direct. It's impossible. Dad is my most challenging opponent. When I was little, I remember Dad and my uncle Art yelling at their father in mixed English and Norwegian in disagreement about their jointly-owned farm near Oso, Washington. Grandpa was deaf, too. I cringed. Anger was something else I didn't know how to handle.

After disengaging in arguments with my father in my late twenties, we didn't share much of anything. Since I had become a minister focused on spiritual growth, however, others at church anticipated my sharing of faith. As I struggled with the words, I realized I had substituted music for emotional expression for years, and shared personally most often with fellow students and peers. I hadn't "given witness" to a congregation since I was at junior high summer camp in the 50s, or the *Cursillo* renewal in the 70s and at church retreats. Suddenly I was mute. I feared that I would lose my cloistered walk with the mysteries of God if I shared all that was in my heart. Why must I? Because faith is the language of the soul, our spiritual heart, a seminal bulwark against the unpredictability of our lives. In these first years, when I opened my mouth, sometimes nothing came out. This was a sign I must be getting somewhere. I felt foolish, but introverts usually take time to think before we speak.

There is typical Ramstad family uncertainty over the Thanksgiving meal. The family now includes my older brother Dave, his daughter Erin, who has a large family of in-laws and a daughter an hour north of town, our brother Lew's widow, her two daughters, and my partner Ardene and me. My folks are the hosts. There are fewer of us than ever: my older brother isn't sure he can come. My sister-in-law pulled a muscle in her back and can't help. Everyone seems to wait until the last minute to see if there is a better offer elsewhere. So in the typical family model of doing too much, determined to bring the whole dinner to the table, I brine a

14-pound turkey in a plastic five-gallon bucket in my parents' basement. The bucket handles the mass; the turkey stays submerged overnight. That's one achievement.

The second is getting it in the oven. I did that early in the morning, driving to Everett and back home to change and return later with Ardene. Now while the turkey is roasting, Mom, Ardene, and I sit on the couch watching the Macy's parade. But Mom can't fix in her mind where the parade is. She asks me at least three times an hour where I work (at church and now at Seattle University) not able to remember my answers. How does she manage to take the 11 pills I've seen her select out of a small plastic caddy every morning and night?

Dad is increasingly deaf. He watches the television apparently uninterested in the commentary. His deafness has been a family trial since he worked in the paper mill without ear protection, machinery roaring (even I did that in a summer job after high school). He cautions me firmly, "You don't have to raise your voice. Just speak naturally; I can hear you." So I speak normally and he stares at me expressionless, not having caught a word. This is not going to get any better soon.

More and more these days, I am struck that my folks' habits put them at risk. They take walks separately in different parts of town. Dad goes to the navy pier on the waterfront near Scott Paper Company where I packed toilet paper at the end of an assembly line after high school graduation. Mom walks around the blocks close to their home. Neither has company and that's apparently what each prefers. But at least twice Mother has fallen along the way and needed help from a neighbor. I worry about her. I worry about them both.

When Mother and I are working together in the kitchen, silently in sync as we've been for years, I'm hunting for utensils, but for the first time I realize Mother can't find them. I ask, "Where's the potato masher?"

"Well, I think it's ... no...." She goes from drawer to drawer, opening each one and marveling at the contents as if they are a revelation. How on earth are the two of them getting along with her memory loss and his loss of hearing?

When I carve the bird and present it on a platter, the white meat is tender and delicious, but the drippings and dark meat too salty to eat. Everything else seems good enough, though, and we enjoy catching up with one another. But after all Ardene's and my brining, chopping, sautéeing, stuffing, roasting, slicing and serving, I watch openmouthed as Dad, his plate clean after one helping, slides his chair back from the table, puts on a plaid scarf and cap, and, without a word, heads out alone for a walk. Didn't he like his dinner? Was he tired of the conversation?

In December, I bought a small Christmas tree on my way north. This holds no candle to the pumpkin. With a grimace, Dad gives me the silent treatment.

"Your father doesn't want a tree, Dear," Mom begins, interpreting what "Dad doesn't want" or "Your father would like," before she offers her own opinion—if she dares even to voice it. Mom rarely shares an opposing view except under her breath to me when she complains about what she thinks she cannot change. She's done this as long as I can remember. That's how I learned what a formidable opponent Dad was. Even my mom didn't engage him with projects she thought he'd disapprove of or argue with him when she disagreed. At least not within my earshot.

"Why not?" I ask. "I'll take care of the whole thing. Put it up. Take it down. You don't have to do anything but enjoy it." She lapses into silence, and I realize she wants the tree but won't say so. She's less spontaneous now, rarely initiating conversation. Since she's been a cheerful conversation partner, her silence sobers me. How forgetful is she?

"How much is the tree?" Dad asks over his book from the corner chair. I say $32, but immediately regret it. "I have only a $20, or I can write you a check." This is too petty to discuss; I should have just said, Forget it. Then he tells me the toilet seal is leaking. The plumber recommended the flooring be replaced. And there's more: "We have to buy a new washer." My empathy is hooked.

"We don't know the salesmen at Sears anymore," Dad continues. Familiar proprietors and friends are disappearing as he continues to live longer than most late ninety-year-olds. Because he was so well acquainted in town, he used to urge us, "Tell them you're Carl Ramstad's child," as if that would open all doors. But Dave and I were too cautious for that. Too afraid of criticism. Dad still takes the initiative, but he can't hear. Mom is afraid to speak lest she say something Dad doesn't like or agrees to something he will disapprove of.

Early in our lives my brothers and I learned that Mother and Dad required our complete attention. I was taught, before I can even remember learning, not to voice my own desires or feelings. Rather, I should first know what others want—especially my parents. They took good care of us, but we learned to anticipate the situations we found ourselves in and to be very careful what we chose to do. Dave and I lived by radar. Vigilance was our key to peace.

It wasn't long before we paid more attention to our parents—and to others—than to ourselves. This led to deference, as many "too-good" children learn, and soon to doing what the adults needed rather than discerning our own developing desires. My first real experience of personal power came with my teaching certificate in English and a classroom of sophomores when I was 23. I liked introducing my students to intriguing paradoxes, encouraging them to question and navigate intractable rules. In the classroom I was creative, flexible, and in charge. Outside it, I was reserved and anxious.

I took kindly to the prospect of teaching since I loved reading and writing and was good at school. I hadn't a clue what else to do. In spite of my musical talent (I sang, played the piano in recitals, for church gatherings, and was a church organist for several years), I didn't want to be a musician forever. My interests were far broader.

Our church played a role. Many faithful people I knew when I was growing up were loathe to say honestly what they thought or wanted. I didn't learn to even recognize dissent. Oversocialized to accommodate all comers, many think being Christian means we have to "be nice." We are conflict-averse. That means we get what we really want only through passive-aggression or sometimes, the threat of withdrawal, and withdrawal itself. This is false modesty: not voicing concerns, not drawing any attention to ourselves, not seeking recognition of any kind or praise for accomplishments (lest we be proud), and not being honestly who we are. Garrison Keillor aptly described the traits of Norwegians in Lake Wobegone: "the little town that time forgot, and the decades cannot improve...." The lives of folks depicted there reflected the values and priorities that I learned as a youngster. Now I laugh about the need never to draw attention to myself or achieve any station higher than honorable mention. "That's quite enough for Lutherans," he says. That was pretty hard for someone who was asked to perform and could sing, play the piano and organ, or speak off the cuff.

I learned through trial and error during the many middle years of my life that sometimes I needed not to be nice. I needed to voice my moods and thoughts, to encounter others and work things out together, and come to the table with a full deck. I couldn't do that if I were paying more attention to everyone else. I had to identify for myself what I felt, learn how to express it, and manage engagement with others whether or not we agreed. This is called claiming our voice.

My pilgrimage began in earnest in the 1990s when I sought to scrutinize the scriptural lessons I had been taught. Emerging self-awareness changed my faith. I recognized that had Jesus, "meek and mild," merely knuckled-under to the powers of his time, clerical and lay, he would never have dared to offend by seeking out the marginalized, healing on the sabbath, and talking of a kingdom that appeared to rival the empire. He was a provocateur. I was trying to spur my partner to recognize we needed both independence as well as dependence. Since our relationship was dying for lack of oxygen, my full accommodation to her needs had to stop. I had to learn to speak, selfishly I thought, for my own needs.

Why, in the church, with Jesus' model, do we admire as well as teach deference and self-abnegation to the extent of encouraging voicelessness? Authenticity precedes servanthood. Servanthood comes by choice and ought not be commanded—otherwise what, exactly, are we asking of ourselves? My meditation and writing begin to tackle this subtle paradox. My relationships reflected my faults just as they did my gifts. I was beginning to find some new keys for resolving conflicts.

> *The spiritual journey entails confronting these*
> *hardened patterns that we've spent a lifetime creating,*
> *patterns that oppose the life of the spirit and obscure*
> *our true spiritual identity.*
>
> ~Kidd, Sue Monk. *When the Heart Waits.*

My brother's widow calls to announce that there is uncertainty about Christmas dinner as there was about Thanksgiving. Apparently there will be no familiar dinner at my parents' home. Both of Lew's daughters are spending the holiday with their in-laws. Brother Dave's two kids are out of town. Mom grieves the loss of her closest friend, Liv, and seems too weary to open the family home. As the winter is upon us, this shrinking family appears more and more fragile.

"Your father has had the flu for two or three days," Mom explains when we have our weekly chat. "I went to church alone last week, and to Liv's memorial service today." Her toneless voice belies deep grief. She seems forsaken.

In spite of over 60 years with Dad, Mom appears to me to be a virtual widow. Maybe she used to speak up, but she told me when her requests fell on his deaf ears. As I responded to her request that I be her best friend (she insisted she had no one else), she named Dad as the reason so many events didn't or couldn't come to pass. Sometimes it was because he was 14 years older than she. Now it is because Dad can't hear her. Even when he is close by, he spends most of his time napping or reading, or running errands in his bright red Chevy stationwagon (which my eldest niece says she's glad he drives because people can see him coming). He is an habitual napper after lunch. But now she reports he naps before lunch *and* after. He is nearly 96, after all. But his Norwegian heritage ensures he looks much younger than he is, and that's my legacy, too.

Now as I observe Mom become increasingly baffled by all but the most customary routines—getting dressed, setting out breakfast, planning the same lunch day after day—the sticky-notes persist. But she doesn't want any favors. When I show concern and offer to help, she assumes her authority to warn me off. Stunned, I realized I couldn't help. Mom and Dad won't allow it.

I can't protect her. So as my mother regresses, if that's what is happening, I can merely look on, anguished, and offer help if she'll accept it…or if Dad will. I think I can accept mortality, we all must; we cannot change it. But this will be the end, then, of a lifetime of being able to "fix" things—things both my parents expected I could, and things I often did. Thankfully I am learning to respect my limits; I cannot rescue them any longer.

"I sit on fire hydrants," Mother tells me one afternoon with a cheerful smile. "When I'm walking around the block, I perch on them to catch my breath." She means to reassure me. Fire plugs must lend themselves to resting. So do the fences around some yards and even stop signs, if all she does is lean. Although she walks by herself, I'm glad she continues to do so. The lack of Dad's arm to steady her doesn't hold her back at all.

She has courage and creative ambition, but Dad's age has always served as one reason some friendships and activities don't work for both of them. Nevertheless, they're inseparable: going to choir together, to church, to nurseries, and to work out at the gym, doing the bicycle, the treadmill, and "something for the arms," she tells me. She says she does her exercises faster than most of the others there. "But then, I do most things fast," she adds, and, "Your dad just talks with the other ladies." One afternoon, she tells me, they had to help her up from the floor after a series of sitting and standing from a chair tired her so that she fell. Without injury, thank heavens.

My parents have been engaged all their lives in church activities, socializing with a group of informed, extroverted couples their age. Now time and inactivity lie heavily. Worried that she cannot contribute to the church-women's circles as she once did, she sadly confides to her friend Pearl that she can't host meetings at her home anymore.

Pearl tells her, "Just put more money in the offering, June, and don't worry about it."

I realized this was a common experience among the elderly. I witnessed it at my church. It was not to be "fixed." The elderly were to be companioned, not chided. All I could do was try to assist, and accept the losses as they occurred. And that's what elders had to adjust to as well.

Mother still worries. What she offers has never been enough. This is a frequent lament in a family living the gospel of scarcity. There will never be enough to go around: money, food, luxuries, love. We conserve what we can, then try to make up the differences, yet never succeed. To overcome the lurking deprivation my family feared, I inherited a try-harder approach. I was learning I could do many things I didn't at first welcome if I just got into them and worked hard. I often surprised myself by the result.

Mom sang in choirs for over 40 years. I began to accompany her when I was only 13. She sang in the Everett Symphony *Messiah* and at the memorial services and weddings of many citizens, family, friends, and church members. She created and directed a cherub choir at our home church, Everett First Baptist. The cherubs rehearsed every week after school (another afternoon lost for me) and sang every few months in worship—decked out in white surplices with large red bows she had made. Mom went to work as an office clerk for Weyerhaeuser the year my little brother, Lew, started school. When she was subsequently hired by the Everett School District, she followed her supervisor through every one of his promotions until he was an administrator. When he was chosen the superintendent of schools, he appointed her Director of Personnel.

Although her highest level of schooling was Rogers Business School, she was bright, verbal, talented, and an expert organizer. When she and my dad met, he worked at Soundview Pulp Company where she was a secretary. He ate his lunch in the company offices. There was another secretary too, but the story is that this co-worker used profanity. Dad chose Mom because she didn't swear—faint praise. She was also a striking brunette with energy and many talents. They dated for six months before they married in 1939 when Mom was 21. Her lack of self-confidence belied her obvious gifts.

How could these fortuitous events add up to scarcity? My parents were extremely fortunate to have had steady income before and during WW II. When they married, Dad had not only a job but a car. They were never without either. But, like many of their peers, they constantly warned against taking things for granted, or trusting that there would be enough. When I look at my own life, particularly the low points, it is hard to find any deficiencies compared to the misery in the rest of the world.

Why in the midst of my blessings would I acknowledge any want at all? Because I was so used to waiting for others to act first or to shine while I took a supportive role. This was a habit I needed to reject. Sometimes I had to sit down and write a list before I could put the elements into proper rank.

We live in a culture crammed with emptiness. We buy cartons of commodities, boxes of false gods: things, appearances, hollow values draped over products, computers, and cat food. None of it satisfies. Each sound bite, billboard image, commercial, and tweet, displays something we must have—so we cannot rest with what we *do* have—nor stop to give thanks. Our culture creates anxiety in the midst of wealth and blinds us to those next door who cannot afford both to heat their home and eat.

Sitting on fire hydrants my mom stops, honors what is, sees beyond the clamoring commerce, and sinks her roots into the true and eternal. In the midst of the parade of what passes for progress, her pauses invite her long devoted prayers.

CHAPTER 4

More of the Same, Or Is It?

❧❧❧❧❧

More than a year has passed of Ardene's and my regular contact with my parents. Eager for a break, we head east on Interstate 90. There is nothing like driving east over Stevens Pass to regain perspective. Nothing like spotting a roadside waterfall frozen opaque in the broken crevice of massive rock cliffs. Hundreds of square miles of dark green fir knit to rock. And on the east side of the Cascade Mountains? Ancient hills frosted with fresh snow sloping to fields nestled by the Columbia River and scored with fruit trees.

Just as sorbet cleans the palate between courses of dinner, vistas of such scale clear my vision. The scope and sheer magnitude of creation reveals itself, providing a glimmer of life eons before our ancestors rubbed sticks together to make fire. In some ways it is all still there. We are kidding ourselves if we believe this is all we have left, the strip from the mountains to Puget Sound, the rest of it carved up into subdivisions just over the ridge. God is in the chaos, not the tilled fields. My mentor, the Rev. Dr. Rodney Romney, said, "The goal of the wilderness journey is … to bring about [the self's] true home, its true freedom….We surrender ourselves to the wilderness of place and the wilderness of self to discover where we are and who we are."*

When I head onto the pristine ski track in the very cold woods near Mazama in the North Cascades, I am all alone since, too cold, Ardene went back to the lodge. I shove off with my poles and begin to step and slide down the trail. Sound is sucked into the sky. I hear its absence, the surge of my blood, the scrape of skis on the trail, the rustle of my jacket.

---

* Rodney R Romney, *Wilderness Spirituality*

One person in the wilderness. Small. Vulnerable. Mystery looms large. Here is the silence and beauty I love.

I grew up on busy Colby Avenue two bus stops north of Everett High. Only when it snowed did the constant traffic noise soften. The truth is that the quiet of the empty church, where I practiced the organ, was more comfort to me than my home, except when I was in my room alone. Was it the sound of absence, was it fullness? Presence of spirit? I owned myself; no one could occupy my mind. I hadn't yet captured it, but I could hear it in the wide spaces cloistered under the expansive roof. It was true, too, that the back rooms of the sanctuary were heated through the week and I could linger to study in an empty classroom quiet and alone in contrast to five of us clamoring for time at home. The fragrance of baking cake or roasting meat for dinner wafted up from a floor below from cheerful women. The church was a refuge.

Ardene and I loved our years of cross-country skiing. Trekking into the snow and woods gave us time to play, exercise, and regroup. She is an affectionate and reliable companion who loves silence as much as I do. When we've had enough of snow, we go inside to warm up and spend hours reading by fireplaces in the lounge or our room. Lodges welcome us in the Cascade Mountains at Lake Wenatchee, Leavenworth, and farther northeast in Mazama or Winthrop. We spend two or three days, which seem to be enough to fill us again with love of the land and ourselves before returning to our work lives.

Once at home again, I increase my visits, noticing that Mom and Dad grow more eager to see me and reluctant to let me go. Instead of stoic indifference, there is warmth. We seem to be living at a more comfortable emotional distance. Feelings are thawing.

"We are so fortunate we are so close to everything here, Darling," Mother croons. "Only a few blocks to the grocery store, the hairdresser, and church, although of course we don't go as often as we used to. Your father is frustrated with the pastor and the folk service. Sometimes we go to Faith Lutheran (a block away), or we don't go at all." Her litany of the routines that fill their week grows more rote.

Which story is true? Who knows? I see them more than anyone, elder brother and sister-in-law notwithstanding, not to mention the four grandchildren. There isn't a soul I can compare notes with since even the church folk don't see them, just as they say. Mother seizes on her stories with energy as if she's relieved she's thought of something to say. This time I find her buried in a paperback romance she bought at the grocery store.

Ardene and I decide to take St. Patrick's Day dinner with us to Everett. We, cruise up Interstate 5, bordered by subdivisions and tall evergreens, to celebrate my folks' anniversary. On our way we had a number of thoughtful conversations about their decline. Ardene assures me that she will support me and them whenever needed. In the very home we now share she'd cared for her own mother for three years until she was 96. I learned the drill. In fact I had accompanied Ardene a number of times on her own visits when her mother was hospitalized, and finally to drive her to St. Helens, Oregon, for her mother's memorial service in 1996, the same year my little brother Lew died. Our sharing has made things easier and brought us closer together.

I know now that in just another year, Mom and Dad will celebrate the final anniversary of their lives together and within a few months, Mother would be gone. As we lay out the dinner, they are delighted with corned beef, new potatoes, and a traditional Ramstad lime-jello salad of walnuts, celery, green olives and grapefruit; they eat with relish. The four of us sit at the teak table adjacent to the living room sharing information about my father's parents. I never met my paternal grandmother, Joakima, who died of tuberculosis when Dad was just six.

I wear 'Kima's tiny gold wedding band from 1894 on my left pinky, a symbolic attempt to connect with Dad's maternal line, a line that had stopped until I was born. Joakima met my grandfather Elias Ramstad when the Severinson family emigrated from Norway to Bella Coola a year after Grandpa arrived there with a group of evangelical Lutherans on pilgrimage from Crookston, Minnesota. Joakima Severinson's bleak experience in that homestead some 600 miles north of Vancouver B.C., intrigues me. Or is the bleakness my projection? As I quiz my father, I am after social and personal history. I have no knowledge of her but what Dad has shared infrequently, and a tiny tinted picture I've misplaced. What could he remember when he was with her only a few years?

So this is a different silence. In addition to the silence of my own parents, silence is one of the few legacies from their parents, too. No letters. No family history from Norway: the reasons Elias, the eldest son, left the farm in Norway near Andalsnes for the United States in 1888 (lack of a future? Poverty?); the reason his younger brother, Ole, joined him 15 years later to settle at a farm on Whidbey Island west of Everett. Mom's heritage is lengthier in the U.S. than Dad's. The McGhees came from Tennessee: descendents of Hessians hired by the British to fight in the Revolutionary war. There is still a town called McGhee there. When Mom married Dad, her mother Kittie (Catherine) refused to speak to her for a year. Compared to Grandma's family tree, Carl was a "foreigner." And perhaps, also too old for her daughter.

I feel the weight of lives caught in dark rooms lit by oil lamps and wood stoves, damp to the core with heavy, persistent rain, and pernicious disease. Perhaps I imagine the starkness of my paternal grandmother's life because I have also known isolation. I assume, since it was my father who lost his mother at such a young age, it is my own grief I feel. But is it his legacy to us? I yearn for wisdom from the past—and from writers and mentors.

Although both Mom and Dad have accepted the friends I've brought home over the years with very little comment, when my friends were women, increasingly women, I assumed they realized that I was lesbian, but they didn't. I never spoke of it. With more than one marriage behind me by my early thirties, I supposed they were glad I continued to be independent, professionally successful, and apparently happy. They had stopped inquiring. None of us inquired much beyond face-value comments. I became my extroverted self at family dinners, regaling them with classroom tales about outrageous teenagers. They laughed.

"The wildest, most dangerous trails are always the ones within."

~Belden Lane. *The Solace of Fierce Landscapes*

Sometime in my thirties, in the midst of earning a second masters in Educational Psychology, a colleague walked me to my car after school. She and I enjoyed spontaneous conversations at early 8 o'clock coffee; I found her quick, bright, and funny. This afternoon she walked me to my car and sat briefly in my passenger seat to confess, "I'm in love with you." The words flashed through my innocence like a shooting star. Instantly, I responded viscerally. *This* is what love feels like! Wow. But I was frightened. Would this recognition change me? Would my job be threatened? Would I have to finesse this "curse" in my life after all my efforts to do everything "right?" Yes, "right," one might say, but with regular human mistakes.

One Sunday after mass in my Episcopal Church, I continued to linger on my knees after the postlude as tears flowed. I felt exposed, vulnerable, and—guilty? My best partners were so natural to me, and now somehow, stigmatized. Painfully aware that my sexual orientation illuminated my marriages, my flirting—posing, really, as someone I wasn't—I was also relieved and hopeful I was grounded enough to make wiser decisions. It was an enormous breakthrough.

But why did I have to discern all these influential issues now? Others didn't seem to have to. I assumed the lives of my family and friends were predictable and acceptable and mine wasn't. I was very naïve. It was the mid seventies, only six years after the Stonewall uprising. And though in sympathy with "their" right to be who they were, I had not taken it personally. Not long after this breakthrough, I fell in love with a stunning woman with whom I was fortunate to share many years. Ultimately, once again our differences were too stark, sadly unnegotiable, and I moved out one wintry weekend to get some perspective. The demise was rocky and upsetting. But it was another step of mine toward speaking my own truths.

In the spring, as I ponder the signs of decline in my parents, I imagine Mom and Dad in their opposite corner lounge chairs in the gold and light green living room, the western sun dimmed by blinds lowered over their picture window. I dread calling. I saw them recently. But this Saturday I did not visit, nor Sunday or Monday. They are so frustrating! Ever composed, they hold their own, defending themselves and obscuring my dad's silent control. They both assure me how well things are going and I nod, approving their defense of the status quo as if I am not aware of the growing need they have for support and oversight.

Mom continues to vent her frustrations with Dad to me, out of his hearing, working hard to avoid crossing him. As much as she tells me she would like to "move to a home," she quickly adds, "but I will not upset your father in his last years." What she's really saying is "I will *never* upset him." Is she that fearful of what he would do? Or is she completely loyal to his will? A will that has controlled us all. Perhaps once that was protection and nurture. It seems fatal now.

Do I know the whole legacy Dad received from his parents? What difference would my knowing make at this late stage in their lives? Someday I will make that trip north into Canada to visit the homestead my paternal grandparents had hewn in the deep forest of the Bella Coola Valley. Grandmother 'Kima, who died long before my birth, is a cipher. The Norwegian village of Hagensborg is some eight miles inland from the fjord. Elias and Kima lived there several years, through the birth of their first son. They lost the next baby, and then moved south to Annieville, a tiny town southeast of Vancouver in the delta of the Fraser River. After they moved south again, from there to Everett, she died of complications from tuberculosis and pregnancy at 34. It was 1910, and Dad was just six years old.

Dad tells about being brought in to stand at his mother's bedside, she as white as the sheet that covered her. "You be a good boy," she said, and I'm sure, in shock and fear, he agreed. And then his world collapsed. He'd already endured her absence of at least two years while she was in treatment at a sanitarium called Tranquille near Kamloops, B.C.

That six-year-old who stood at his mother's death bed is still grieving. How can I not factor his loss into his apparent inability to allow even himself flexibility, understanding, or forgiveness? How much has that been my legacy? He holds everyone to an impossible standard. I grow in my ability to forgive myself and my parents enough to credit their certainly well-intentioned care of their children as "good enough." I stood on the shoulders of many people in my childhood, but chiefly my parents' faith and love of music and art. As my parents become infirm, if that is what's happening now, how much will my knowing their story affect my ability to help?

Mom played 78 rpm records for Dave and me when we were just toddlers, explaining the *Toy Symphony* by Haydn as we sat on the floor together, listening to that and the William Tell Overture. We went regularly to church and choir concerts. More music. And silence. I absorbed the hymns, loved singing with the congregation, and volunteered for youth activities and choirs. They took us to the Seattle Art Museum at Volunteer Park often and once checked out a series of art slides narrated by Vincent Price that we watched after dinner. Everett presented community concerts as well, including soloists, pianists, and once, an opera. These made up a rich experience, including my accompanying my mother to her voice lessons. When Jim, her coach, suggested she use her diaphragm more, my 6- or 7-year-old self came in from the waiting room full of comics and heaved my belly in and out saying, "See? I can do it!"

Mom and Dad were so afraid of doing something wrong that they worked too hard on the letter—not the heart—of the law, always looking over their shoulder, finding judges, not advocates, then turning to judge others. The first discovery I made of "heart," laughter, forgiveness, was in my lively, talented piano teacher, Bernice, Jim's ebullient wife. Tragically, she died of a brain tumor when I was 12, and I was heartsick when I was thought too young to attend her memorial. Then Frances, a tireless advocate for our church's youth, and later many other adults—like Florence, Frances, Rosie, and Edith, Esther, the Eders and Sanders, even "Grannie,"—who reached out to me and softened the edges of the realities against which I so stiffened in self-defense.

Now, even as the circle of their lives narrows around their home, my parents keep their feelings close. Mother shares hugs and smiles, praise and admiration. But Dad's lips are tight with the need to keep all emotion in check, from joy to lament (except for the remarkable disclosure about his favorite Bible verse last fall). I know this is not from anger and fear alone, though there is some; nor is it from self-pity, though that, too, is there. I am beginning to see their own losses, the austerity my parents struggle against. Shutting it in kept them free to create a new family life together, and not without joy. But I cannot entirely forgive the rigidity that made my brothers' lives and my own so difficult when we were young. The judgment we strove to avoid generated our judgments of other people, and laughter never much lifted our low self image.

Today, their refusal to reveal their vulnerability seals their own hearts from each other. They cannot reveal their own pain, and thus cannot comfort one another or ask for help. I simply couldn't accept that they didn't know their own souls well enough.

"What holds your dad and me together is sex and the church," Mother sometimes declares as some sort of justification. I still don't know what she means. Faith and sexuality are fine, but what is she leaving out? Friendship, partnership? A meeting of the minds? I never hear more examples, what else they share—like the garden, or what they choose to avoid. She did tell me they closed the door on their prior life experience when they married.

To be fair, their own peers may indeed live the same reality. Baring one's soul was simply not done in those generations during and after the war among the elders I know, and probably a number of other Northern European cultures. Nevertheless, it is obvious how highly Mom and Dad esteem each other. Together they have woven a comfortable, caring, and deep reverence. Since my early adolescence it simply does not admit of overt affection, humor, or perhaps even forgiveness.

The routine is becoming more and more comfortable when, with Ardene's blessing, I take the time to drive up to 47th and Fowler to check things out, to assure myself the folks are okay. Dad is at the door and, just inside, Mom is rolling up out of her perpetual niche in the recliner in the corner. We embrace.

"Your *Spirit Stones* are like a journal, aren't they?" Dad says. He's been reading the weekly reflections I send out on email.

Yes, sort of," I answer, bracing myself.

"The prose is beautiful."

Stunned, I manage to thank him.

He's a fair judge of prose, but it's rare that he likes what I write. Dad reads extensively and it was his subscription to the *Saturday Review of Literature* that revealed literature and criticism to me while I was still in high school. Now, pleased and shy after his praise, I am silent. Mom quickly introduces a new topic: the arrival of a new great grandchild. Should we send a gift, she asks. Dad isn't interested, or doesn't hear, and has already turned back to his book.

I give her a hug and turn to the door as Mom says, "Here," putting a folded $20 in my hand. "Your father doesn't approve of buying baby gifts for great grandchildren," she whispers. There she was, defending her children in spite of Dad's inattention. I stuffed the bill in my pocket and when I got home, sent a check on their behalf to my niece for her second child, a boy named Owen.

Women—and men, sometimes—find church both life-giving and death-dealing, enthralled with worship and weary of the control, not to mention ethics, of leaders, pastors and priests. Disillusionment is not a bad thing. We need to be realistic and see institutions for what they are and what they are not. People are people—ordinations notwithstanding. Temptation lures the holiest of us to take the low road. The Northwest is notorious for the lowest church attendance in the nation, and the number of "Nones" is growing nationwide. I grew up with male pastors in all the churches I attended, listening to the *He* and *His's* in Scripture, anecdote, and sermon. Twelve sober deacons in black suits walking two-by-two in step down the center aisle to serve communion. The "deaconesses" prepared communion, but never served it.

I had rarely seen women in pastoral leadership until Laura Fraser was ordained in 1970, the first woman Episcopal priest in the Diocese of Olympia, here in Seattle. When she stood before us after her ordination, I saw a visible scrim rise over the scene as a lighter semicircle inscribed itself 180 degrees from left to right to complete a full circle. Men and women priests! What a concept. I was thrilled. When I was a child, a woman visited from our Baptist Association headquarters whose name was Ardith Reike. I admired her, and wondered how to be like her. I suppose I could have felt a call to ministry; but in those years, the expectation was that we marry a pastor. That was it.

Some still doubt that women have the "authority" to preach the Gospel, and this in spite of Jesus' own relationships with women in his itinerant ministry in Galilee, and those of Paul on his missionary trips and in the newly-established home churches throughout the Mediterranean. Most women in churches find a vacuum where our lived experience should be. The writer of this text believes we need to honor our experience, our sense of call to vocation, daring to name it in the presence of the very tradition(s) that threaten to deny us.

For me, naming my desire for ministry seemed to tempt fate. I had not presumed to speak truth to the powers for such a long time, I lacked confidence—afraid when I spoke up, I would lose the shred of hope I had left. My faith had buoyed me through many crises and made me eager to enter the School of Theology and Ministry at Seattle University. In the face of what would be considered the natural result of seminary, when I, a lesbian, proposed to stand in a pulpit and proclaim the Gospel, I felt I might be going a bit too far. My father's scant praise didn't help, but he already had begun to show me that he saw more than he let on.

I remember the shock of my pastoral-supervision professor when I said that naming my goal for a pastorate induced fear. "Might it not be excitement?" he asked. "Anticipation?" No. I was afraid naming my goal would risk losing it. I used to joke with a friend that once things were going well, "God would yank the rug out from under you." Some faith. Yet this dread came with memories of exactly this reversal.

Some of this came from unexpected discipline when I was young, surprising me with a mistake I had made unknowingly. Doubtless that cynicism was confirmed when I was a senior in high school and aspired to a fine liberal arts college. Although I qualified, was accepted, and award-ed a scholarship to Whitman College in 1961, my father withheld his blessing. Dad had decided on my attending the junior college in Everett. My desire didn't really matter. His mind was made up. We could have considered any number of other reasonably priced schools had we been able to discuss them. When I thought we could, I lobbied, argued, and advocated for myself, only to come up against his closed mind.

I had misjudged the Ramstad silence, expecting that my obedience, my academic and musical achievements would all manifest my worthi-ness. I had done everything right. I had thrown myself into the illusion of debate with a passion, but there had been no debate. My parents (my mother?) should have been clearer. Why didn't someone just say, "Give this up! You don't have a vote." No one but Dad had a vote.

Dad seemed pleased to offer me room and board without charg-ing me rent—and even bought a '47 Chevy (repainted an odd shade of green) that I could drive to the local community college. I should have been grateful I didn't have to pay him.

While peers went to Stanford, West Point, the Coast Guard Acad-emy, Whitman, Reed, Willamette, Linfield, the UW and Washington State University, I entered Everett Junior College (Everett College), sink-ing into a depression I didn't escape until I completed my B.A. at the University of Washington and began to teach English at Cascade Senior High School. By then I was also committed to a short-lived marriage. At college I was befriended by two or three encouraging professors, espe-cially the ebullient Marjorie Day, who read my poetry and listened to me for hours on end. The friendship extended by both Marjorie and Russell was life-giving.

From my sense of betrayal I fell into the arms of an admirer not at all suitable to the woman I might become. Scott listened to me at first, and oh my, did I have a lot to share. I poured it all out: my closest friends had moved away and I had few friends left. I was so lonely! An alliance with a boyfriend seemed a way out of the time-warp my home had become, and this, too, proved a disappointment. Soon after we married he transformed into someone who insisted on going his own way without exception. "Don't you want me to be happy?" he'd ask, smiling roguishly as if he knew I couldn't stop his escapades with his single friends, his hunting trips out of town, his emotional distance, his quick anger and rigid gender role. He had been the soul of kindness and patience before, hadn't he?

I felt invisible. Sex became meaningless. My husband's inability to listen appeared more and more like my father's in the difficult, contradictory home I had just escaped. My parents and my husband saw what they wanted to see in me: a dutiful daughter, an agreeable wife, an assistant rather than a player.

Though married, I was on my own, and of course, limited by what I could afford, so the futility in my marriage solidified into an impasse. The only thing I knew how to do was to create distance, so I separated from Scott. After my divorce, I began to focus on my own life by responding to the encouragement of professors, academic degree by degree, relationship by relationship. After earning a BA in English, I began an MA as well.

I had not experienced noticeable failure before, not in any commitment I had made—maybe once when I had been directed to go blackberry picking with a neighbor but walked bald-facedly home to refuse. But after my divorce, I sank into further depression, living as if in disgrace.

The only things that kept me going were prayer and music. And hope, really. Fellow teachers at Cascade Senior High and friends in the Seattle Chorale buoyed me; I thrived on worship itself as a participant, practicing the organ through the week and playing for worship, memorials and weddings. I stayed within my reach, constrained by apprehension and reserve, balanced with occasional extroversion, which was, of course, "the performance" I had known all my life. Since emotional intelligence was not yet one of my gifts, I could hardly identify my feelings until I knew what I *didn't* want.

Disillusionment tainted everything. But inevitably or not, I slowly saw a bigger picture. I learned as I taught at Cascade Senior High in Everett, then Garfield High School in Seattle's Central Area in the height of the Civil Rights Movement, and then at Roosevelt High, informing myself on many levels at once. I knew no other way of coping except to try harder, working doggedly through any situation that was not positive. Now I knew, without naming it, that my parents were facing disillusionment themselves as Dad (or Mom?) considered how to deal with their needs to address my mother's failing health.

Later in the spring Mom laments, "I talk to the Lord all the time." Her faith gives her a loose acceptance of her condition, just no personal agency. "I wonder how long I will stay in this veil of tears?" She smiles wanly, but this is a sadness familiar to me as well as, "We are just pilgrims passing through." Suffering from arthritis since her forties, and high blood pressure for just as long, she is often in pain. She rests for hours against a heating pad in her recliner. I am powerless. I can't encourage her to move to the "home" she imagines would solve the challenges of grocery shopping, cooking (or heating meals), washing clothes and bedding, or cleaning the house, because she will not win the argument with Dad to achieve it.

I can't blame her. I can only own the part of me that is just like her, like them, and confess my own fears. How can this end?

And what if God is waiting here in the wings for me to figure this out by myself? In a recent sermon I had spoken of someone calling out to God for help when their world was shaking, only to discover that it was God doing the shaking. What if I had to make the move I was waiting for? And what if it is I who will be the primary respondent to my parents' needs?

"Some of us have begun a search for the feminine face of God and found ourselves in the path of a tornado," I said in a 2001 sermon.*

"Kristen Johnson Ingram writes: 'The Hebrew word for the Spirit of God is *Shekinah*, like the pillar of fire and cloud that guided the wander-

---

* *Encountering God.* Fransson. Luke 1:46-55. Dec. 16, 2001

ers in the wilderness. *Shekinah* roars into our lives unpredictably and un-predictable, full of demand and violent love.…She [comes] not as Lady but as Wind, as passionate intuition, as blinding light and breath-sucking presence. She came not as a gentle Mary-like handmaiden but as a queen, not whispering but crying out like a hoyden in the streets, bringing not consolation but urgency.'

"This is more like it!" I said. "Not this namby pamby spirit of gentle-ness, but a spirit of real life: *Ruach*, the breath of God; She is Life-giver, the Paraclete, the wildest force known to God.…*Ruach* rested on the proph-ets and anointed them so that when they opened their mouths, words fell from them like fire… *Ruach* is in the mouth of blessed Miriam.… [it] vaults to glorious Deborah and gives her an army and a song.… And *Ruach* swirls over a young Galilean girl, lining her womb to prepare it for a salvific miracle.

"Ingram concludes, 'When *Shekinah* comes into your life, she ruins it.'*

"And how else could we view the conception of Jesus in Mary of Gal-ilee? We still denigrate women who conceive without the support of the father of their child, as if they alone were responsible. Since our culture touts sex as the single signifier of true love, erroneously named intimacy, it is still a terror to single women to discover an unexpected pregnancy. Two thousand years ago? Mary was fortunate not to be stoned to death.

"Why else would Luke put words in Mary's mouth that sound like preparation for battle?" I continue. "Words that echo her brave kins-women from thousands of years before? Warriors, not handmaidens who shrink from the challenge of peasant village life. Warriors like Deborah who led a coalition of Israelite tribal militias to victory over a Canaanite army commanded by Sisera and, named prophet, sang of her victory. Mary needed the strength of a warrior to answer the call of God."

In June, Dad announces, "We're taking out the rhodies and azaleas in the front yard. They're too ostentatious." He had said the same thing about my dark red '86 Supra, clearly drawing attention to itself (and his red Chevy didn't equal my hubris?). The red and fuchsia plants resplen-

---

* "The Hunt for Shekina," Kristen Johnson Ingram.

dent across the front of the yard are gloriously in full bloom. How could they possibly offend?

"That would be terrible, Dad! Awful. Why would you do such a thing?"

He glowers at me, ending the conversation. But I had spoken up! A small triumph. All family members caring for other family must find ourselves in what we're doing, find our own voice in what becomes our responsibility. Otherwise we will continue to repeat family patterns.

When I arrive the next week to take mother out for her birthday, Dad, looking askance, says, "I don't know what to say to you. How could you have said what you did to me last week?" I am relieved he has spoken, although he seems hurt by my "defiance." This is a good beginning. Perhaps this is just the first time as an adult I had spoken something against his plans, but I thought that safe enough to do. Why wouldn't I disagree if I truly didn't think it wise? My brother Dave and I will have to pick up after him, caring for the property when he becomes unable to do it himself, so I don't want the property devalued by the removal of these stunning plants.

The next week he says, "It's none of your business what we decide to do," which is a pretty spectacular thing to say to his daughter whose care he will ultimately need. "We didn't take them out, anyway; we pruned them back." Oh, I notice. They are half the size they were the week before, but at least they are still there. "I'm sorry I upset you," I say. "But don't you want to know what I really think?" He says yes to that. In itself, a revelation.

During my studies at STM I became more aware of Murray Bowen and his work with family of origin issues: studies about how emotional connections move from one generation to the next, something I recognized was effectively at work now. Bowen posits that the family diagram is greater than our map of ancestors itself. It represents profound emotional connections. He concludes, a family's past lives in the present.[*] I persuade Ardene to join me on a trip north to honor my heritage, traveling on a Canadian ferry from Port Hardy, Vancouver Island's north port, through Queen Charlotte Sound en route to Bella Coola. Glad to be alone together and in a completely new environment, we rest as we thoroughly enjoy the scenery outside the large windows. Ardene and I

---

[*]   The Bowen Center for the Study of the Family, *thebowencenter.org*

met when we were both colleagues as high school counselors traveling to college conferences. We discovered we had much in common beyond work—significantly, faith. She is quiet company, taking in much of what we see, enjoying the contrasts from home.

On the *Princess Louise* in 1894, one of the immigrants to Canada commented that the rivers were "black with salmon." Certainly they noticed the swarms of salmon swimming up the Bella Coola River to spawn. In the 1890s, the shore would have been chock full of crab, oysters, mussels, and clams. But the settlers' first winter saw one of the worst flood-years along that coast. The little party camped near the native Nuxalk village till summer on the inlet before moving inland. Watching the Bella Coola river flood, whole trees and boulders roaring down with it, one pioneer remarked, "We don't have to go up the valley to see our land, the river is bringing it down to us."* I let my mind wander, wondering how my grandpa *Elias* (*Elijah* in English) felt about the same trip over a hundred years ago.

What beckons us into our past? Geography and spirituality, landscape and the love and belonging of generations. All of it contributes to who we are. Once I remarked that my attraction to the center of Seattle could not possibly interest God. "God didn't do geography." But my spiritual director Alexandra enlightened me: God is in everything—or, everything is in God: geography, feelings, vacations, treks, homes and homelessness—a concept called *panentheis*. Nothing is out of bounds. We live in God, the Mystery that spins the cosmos into perpetually renewing life.

Rod Romney, author of *Wilderness Spirituality* writes, "Until we make friends with the wilderness of our place, we will never be able to make friends with the wilderness of self."⁊ Clarity arrives slowly, much as the glacial melt sinks out of summer rivers to return them to deep green in midwinter.

The first Norwegian-Canadian Ramstads are no longer in the Bella Coola valley. But during my visit, I could see that they surely must have passed many moments here among the stunning peaks, with glacial-fed streams, first-growth cedar, and salmon for the taking. That is, when

---

* Cliff Kopas, *Bella Coola.*

⁊ R. Romney, op.cit., p 26

they stopped from hewing down huge fir and cedar to build their cabins. What they tried to grasp was as illusive as the silt suspended in the bay.

In the fall, after the destruction of the towers in New York, my head will not work. I sit down to write, think of something else, tackle that, and give up. I can't concentrate. The things I should do I can't marshal the energy or initiative to begin. Too much has broken. How do I pick up the pieces? Colleagues and I went to noon mass at St. James Cathedral the day of the attack, and shared leadership of an open prayer meeting in our sanctuary the following evening.

God did not promise us seamless transitions and closure in our ventures, relationships, and communities. Death is real. Betrayal is real. Paul puts it best in his letter to the Corinthian church: love prevails. "There are, in the end, three things that last: faith, hope, and love. But the greatest of these is love." (*1 Cor. 13*) In the ancient Hebrew scriptures God offers us a choice between life and death. A choice to thrive in faith with care for our neighbors as well as to focus on the common good. "I set before you life or death, blessing or curse. Choose life then, so that you and your descendants may live" (*Deut. 30:19*). A number of things have ended now and will continue to end in our hopes, the nations, and our neighborhoods. I struggle to accept the vision of crumbling buildings by trying to bring order to other parts of my life.

Driving to the home of a friend and confidante, I head north and then west from Stanwood to Camano Island. Just as I cross the northern bridge from Everett over the Snohomish River, I appreciate the rich green valley of its spreading delta, the Cascade Mountains on my right, Puget Sound on my left, inspiring a deep breath as I pass the mushrooming housing settlements toward greater acres of farms amid random country roads disappearing into the rural countryside. It takes about an hour to reach Sue's home, a refuge on Saratoga Passage on the west side of Camano Island. Here heron croak hoarsely in the woods, eagles chortle their high scales, soar, and—if no one is running a chain saw or mower—the silence is deep and comforting. She and I readied wood for her winter stove, stacking cedar fence scraps to be split for kindling. Fitting the pungent, odd-sized pieces together on shelves in the shed made sense, as if we could order the world through our work. Fragrance bloomed as sun shone through the old maple, warming the scraps, dappling the ground. Prayer came more easily.

Creator of this amazing Universe, teach us how to love one another—even our enemies. Help us live into the love that will not let us go. And help us strengthen each other to come together in common understanding, so that we may contribute to the wholeness of this planet rather than destroy it piece by piece. Comfort the grieving, give peace to the lost, "drop your still dews of quietness till all our strivings cease; take from our souls the strain and stress, and let our ordered lives confess the beauty of your peace." (Fransson; end quote from John Greenleaf Whittier)

Two days later I sit with my parents, my eyes filling, as I realize how frail they are, how shaken by the ruthlessness in New York and its reverberations across the world. I should have come here first, I realize with remorse.

"We don't hear from the kids, we don't know what anyone is doing or when we'll see them," Mom laments. Dad looks uncomfortable as he tries to hear what he can grasp from her tone, his ears, in spite of the aids, no match for the conversation. I listen and nod. Suddenly I realize it is my younger brother's birthday, September 13. Lew would have been fifty-four today.

Five years my junior, Lew developed diabetes when he was 13. Fearless, creative, and unpredictable, he lived large with his many friends, his wife and two striking, athletic daughters. He went to college late, then graduated with two degrees from the University of Washington in art and communications. In his last years he painted portraits, Everett's historic houses, and his moods, volunteered for the Everett Historical Commission and dabbled with the antiques he had spent so much time rebuilding and refinishing in our folks' basement, keeping up with a limping cat he called "Lumpy."

Mom and Dad grieve more than a national tragedy. Lew succumbed to a fatal heart attack five years ago. It isn't long before one loss piles upon another, complicating its burden of grief, darkening our outlook so that we can barely put one foot in front of another. I share my parents' anguish, and, of course, theirs includes their youngest son and many more of their friends than I know. I am very, very sad.

As I prepare to leave, Dad walks over to his handmade cedar mantle, beautifully measured and fit-together into shelves and niches for books, a fragrant Chinese brass-covered wooden box and a portrait of his parents.

He insists I take the 300-day clock sent decades before, lifting it carefully off the shelf and packaging the glass bell for safe travel. Then he adds a framed collage of our oldest family snapshots from Norway: my grandfather Elias' parents, a postcard of a fjord Grandpa sent home from his visit to Norway after his wife's death and, lastly—the tiny, faintly tinted picture I remember of my grandmother, Joakima Antoinette.

CHAPTER 5

The Order Comes Apart

∽∾⊙∾∽

We grow spiritually much more by doing it wrong than by doing it right.

~Richard Rohr SJ. *Falling Upward.*

Although it is October, the cedars haven't lost their orange needles. The vine maple by the back deck is stunningly red and gold, projecting a warm glow in our kitchen. Early in the evening Dad calls. That's twice in a month, unusual because he's never called me just to talk. The previous week, when I was there for lunch, he touched my arm as I was leaving and, looking me in the eye, said, "Thank you for coming." Surprised, I was moved.

Several days later on a Sunday night, Ardene and I take chicken pot pies from a deli to their home. It is her idea to take them a meal, and I quickly agree. But when we arrive, my mother reveals, "We thought you had forgotten all about us," enthusiastically ushering us in, hugging us both.

"We said we'd come around 4:30," I say cautiously, taking off my coat, dropping it on the blue chair they received as a gift at their wedding 60-some years ago, heading for the kitchen.

"Oh, we thought you said 1:30, Dear. But never mind. Now you're here." All smiles.

I sigh. Unsurprisingly, she gets it wrong, and instead of being there for lunch we are indeed, very late. To a failing ear, 4:30 *can* sound like 1:30. And they must not have eaten! Things get worse. Mother had gotten lost on the way to her hairdresser a week ago. I am relieved to hear she returned safely home. The Monday following Dad tells us he took Mom to their general practitioner, Dr. Palmer. Why?

"What am I going to do with this growing evidence of their decline, and all the things I *don't* know?" I ask Ardene as we turn off Fowler Street on the way to the freeway.

"We don't know enough yet, and neither of us knows what each of them would actually accept," she says.

"Yes, but simple inquiries don't help. We learn a little, but not enough to know what Mom and Dad really know, or how things happened. I am growing more worried about their being alone." Ardene readily agrees.

Mom and Dad have loved how they simplified their lives in this home since 1964, never tiring of the yard work. Now the yardman mows the grass, but Dad still tinkers with his evergreen shrubs. Mother's garden spilled over with gladioli, pinks, iris, ivy, tulips, carnation, dahlias and daisies, the cut flowers forgotten now. In contrast Dad's beds are neatly trimmed and studded with rhododendrons spaced carefully in clean, weeded beds.

My father's on the phone again. "Your mother's not feeling well. Could you come up and see what's wrong?" It's a cold, sunny fall morning. I grab my jacket and hop in the Supra.

After our hellos, I discover that Mom is ill. I look for rubber gloves to clean their room and the bathroom on the spot, changing the bed. I notice that the bath fixtures are moldy and spotted with toothpaste and soap scum. It's obvious they are behind on the chores but do not see what's needed. Nor would Dad accept my help, which he'd hear as criticism.

A couple of hours later everything's back in order and they're both grateful. Since I am busy enough with my part-time roles at church and Seattle University, might they be ready for professional help with housework? I wonder, as I strip off my gloves. My father, who had been happily ignoring me, looks up from his book. I take a deep, soulful breath, and say, "Mom needs more help than she's getting, Dad. Could someone come in once in a while for the heavier work?"

"We're doing fine, Honey," he said in a dismissive tone. "We can take care of the few things that need doing," turning back to his book.

"Dad, I cleaned things that obviously have been forgotten. I think someone coming in every other week would be a great help to both of you. There's the bed, the laundry...."

"No, no, Cathy. There's nothing amiss. We. don't. need. help." Full stop.

I was not about to further the discussion. But how much more will I need to do to ensure that things stay this way? And how would I manage that, if Dad thinks the two of them are just fine? Dad is asking for help now when *he* finds it necessary. Without sibling input (no one sees them as much as I do), I am the one who can respond. Am I supposed to leave them alone, but rush to see them on demand? There is an endless conversation in my home about how to support my parents without decreasing their independence. That is a classic conundrum. We have no answer. It's time we did.

> *"So I wrote down all my fears, and as I folded up*
> *the piece of paper, I said to God... 'Look, I am putting*
> *this in your in-box, and I'm just going to wait*
> *for my next operating instructions.'"*
>
> ~Anne Lamott. *Operating Instructions*

My parents' increasing needs are hard both to anticipate and meet. Maybe there can't ever be good timing. How do people do this "sandwich" thing? Kids in school and aging parents? Demanding work and distances? I am free of kids, but I have two engaging positions 30 miles from their home, and no one but Ardene and I seem to be offering help.

Teaching Pastoral Communication Skills with my instruction partner, Gretchen, to graduate ministry students at Seattle University is stimulating and engaging, but it's church ministry that calls to me. I need longer-term relationships than a quarter here and another there. I have simply walked into my congregation and been drafted by the senior pastor who then retired. I don't even have a job description. The unknowns of my life outstrip the knowns. I am fortunate to have any time at all to respond to my parents' needs. What should come first? I recall that verse Dad quoted to me: "Though the fig tree does not blossom and there is no fruit on the vines....yet I will trust in God...." [*Hab. 3:17*] Is trust enough?

Back at home I lament, "How on earth am I expected to run to Everett every time Dad calls? Who else is he asking? And when he said, No, they didn't need help, that leaves it to family when much of the family is estranged." Ardene nods in sympathy.

"We've got to try," she responds, asking the questions and questioning the answers until some clarity emerges.

"When should we begin to look for a place for them to live? How will we know? If they don't accept help, do we have to wait until they're carried out on a gurney? Can we each offer time to try to pick up the pieces at a moment's notice?" I list whatever comes to my mind, Ardene nodding with understanding, because she had moved her own mother into her home in Edmonds while she herself was still working. Her mother lived there for two years until her osteoporosis finally necessitated a nursing facility. Ardene had offered "assisted living" herself in her home, but even at that her mother was alone all day as she worked. And *I* felt sorry for Esther. Ardene knew it couldn't be helped. She did everything she could.

Out loud, Ardene concludes, "I doubt there is much to do right now. Your father won't permit it. How about your brother or sister-in-law?"

First, I laugh. Then I say, "I'll ask. But until we know what's needed, we can't ask them anything, except to be ready for everything."

Talk about living in the moment. But managing it a day at a time in a 30-mile radius is impossible. Bemoaning what is, I pray with Anne Lamott: "'… so I am putting this in your in-box, and I'm just going to wait for my next operating instructions.'"* Ardene and I had both had long relationships before we met. She was separated, and within a few years so was I, trying to make new lives on our own in our fifties. We had both been counselors in high schools in Seattle. We met at conferences and college tours, discovering that our shared faith was important, as well as a love of music and literature. We took years to make a permanent decision. Adults who have accumulated furnishings and paintings, sound systems and plants, annuities and financial plans, not to mention debts, children, values and boundaries, have a lot to discuss before merging households in midlife.

Ardene's adult daughter often dropped in. But the first time I opened her refrigerator I found only a bottle of water and an apple. No leftovers, cheese, or wine? No munchies? I was astonished. My fridge was full of

---

* Lamott, Anne. *Op.cit.* p 39.

wine, cheese, chicken, avocados and romaine. She took main meals out. We took our time.

In her absence I realized I missed talking with her about…whatever I was thinking. I missed her. So after a time of gauging how best to protect each other's autonomy, we were delighted to blend our lives. Dr. Romney offered us a beautiful blessing at his sunny home overlooking Puget Sound surrounded by her daughter, my brother, and a few dear friends. In a few months we adopted Tully, a striped tabby who kept us both very busy keeping rodents and birds out of our house.

*"Talk about God cannot easily be separated from discussions of place."**

~Lane, Belden. *The Solace of Fierce Landscapes*

On my way to visit my friend Sue, I drove at full speed north on I-5 until the bridge over the Snohomish River to the straightaway to Marysville gave me a glimpse of peace ahead, breathing more deeply now as I drove further away from the city and into the woods, farms, beaches, and mountains. During our visits, Sue and I had fallen into a crab-salad routine, and we enjoyed that while she plied me with questions about my work and my folks, whom she loved. We had a glass of wine and relaxed while the sun fought the clouds and lost.

Then we walked down to the beach and kicked a few rocks into the wavelet surf. Sat on the bulkhead just watching the wheeling gulls and boats heading north through the blue and white chop toward Deception Pass. Not much traffic today. Sue talked about clearing another couple of yards of blackberries and planting fern. And as I often do, I lost track of time and would be returning after dark.

Since it had rained, I steeled myself for a highway obscured with road spray. But to my delight the sky had cleared, and as I ascended the steep rise of the hill heading east from the west side of the island I found myself in the midst of a dome lustrous with stars. Astonished and fascinated, I guided my dark red car to the shoulder at the top of the hill, turned off the engine, and stepped out into the night.

Heaven itself had descended. I was surrounded, held by a million brilliances in galaxies light years and millennia away. The great expanse

---

* Lane, Belden. *The Solace of Fierce Landscapes*

of space offered silence; but presence radiated within it. I wished for all the world I could fly into its midst. But I needn't have moved an inch. I felt known. And as safe as if no single event, person, or trouble I knew on earth would ever dislodge the serenity of all. How small I am. Yet how loved. When she felt something very similar to this awe, Medieval mystic Julian of Norwich wrote, "All shall be well, and all shall be well; all manner of things shall be well." For a blessed moment I knew everything that troubled me was known to God, as every hair on my head was known, the sacred resting ever so lightly around me all of the time.

It is December. Christmas approaches, the time of my winter birth fifty-nine years ago. I was two weeks late, arriving on the afternoon of the Christmas concert at church. I used to joke I hadn't wanted to arrive at all.

When I call to check in, as I am now used to doing, Dad got on the phone in his "official" voice to thank me for the red and white poinsettia I'd sent. Nice. As I was readying to hang up, he added, "At least it's better than a tree." I laughed. He wouldn't miss the chance to tell me what had been awry. Perhaps he's trying to be helpful.

On my next visit Dad makes a wide gesture at the room. "Notice anything different?" I look. The gold rug had been vacuumed? I walked to the kitchen to see that surely the sink had been scoured whiter than I'd ever seen it. As I was about to compliment him, he broke in with confidence, "No need for anyone to worry about us. We can take care of ourselves." Quite proud of himself, he had hired a maid service. Two people worked three hours to clean the house top to bottom. See if I offer to do anything for *him* in the near future.

On my birthday, the 20th, a large bouquet of red carnations and white gladioli arrives. My father is trying to impress me. Not a bad thing. I rebuke myself for my suspicion and mistrust. As I respond to my parents' growing needs, I should be kindhearted. They have every right to remain as independent as they can. I don't have an official capacity to direct their lives, anyway. I'm just trying to be helpful. (Prescient words.)

They have been independent for the thirty-five years since their children moved out on their own. They know no other way of being. Even asking for help challenges their concept of who they are. Do they even think of asking? They appear not to want to move. So that means they will stay in their home as long as they can until one of them falls or suffers an illness. And they're not talking about that because in itself, talk is a harbinger of death. No matter the precedent that his own father moved to an "old people's home" in his late 80s and lived to be 94. But Dad isn't ready to let go of his home, which equals his independence. He wouldn't know who he was.

On Christmas Day I drive to Everett and, leaving my car at their place, drive them back to our home about 18 miles south in their car. Once we arrive, Mom and Dad walk up from the driveway to climb the five stairs to the porch of our split-level and then six carpeted steps inside. Not used to stairs and surprisingly frail, Dad pulls himself up hand-over-hand by the balusters. I am stunned.

Ardene and I have knocked ourselves out to serve them a deliciously juicy Spencer roast of beef, perfectly done medium-rare, with mashed potatoes, green beans, and aspic. Mom loves our dinner and our home, the candles, my hand-made crèche from Provence, and the tree decorated with silver and crystal ornaments. They are picky eaters except when we fix them a meal (corned beef and cabbage on their March anniversary, turkey for Thanksgiving, beef today). True to form, they clean their plates and leave room for dessert.

"Ever notice how much they eat when they're here?" Ardene asks. She's right. How fortunate we are to have found each other in middle age and recognized common values: faith, walking, music, keeping a house. Reading, independence, interdependence. This dinner was an idea we visualized together, and I'm glad we could share it.

"…their plates were clean, weren't they?" I say, and she nods.

It is harder to get their attention. Dad, merely polite and as deaf as ever, is missing much of the conversation and Mom is bewildered by our house; she is not really sure where she is. She gazes at the tree, its light reflected in her brown eyes, pets our striped tabby, Tully, and enjoys a number of sweet hugs. Dad presents us with a Christmas card. Inside are two $20 bills—one for us each. I am instantly transported to my twenties, when $20 was a substantial gift.

Before I can respond, he asks, "Do you still have the print I gave you?" He framed many of my prints in his Custom Frame Shop on Hewitt Avenue, no doubt remembering most of them.

"Of course. The Elton Bennet is downstairs in my study. Want to see it?" I have collected a number of prints he has framed for me for no charge, which is saying quite a lot.

"No, that's okay," he says, although I think he'd like to. He's afraid (and I am afraid) he won't be able to get down the stairs and back up again. After marionberry pie, all four of us pile back into their car and return to Everett. They are tired—too much new information, too much company. Once they're safely inside their cozy brick home, we say goodnight. But as Ardene and I drive away, I say, "I feel irresponsible leaving them alone in their house on a dark night." She comisserates. How do I let go of my constant worry of what could (and has) gone wrong in their home? "Well," says Ardene, "your dad hasn't yet given permission, and so far, we haven't met a situation that required it."

I am thinking it cannot be very far ahead of us—and them.

We lived by habit when I grew up in Everett, circumscribing the world, shrinking it to fit. To be with my parents now is to see how small it is to them still, though I know some of that is fatigue and forgetfulness. I feel protective and wish there were something I could do. Given how they limited my own aspirations for college and rarely inquired into my subsequent relationships and professional pursuits, it's a wonder I am so solicitous of their needs. This might be compassion, or obedient attention to putting them first. They display a not uncommon lack of authentic intimacy among families like ours. Nevertheless, I am the only daughter, and the one who shares their interests in faith, in art, and music. My older brother keeps his distance and though he is a bright, sensitive man, he has maintained this space because of his early parenting. I don't think he can be helpful now, and moreover, I feel protective of him and the tension between him and his father. So what does that mean for Ardene and me? I think we know. No one else has appeared on the scene, and the circumstances here tell us the time is now.

Expect the unexpected.

~Heraclitus

On a crisp January morning in the long-awaited new year of 2002, I stop in unannounced, only to find no one home. Rare. Knowing how tightly Dad controls their affairs, I pause, and then take the chance to look through the papers in Dad's roll-top desk in the den. He's very neat. Cancelled checks, lists of contributions on lined paper, bills to pay, all in pigeon holes and all up-to-date. Not much else. A few folders lined up in the bottom right hand drawer. I am surprised there aren't more documents here. You'd think there would be at least last year's worth of bank statements or medical receipts. Without disturbing anything I can't replace quickly, listening for their car in the garage, I pull out a file labeled "Will" and open it.

I read enough to see that the only time my brother and I are named is in an item noting that if both of our parents die, we would each receive $1,000. Not 10,000. One. Astonishing. Everything else—proceeds of the sale of this house, their bank account, and a few investments—are bequeathed to a local foundation. I find a recent statement, quickly add the other approximate assets to that, and make some calculations. We have been left out.

"I'll be damned!" Dismayed, hurt, and angry, I stop cold. For all my striving to get my parents' attention, especially my father's, all the achievement that I imagined would someday garner some sort of blessing (*Well done, good and faithful servant....*), it turns out that I will not share any significant possessions or assets?! I have never tied my own work ethic and achievement to a monetary award or to Dad's approval. Unconsciously, of course, yes. Wouldn't any daughter? Dad's approval? Tears well in my eyes as I stand and walk to the window, feeling betrayed. I can hardly breathe. My sense of peace? Shattered. I feel as if I've been socked in the stomach. I work hard because I have high expectations of myself. I find my work deeply meaningful. Frustrating and endless, but meaningful. To find my father turning his assets over to charities alone (his hand is written all over this; I doubt my mother had a say) flies in the face of what he might have been proud to share with his remaining children. I feel like raging and crying both.

Why should I continue to engage with a man who, after 62 years of marriage and fatherhood, still can't communicate with his two remaining kids and daughter-in-law? A man who never paid for a single college course of mine. Never wrote a check to get me, or my brothers as far as I know, out of a jam, certainly not to give us a stake in anything. I used to think Dad helped my brothers from time to time, doubtless because both of them had children, or perhaps because they asked for it or seemed to need it more than I. He never offered me much. Oh, a mature fern he didn't want any longer—and a half-barrel he bought for his yard but didn't like and charged me $35 to take off his hands.

Why do I keep trying? Faithfulness to my mother, even protection, and respect for my elders, even those I do not like. But there is something of misplaced duty here. Has he done just enough to show up at my home when I lived alone, or urged Mom to accompany him to visit the churches I've served?

Scripture declares that Jesus came not with peace but a sword. A sword between the generations, fathers and daughters, for example. Perhaps I'd glimpsed beyond his expressionless face to his inner motivation, thinking what he did was love in action, rather than in words.

Well, this is something he has done. And it's certainly not done in love. Damn!

I am reminded how, to my dismay after my first year of teaching, I discovered I had had too little income withheld. I owed $200 to the IRS. I asked Dad whether he could lend me a couple hundred dollars. My annual salary was $5,000; $416 a month. Imagine! And there was a car payment and ongoing tuition to pay. I was still taking courses at the UW for my fifth year. I played the organ twice a week to supplement my income, so I had only one day a week for myself, when I corrected papers.

"What do you have in your savings account?" he asked.

"Oh, about $400," I answered truthfully—hard-earned, scraped together, hold-my-breath and hang-on-for-dear-life savings.

"Well, that's what savings are for," he declared. End of discussion.

I did not argue with him. I just went away believing I hadn't made the grade. When you ask for a favor from your dad, and he says no, what are you supposed to think? That the denial is in your best interest? It was a small amount, but it was a token added to an already large storehouse I had of being slighted. I felt rejected then. And I feel *persona non grata* now.

I perch on the chair in the den, alone in the empty house, and ask myself: "Will I always be on my own without his blessing? What will it take? Dad apparently has begun to rely on my support without—so far—responding graciously in return. Is he taking advantage of my generosity? Why am I so considerate of my parents? Not for money, of course. Because of common faith? How can it be common if our values are so far apart? To see that in the final analysis, charity means more than his children and grandchildren—none of us is named in his will—I have to reexamine my priorities."

I quickly put everything back where I found it, walk to the kitchen to write them a brief note telling them I was there, and head out to my car.

I need to fire my father.

My next sermon captures some of my own surprises. "The spiritual life does not progress the way a worldly life does, its sign-posts say paradoxical things like 'what appears to be a detour may be the most important leg of the journey.' They say 'sometimes we travel furthest by sitting still.' They say 'enemies' and 'aliens' may make the best traveling companions."* I continued, "On such a journey we can see our progress sometimes only by the wake of our boat, trailing off into the fog behind us. That means that when we outgrow our image of God, we invent a new one to fit. That means that when our foundations are shaking, we learn that God embraces even the shaking and brings something new to our lives.

"The most widespread God language is metaphor. In a lucid moment all of us might agree that God is not literally our father, but a figurative father, a god who acts like a father, protecting and nurturing children. So of course, God can be mother as well. God is like a father, like a mother... and not literally either. Remember, 'We cannot think God; we can only know God,' Chittister said. We can know how God feels to us.¶

"So the invitation is, if we haven't done it for years, we had better get acquainted with God anew. Because this God, who may shake our foundations, I suggest will never shake our faith. If we know who our God is, then terrorist attacks may shake our foundations, but they will not shake our faith. If we know who our God is, then conflict and opposing opinions will not shake our faith. Sexual abuse of children will certainly shake our foundations, but they need not shake our faith. Our faith in God can withstand even the failure of the church. By this term I mean

* "Paradox Road," *Weavings,* Judy Cannato

¶ Joan Chittister. *In Search of Belief.*

only the bureaucracy we have built. Because a church that is enlivened by a real God in relationship with us, can never fail."*

On a Saturday a few weeks later, I'm attending an all-day seminar in Seattle on handling reports of sexual and domestic violence. Ardene calls to tell me Dad telephoned asking if I would come up. Ever faithful, after church Sunday, I do just that: drive to Everett, sit down on the couch in my usual place between Mother, on my right, and Dad, on the far side of the gold-carpeted room. He is smart-looking in a blue shirt, navy blue suspenders, and chinos. Mother is in comfortable purple slacks and a blouse. What's on his mind? I don't trust him. The house is heated to 78 degrees without a breath of air in the place. Mom seems at ease. We talk, but it is of no consequence. No news. No announcements. No questions.

I spend a respectable time paying attention, questions forming in the back of my mind, accepting a glass of wine. Then Mom and I head out east to visit a friend who just moved into a new house. Dad says he is feeling weak and chooses to stay home. So it's the flu. When Mom and I return, they both see me to the door and wave as I drive away. He made no attempt to tell me anything.

The very next day, I pick up the ringing phone and it's Dad once more, asking me to come to Everett. The mystery is too much, so I ask Ardene to come along. She is just as curious, and it gives us time to talk.

When we park at the curb, Dad greets us, and says with an edge in his voice, "I feel weak." So it's *not* the flu? He has no other descriptive words for his feelings. He never has had. I had a dearth of vocabulary for feelings as well, but as I've grown and changed, I have added thousands. He adds, "I'm exasperated with myself." Is he malnourished? Dehydrated? A number of months earlier his doctor suggested he stop eating only English muffin bread (his favorite), then splitting Lean Cuisine with Mom for dinner. When we learned they needed more nourishment, we had begun to stock the fridge with Ensure and whole grain bread. We add a few groceries every visit.

On the day following, Dad calls again, saying he's feeling better. What is going on? This is the third day in a row he complains about

---

* *The God who Holds us Back*, Fransson sermon May 26, 2002. Trinity Sunday.

weakness, but doesn't ask for anything. What can he mean? Why call to tell us? He is 97; he could be nearing death. Every time I've thought this, however, based just on his age, I've been wrong. I've bought two smart black suits, worn them on Sundays and at memorials, and then, as my figure and fashion changed, exchanged them for newer styles. Carl is still with us; he persists.

It's odd that the family somehow expects my father to precede my mother in death. He's actually healthier than she is. But Mom has always expected (hoped?) he would die first. Most of my life she's said, "When your father is gone, I'll travel, visit friends, eat out…." (fill in the blank). She wants to move to a retirement home. Dad's always been robust, but Mother says behind his back, (and perhaps just because of his age), she wouldn't mind if he "just slipped away." I doubt that's even possible. But then she would have the company she wants in assisted living, her meals prepared, her daily needs taken care of. She'd be the belle of the ball in such a place, wouldn't she? Maybe Mother is starving him!

Ardene and I are now in daily contact with Everett. Today it's Mom calling at 8:10 in the morning. I leave my habitual journal writing with a sigh and answer in the kitchen.

"Your dad has been taken to the emergency room. Can you come up and take me to the hospital?"

Alarmed, I ask, "What happened?"

"He's still weak. He thinks he's dying," she says, not without a little sarcasm. Since I know further conversation will get us nowhere, my only recourse is to drive up and see what is going on for myself.

Ardene quickly joins me and we meet Mother at the back door in her gray blazer with a lavender chiffon scarf arranged at her neck, her eyes fearful. She climbs in the car and we drive the short distance to Providence Medical Center which overlooks the Port of Everett. The Kimberly Clark plant (once Soundview Pulp Co. and then Scott Paper Co. where Dad worked) steams away in the distance against an early blue sky, and the ships of the Naval Depot are quietly moored at the piers. It is 9:40 a.m.

When the ER admits a man of 97, they make assumptions: he's nearly dead, he's incoherent, or both. Of course, since Dad is deaf, they can draw all the conclusions they want and he can't contradict them. That's a major problem, too, and I try to negotiate what he needs. I find myself at once sympathetic, and then unreceptive to what he says because he has been so callous to me. But I keep trying because I have eternal hope—not in him, but in the universe. I hope I am not unrealistic, too, but I try faithfully to offer love where there is nothing but impassivity or anger. This is my father! Friends and church members are one thing. But he is the one I was about to fire.

He lies pale beneath slim cotton sheets on a narrow gurney, his face a mask of misery, feebly accepting every test they offer, hearing virtually nothing of what is said. They run through the basics: heart, lungs, kidneys, bladder (he'd had some sort of procedure in December for bladder stones), blood and urine labs. Nothing. The doctor, younger than I, heartily and loudly announces to Dad, "Your heart is better than mine."

Dad is not pleased. He wants to stay where he is. He is disappointed to be released. In hindsight I recognize he's so tired he can't imagine coping, but apparently he is not ill. He is just tired. Ardene and I suspect my mother is harder to keep up with than Dad will admit. This explains not only the sticky notes but my father's fatigue. But he can't say he's tired. "Tired" is translated as weak, and weak is disgraceful. He's hoping for diagnosis of some real condition that would grant him a rest. He needs an excuse.

I had no real grasp of my parents' medical conditions beyond Mom's long-endured arthritis and high blood pressure and Dad's failed hearing. I knew about the outpatient bladder procedure because my sister-in-law informed me that they told no one about it, and it took all day at the clinic where Mom waited alone without eating. She was too confused to ask someone for help, and finally called her. My sister-in-law brought Mom a sandwich. After that, I told Dad I was upset I hadn't known they needed help, and that he had asked no one to look after Mom. It is time I know more than they're willing to tell me. He apologized, thankfully.

Dad is exhausted, but, as we soon learn, unable to say so to someone who might actually help. It's the old struggle between his image of strength and giving in to the truth. Mother croons over him as he lies there, hoping something tangible is wrong. "Come home, Carl, I'll take care of you. I love you." She smooths his graying-blond hair, kisses his forehead. Tears come as she thinks she might lose him. I watch them closely, swallowing my own tears.

Then Dad winks at me. Really? When Mother moves away from his side, he beckons me forward and whispers, "She can't take care of me. She doesn't know what she's doing." He's pleading for help. But what does he mean?

When he is released the four of us pile in our car and journey home. It is not long before I understand what he meant to say. Mom is not able to handle even their long-familiar routine. It appears she can no longer manage the household as she has done all their married lives. Dad feels vulnerable and overtired and is finally (finally!) reaching out. He has to remind her what time it is. She can't remember when or how to put food on the table, even though their schedule is so fixed that the times and the menu have been firm for years. She forgets where he has gone when he runs errands. The notes proliferate. And he is exhausted keeping up with her. By observing more closely, I begin to understand. If you're paying attention, the decline of our elders is told in fits and starts, in details after long hiatuses and ever-growing evidence. This is all we have if they're not going to talk about themselves.

Once Ardene and I get them safely in the house, the two of us go on a shopping trip for groceries. They clearly need more than this: someone to fix their meals at least three days a week, clean the bathroom and kitchen, change the bed. I'm about to look for resources. Suddenly Dad seems open and ready for support, and yet I wonder. I ask myself where my own altruism is coming from. I had been ready to fire him, so how can I honestly offer him what he needs? I can support my mom, but my dad? This, no doubt, is a theological issue—the call to love my enemies. A very difficult thing to do.

There are countless stories throughout Scripture about welcoming the stranger, not tolerating, but loving our enemies, and turning toward rather than away from those who hate us. I am more convinced that the very things that alarm me I need to pursue. If we are to live an abundant life, we need to take risks. My very life is at risk in this culture, even though it is changing as we speak. I don't talk a lot about the gay world because my very presence in the pulpit is a statement by itself. Sometimes the silence in others, probably even in my dad, is a sign of disapproval or, at least, doubt. I need to meet that flat affect to test out its truth before I walk away doubting myself. He's given me a lot to test my ability to take risks. Now is a time of true encounter: make or break.

"The basic requirement of the spiritual journey is to pay close attention." I said, as I launched into *The Rules of the Road*, my sermon on Romans 12:1-8 in August of 2008. "'In the beginning, you weep… The starting point for many things is grief….' writes Belden Lane."* I was at a loss when I entered Seattle U in the summer of 1996. I, too, wept.

"The language of the spiritual life is paradox," I say, returning to my sermon on the rules of the spiritual road. "I find God through Mystery, not definitions and rules. Somehow when I have given up the need to know, I begin to learn. What may appear to be a detour could be the main road. When what you do is interrupted, that very juncture maybe be the most blessed moment of the day. Being too careful will keep us from risks that may be well worth it. Sometimes we learn the most by sitting still. Instead of covering distance, to learn to ponder, to reflect, to mull things over, to wait, and wait…and wait more. St. Paul sounds like a coach exhorting his team before a game. His words are full of intensity: 'have genuine love, hate evil, cling to what is good. Love one another, rejoice in hope, be patient in suffering, persevere in prayer.'

"There is nothing wrong with these exhortations. They are just darned hard to follow. Practice is the way of this life; it isn't achievement. It's not a rung on the ladder to success or heaven. We have already arrived when we thank God—or Mystery, or Spirit—on waking, and set ourselves to one day, one moment, even, of practicing love, joy, peace, patience, kindness, gentleness, and self-discipline. One. at. a. time. And forgive ourselves all the time. '….sometimes, courage is a voice at the end of the day saying, I will try again tomorrow,' writes Mary Ann Radmacher."⸿‡ A week later I visit with my parents at our usual places at the kitchen table. They seem to have returned to normal. Then Dad asks me to take him to his doctor's appointment with Dr. Palmer, his primary physician. Not only that, he asks me to drive. This is a request I never anticipated. Feeling awkward, I get into his Dodge in the driver's seat. He seemed relaxed.

---

* Belden Lane. Op.cit. p 25

⸿ *The Rules of the Road*, Romans 12:1-8, August 31, 2008

‡ Radmacher, Mary Ann

In the waiting room Dad sits silent beside me. I notice a number of elderly people sitting alongside others like me who are their parent's companion. I am part of a new social class: middle-aged children accompanying their aged parents. Who knew?

"This is my daughter, Cathy," Dad announces from the examining table as the doctor enters the exam room. I stand and greet the doctor, then sit again, called like an acolyte into Dad's presence when he is completely vulnerable. He has unbuttoned his crisp striped shirt to reveal his pale Norwegian skin. I have never been this close to him when he's not in charge. He is calm, innocent, seemingly without an agenda. When have I ever experienced him without one? Comfortable, too, as if I am always with him. I am hyper-alert.

The doctor pronounces most of Dad's concerns easy to handle, so without learning much, I drive us home, park the car in the garage, and we go upstairs to return to Mom. After we settle into the living room while Mother is making lunch, he turns to me to ask, as naturally as if it followed the doctor's appointment, "Would you like to see the will?" I'm damned if he doesn't leave the room, then return and hand it to me. We have crossed some sort of threshold! I am speechless. It's as if he read my mind.

"You and your brother will each get an equal sum," he said. "but you might not want anything, because there are so many people in greater need than you."

Ah, he's not kidding. I do not respond. With what I now know, he assumes the two of us need/or want nothing, especially in relation to the great needs of the poor, the hungry, the homeless and those in prison. Ever the faithful Christian to everyone except his family. He provided well-enough for us and we've been on our own for years. But how on earth could he think he could leave us with only a token of the mutually-owned estate? Never asking us anything about our lives? Or does he simply prefer to give to foundations more than to his children and his five grandchildren? Parents do that. A broker has told me similar stories about her clients. Dad continues in a matter-of-fact tone, asking me, "Do you want to be the power of attorney, and have a key to the safe deposit box?"

No! He has decided to ask me to be his DPOA? Chosen to show me the will? Take me to a meeting with his attorney? I am stunned, trying to nod, helpful but full of conflict with my inner self—the one who's shout-ing, "My brother should do it. My brother should!" That role ought to go to his eldest son, shouldn't it? Ironically, given their enmity, I still have expected for years to defer to Dave, even though he and Dad have been at logger-heads for as long. I'm saddened for my brother, but he may not want to be burdened by this role. Easy way out, Fransson. Wait till someone else steps up and avoid the risk. Frankly, I don't know how Dave and Dad would ever come to détente. I must have nodded, or simply not disagreed, because he's way ahead of me now. No process, obviously, no give-and-take. No discussions. No asking if I am willing… for God's sake. Is this how he operates with things this important? I feel sorry for my mother.

"I'll call my attorney and we'll make it official."

Done. That was that. In a very short time, I have come from total shock at Dad's lack of foresight for his heirs to being named his legal advocate. I can't find any of the words that I usually do with colleagues and clients. I become something of a willing subject in his empire, afraid to engage with him, and still afraid to speak my mind. Obviously, his last trip to the ER helped him turn a page in his life: since he needed help, I was the apparent choice.

It seems that those of us who decline to step into our own power, preferring to defer to those who wish to control us—stronger or not—tend to back into the shadows of the main scene, letting others speak for us. We're used to it. So used to our self-effacement that we gladly allow others to propose action, arrange for help, buy the tickets, choose the destination for the journey.

I tell Ardene, "I must admit that I wished my brother had taken charge of these issues. I've never done them before except for myself, and I have no confidence I could make the right choices for my parents—es-pecially my father. I feel exposed." On the other hand, I think, now that I've committed to honesty and forthrightness, I need to accept Dad's of-fers or clearly refuse them. He is treating me an as ally who is able to take on the procedures needed in the next however-many years. I've always felt invisible to him. I'm having a hard time adapting. And it's a big job, though clearly I have his support. So, I take a deep breath, hold it a mo-ment, then let it out very slowly.

I await new operating instructions, awed at what is opening up, fearful of censure. I want his choice to be real and to last, and I don't believe there isn't some catch. Is this the way blessings are bestowed? Is it a blessing after all? Why? Why now? What has Mother had to say about it?

CHAPTER 6

Trial and Error

❧❧❧

Dad climbs comfortably into the passenger seat, not having driven for a month—is he losing the will to live? Certainly he is without the energy that he—and I—are so used to. We park near the health clinic and he takes my arm as we walk slowly to the entrance. I am quickly recalculating our relationship, adjusting to his demeanor, and his reliance on me. This time, he gets no satisfaction from his visit. I learn nothing, as well. But we are getting used to walking together. I am surprised, even pleased.

Two days later Ardene and I are pondering how to deal with Everett. She has just retired from her position as a counselor-supervisor in the graduate program at Seattle Pacific University. But I am driving to Seattle four days a week, both to SU and church. Mother calls and leaves us a message: "I can't do a thing with him!" She thinks I can? When Ardene calls her back, Mom says with fervor and distaste, "He trusts Cathy. He only wants to talk to Cathy." I don't believe it. He's never asked for me before. Never for himself. I ask Ardene, "Did he never need to? Has he always trusted I would be there for him when he needed to ask? I am amazed."

Ardene answers honestly, "Whatever the reasons, this might be the chance to grow closer to your dad—if it's possible. You need to say yes."

What he has done is make me his Durable Power of Attorney. He didn't ask me; he appointed me. And, unquestioningly, I accepted what I had believed was my brother's birthright. A few days after this doctor's appointment, Mother, Dad, and I file into his attorney's office. There are musty-looking, well-thumbed files stacked akimbo on every flat surface, including a desk which looks as if it's built for a larger man.

With my encouragement, Mom suggests changes in the will. She is eager to have her remaining children included in a proportionate way along with their legacies to the charities they support. Dad is unusually quiet. I assume he can't hear well enough, and perhaps he isn't feeling well. With almost no discussion, we are done. I am now the power of attorney with the responsibility to take care of Dad's affairs at his direction, and my parents will have a new joint will.

Through it all, Dad is not mute, but unresponsive. His silence may be due to his reluctance to disagree openly with his wife, especially in front of a respected friend. That is, if he could even hear her. His eyes are cast down much of the time.

The very next day, Mother calls once more. A month of surprises.

"The paramedics have taken Dad to the ER. He couldn't pee."

Dad had a Foley catheter inserted and was already released. I find him at home with my mother and brother in the living room. I am hoping I won't have to drive up here every day from now on. I shrug out of my coat as Dave and Dad stand in the middle of the living room attempting to attach the tubing to his leg.

"I don't think I can figure out how to work it," Dad says, half-dressed, as he and my brother fuss with tape. Mom and I look on. I am about done with how much I now know about my dad's anatomy.

> *"There are some things that we must simply wait to receive.*
> *We live our questions and wait for the knowing to happen.*
> *Like the tree, we wait for the sap to rise."*
>
> ~Sue Monk Kidd, *When the Heart Waits*

In a rare meditative moment I pick up my hand-thrown cereal bowl and reminisce about my teaching English at Garfield High School in the late 60s, an inner-city school in Seattle's Central District. When the demonstrations for African American civil rights were in full blossom my English classes were chaotic, hard to keep focused, often interrupted, and sometimes canceled altogether. In only my third year of teaching, I was exhausted.

To find order in the chaos, Garfield tried several new class-period strategies. One was eight-periods spread over two days: four classes of two hours each on two different campuses: A day, and B day. (Planned to confuse everyone.) I could productively handle a two-hour preparation period, but a two-hour class of juniors whose attendance and attention were at best erratic? Yikes. I began to find solutions only in my relationships with my students, many of whom I still remember with fondness.

I followed one of them to the pottery lab a block north of us at an old empty elementary school. Kevin taught me to throw clay on a wheel. I loved it and the skill it took to pull a recognizable thing out of the mud. Throwing pots healed my tattered spirit. I use my handmade bowl nearly every day for granola and yogurt, berries and cream.

I hold this, and still prize the other misshapen bowls for the health I found in making them. I have only several that survived the last thirty-plus years; this one takes me back to the time I found solace in the silent, mystifying exercise of letting the pot make me. On very cold Saturdays in the winter I entered the only unlocked door in the school and made my way to the pottery studio. I felt seditious, like the roots that burrow energetically yet unseen in winter's ground. The chunk of clay I circle firmly with my hands smooths slowly while it accepts my pressure. Maneuvering the clay is like digging in the dirt. It is grounding. Choosing a glaze was guesswork, depending how many glazes had gotten mixed up. The result? A marvel. Almost magical.

In the garden, too, more is going on than we can either see or imagine. Trees experience their greatest root growth. All their energy is turned inward, with a resultant plunge of roots deep into the soil to find hidden ground water and to support greater spring growth. Scripture speaks of trees planted beside flowing waters. Those who keep the faith "bear fruit in every season." (*Psalm 1.3*)

Think of those wounded souls in the gospels who finally encounter Jesus after years of wretched pain and isolation: the man by the pool at Bethesda (38 years), the bent-over woman (18 years), and the woman with the hemorrhage (12 years). They eventually generated enough hope and trust, with Jesus' invitation, to attempt the challenge of a new life.

During the months, years, and decades of stasis, revolutions brew underground. The Spirit works in our lives, weaving, stirring, teaching, until suddenly a whole person or a whole people takes charge of her/their life. Who can explain the years of waiting? The time underground? But who can deny the emergence of new life from what appeared only to be winter? I muse about the changes in my father after nearly 100 years of implacable silence, iron will, steadiness, and autonomy. And I pay attention to the mud; it is full of new life.

The phone rings. Seven p.m. Ardene and I look at each other. "Incoming," she says, as if we were a MASH unit. This time it isn't Dad. It's my mother. He has taken her to Providence Hospital because she couldn't catch her breath and was quite confused. Oh, God! One of them is quite enough, but both at once?! The unpredictability is debilitating. If I had had more wisdom I would have tried to get them moved. Either of them could fail. And it's already begun. We have no choice but to respond right now.

Mom has been given a diuretic and is stable, clearly unhappy having to pee all the time and, having forgotten why, insisting there is nothing wrong. Dad is slouched in a chair in the visitors' waiting room fast asleep, snoring, mouth gaping. Unfortunately, we have to wake him to take him home.

That's exactly what I need, too: a good night's rest. When will that be possible? What if Mom's dying? We are not prepared, and I am the designated hitter when the folks need help. I drive up early the next morning in the rain to sit with Mom while a technician administers an echocardiogram. Black and white flickering heart valves open and close on the monitor while he freezes frames systematically, measuring the chambers without uttering a word. Is she okay? How far off normal? Mother has had high blood pressure a long time; surely there is damage. I have never taken the opportunity to find out, nor has it been given. They've been taking care of themselves for 60-some years without sharing.

Because my parents have been so self-contained, so able, always keeping the details of their health and financial issues essentially private, I am less informed than I would like to be. They have simply waved off my interest and not wanted to say more, and I have avoided prying. Privacy is a high value in this home. I know they have living wills. They've talked about them, and appeared to be sharing what they had arranged, including funeral expenses, in case either of them dies suddenly at home. That's not usually the case anymore. But I have had no access to their records or permission to talk to their doctors. With my new capacity as Durable Power of Attorney, I am suddenly a committee of one. My brother and sister-in-law dropped in earlier, but I am on my own now.

A social worker, asking to speak with me, leads me to an upholstered bench along a glassed-in passage-way with a constant succession of people walking through admiring the lighted garden outside. She leans towards me conspiratorially.

"Your parents really ought to be in an assisted living facility," she begins. My eyes widen in disbelief.

"They're too fragile to be in their own home any longer. We're sending your mother home with a walker. She should use it whenever she gets out of her chair. And you must see that the access to the stairs to the lower floor"—where the laundry is, I immediately think—"is blocked. She shouldn't be going downstairs."

"Blocked?" I ask tentatively.

"Yes. She's too weak to be using the stairway or walking any distance without a walker."

I cannot quite see how to make this happen. I tell her, "My parents still live independently in their own home." As I am about to say, "We couldn't possibly limit their activity when we don't live with them, or close to them," silently I think, I am working in Seattle, for heavens' sake! And I am not Kesey's Nurse Ratched!

The social worker has simply gone on listing the limitations that will make my parents safer. I couldn't possibly make these adjustments for them, who still rule the roost as they have in our home since I was a child. No one else would get near the scepter while they hold the throne. I don't know what to do and I'm afraid. Since we (their children) have not addressed these issues, we have no leg to stand on now when it appears the time to do just that—take a stand. How do dutiful (read, *obedient, good little girls and boys*) take charge of their parents without their asking us? We need to appoint a caregiver, one who has the time and the resources as well. Now I am not so worried about the folks as I am about how we do something the family never has addressed and has no—or will have no answers for? We haven't visited this scenario at all, and now it is upon us. I fear failure.

"...and they should not be driving," she continues in perfectly measured tones while my imagination flies to the four compass points in amazement. I do have two jobs, even if they are part time, and I do live 30 minutes south of them. Now that I have clear responsibility in the matter, I am not sure whether to thank God for the opportunity or slay a lamb and lay out the entrails to discern what to do.

"I am relieved," Dad had said at the law offices when the DPOA papers and new will were signed. Little did I know then how close he was to handing over the reins. He is still adamant that he "would fall apart" if he had to move from his home where, from the back patio, he can see the stand of tall fir to the south and recall his years in the forests.

Meanwhile—with Mother safely at home again with her new walker, me with my official family position—work urgently beckons. It's not work, really, it's my passion, except that I feel as if I am trying to walk on a swinging tightrope in the fog. I have been asked to offer two back-to-back seminars for a career day for alumni at Seattle University tomorrow. The handouts are ready, and I need to prepare. My head is in Seattle, imagining how I will approach the former students who are have lost their jobs in the current recession and are looking for new work. The seminar is called "Changing Directions." My workshop? "Your One Wild and Precious Life" (a line from Poet Mary Oliver, apt for midlife adults). My heart is with my parents struggling under failing conditions. When this career day ends, I will drive back north on an increasingly familiar Interstate I-5 to take Mother to her best friend's birthday party. Suddenly my life stretches from Seattle north through Edmonds to Everett in a constantly turning circle: from Edmonds south to Seattle, 15 miles; then Seattle north to Everett, 30 miles, and finally returning south to Edmonds another 18 miles. It's not Seattle to Southern California, but the worlds are so different that they might as well be.

Our Interstate 5 north and south roughly borders Puget Sound, but it's not a coastal route; one cannot see the water because of hills and subdivisions assembled between it and the beaches. Or the elegant view homes. Evergreens march along both sides of the freeway with a few deciduous trees punctuating the green. As I drive south into the Seattle city limits, there is a spectacular view of Mt. Rainier, the Northwest's touchstone to the Cascade Range—spanning from Mt. Baker in the north to Lassen in northern California. Someone remarks every day whether the mountain "is out," or lighted by sunrise, moonrise, and clear skies. East from my parents' backyard the Cascades can be seen, and not far from my home the view west is of the Olympic Mountains on Washington's Olympic Peninsula. It's not a stretch to say we are surrounded by mountains, and it's not unusual that in the 1920s my dad had college work driving tourists into Mt. Rainier National Park.

For the Career Day seminar, I distributed Mary Oliver's "The Summer Day," as a starter exercise. Very familiar now, I love it because it perfectly captures for me what prayer is: "how to pay attention." I also quoted Frederick Buechner.

> *"The kind of work God usually calls you to is the kind of work*
> *(a) that you need most to do and (b) that the world most*
> *needs to have done…. The place God calls you to is the place*
> *where your deep gladness and the world's deep hunger meet."*

~Frederick Buechner, "Vocation" from *Wishful Thinking: A Seeker's ABC.*

Buechner's definitions above distinguished for me the difference between a profession and a calling, or in the Catholic church, a vocation. And also what "deep gladness" ought to feel like when invested in a dimension of the "world's deep hunger."

Sometimes I preach. Not often, because there are four other pastors: an interim ministry couple, and two other part-timers like me, both male and more experienced. Although I resisted preaching at first, Dr. Romney insisted I do so at the very end of my internship. I love now to wrestle with Scripture, even seeking other churches or retirement homes for practice. I also write reflections on spiritual themes—not Scripture necessarily, but often the weekly designated passages for Sunday. I send "SpiritStones…a touch of the Divine" via email to a list that approaches two hundred people as I explore my experience, what I know, don't know, and am learning.

After the seminar, Frances' birthday party, and church on Sunday, Dad was admitted to Providence Hospital. Same song, fourth verse. Mom explained to me he fell Sunday night, lacerating his head on the glass-topped coffee table—again. (There is still blood on the rug.) The paramedics came but couldn't persuade Dad to go to the hospital. After ascertaining he was stable, they left. But early this morning, Mom called my sister-in-law and asked her to take Dad and her to the hospital after all. She had already spent several hours with the folks by the time she left me a message that she'd like to be relieved. I headed immediately to the hospital.

Dad was still in the ER. Doctors had diagnosed a low sodium level and a urinary tract infection (UTI). (How did this escape diagnosis a week ago?) The plan was to suture the cut on his forehead, put him on antibiotics and transfer him to another hospital campus where he could stay to regain his strength. I think, since he is nearly 98, this seems rather optimistic. Filled with sympathy, I hold his hand while the doctor sutures his cut. Dad worked so hard at being the patriarch that I never observed him needing support. I step into the role with awe.

Much later I brought Mother back to her home and fixed her dinner. It was probably one of the few nights she'd spent alone without her husband in 62 years of marriage. But it's not going to be the last. Mom was confused when we got home, asking for Dad, then quickly asking again, not remembering the last answer. I decide to stay the night, ask Dave to cover tomorrow and then return later in the week. I must be at SU tomorrow but my partner will have to lead our usually shared class. It is Gretchen's turn to offer the lecture anyway and she's eager to be supportive.

After a late dinner of chicken from KFC, I hoped Mom would grow calm and fall asleep. With the assist of a glass of wine and the meds she takes methodically from her pill caddy, she is snug in bed. Their house is quiet. The familiar click of the 300-day clock is missing: it's now at my house. Possessions have begun to change hands.

I take a deep breath realizing how close it all was, but I made it through the seminar at SU, Frances' birthday party, Sunday morning worship, and making this temporary move to Everett. Taking another, deeper breath, I pledge I can do this. Right now it seems I must. I make the bed in the guest room and try to snuggle in for a short night.

Saturday afternoon in their home before this emergency occurred, Mom modeled several blouses and sweaters for my appraisal. How should she dress for Frances' party? She chose a paisley silk blouse and a loosely-woven shrug-shouldered charcoal sweater with black slacks. She didn't look eighty-three at all. At Frances's condominium we saw Frances, of course, as well as Grace, Mary Elaine, Eloise, Delores, Roberta, Florence, Lyle, and Virginia and Frank—all still members of Everett's First Baptist Church. Mom was completely at ease: sociable, gracious, and talkative. This was a complete break from her solitary life as Dad's consort and her confusion of a few days before. She talked with her old friends individually with great animation and warmth. Since many of these people mentored me in the forties and fifties as well, I loved seeing them again. My life had changed, however, and I imagine they were curious. No one said a personal word or asked a question. It was Frances's birthday, after all.

There was a world of difference then between Seattle First Baptist and Everett First Baptist. Everett had been the paragon of large American Baptist churches for a number of years since my childhood, and before I moved to Seattle in 1968, but in the mid 70s they called a more conservative pastor who encouraged them to return to more credal theological rubrics. Rather than continuing their pairing with Seattle as a sister church, they became deeply critical of us for not upholding Biblical precepts. Of course for those who knew I was gay, my being called as pastor at this church must have been shocking.

But these friends loved Mom and me, and although they surely wanted to know how I had "strayed" from the Gospel, they seemed delighted to see us both. I wished there had been time and they had been open to a dialogue.

As we said our goodbyes and took the elevator down, Mom turned to me and asked, "Who were all those people?" Incredulous, I smiled at her in surprise, sighing. "All your friends, Mom; all your friends from First Baptist." She had been a Lutheran with Dad since 1962. He was a cradle Lutheran. But this reunion felt to me as if we had never left the church where she and I grew up.

How strange it is to step outside my life like this, especially here in my parents' home. It's not the home I grew up in, but one new to them when I was finishing college and had been married just a year. Two bedrooms on the main floor of this one-story house were a godsend to my mother, tired of running bedroom to basement, up and down two full staircases in the house on Colby. In one of their bedrooms now was a chute for dirty clothes that went directly to the laundry. "Luxury,"

Mother exclaimed. The Fowler Street neighborhood proved to be quiet (no Colby traffic). They saw generous glimpses of the setting western sun, as well as early morning rays at dawn in the east. The large yard offered ample room for evergreen shrubs as well as croquet space for the grandkids.

The next morning, after sleeping for perhaps six hours, I am sitting in the sun-bright kitchen spooning raspberry yogurt and drinking the coffee I brought with me (they still drink tea). Sunlight streams in from the Cascade Mountains but fails to melt the ice on the rhododendrons.

Mother is still in bed, but I hear her stirring. When she wakes, we'll drive up to the hospital to visit with Dad and see how he's doing. I suspect this is the beginning of the end, and we'd both better prepare ourselves.

We're told Dad will be released to a nursing home. I imagine once he's returned to his normal self, it will be time to find the two of them that "home" that Mom has so wanted to move to, a place where they can regroup as he grows stronger. I am forgetting entirely, of course, that Mom had her own emergency a few weeks ago and that her heart is certainly no better. But there is no time now to research retirement facilities, as well as take care of Mom's immediate needs for meals, laundry, and hair appointments.

The tasks are not difficult; they live a simple life. But I have a whole life of my own a city away! I look forward to a long talk with Ardene about what we can do together, and what others can do to help. I can't quite grasp being encumbered by them while I have such compelling opportunities ahead of me. This is mere wishful thinking. It is with not a little annoyance that I remind myself....

> *"Forget the things of the past,*
> *ignore the things of long ago!*
> *Look, I am doing something new!*
> *Now it springs forth—can't you see it"*
>
> ~Isaiah 43:18-19

...I hope I do.

CHAPTER 7

Betrayal

❦

I betrayed my mother. The two of us face each other in the social worker's office at Rocky Glen, the nursing home where Dad is already placed. Mom's red blouse and charcoal sweater punctuate her anger, always dreadful for me. My mouth is dry, my face blank, hiding fear and deep sadness. She has visited Dad here once; she knows where she is, and she knows it's not her home. She frowns at me, leveling her dark eyes, adamant she will not be admitted against her will.

"This is just for a short while, Mom. It's not safe for you to stay at home alone." My voice is soft and trembling, but full of what I hope is compassion and understanding. She has only rudimentary understanding of what is going on. "When Dad is stronger, the two of you can find a retirement home together." She glares.

Now in possession of and with the authority to use Dad's checkbook, I pull it out to write her first month's room and board of $5664. Still not sure of the full details of their assets, I wrote a similar check for Dad just days before. I blatantly transact this business in front of Mom, feeling careless and rude. The director waits for the check. There have already been hours of paperwork at home preparing for what I've arranged.

"I don't want to stay here," she is inflexible.

I repeat my promises, not realizing I am lying, then sign the check with the notation "DPOA" after my name and hand it to the social worker.

Mom folds in on a fierce silence.

When we walk together back to Dad's room, he is no comfort. He lies passively behind the washed-out rose curtain that separates his space near the window from his roommate's bed. With nothing on his night stand he still refuses that I bring his Bible or magazines. Then he asks me to cancel the subscriptions to the three newspapers he subscribes to: *The Everett Herald*, *Washington Post*, and *Seattle Times*. He has no energy to read or walk, although he seems to be growing clearer as he sleeps most of the day. He needs the rest.

In a few days I'll find Mom sitting with him, but now she is assigned to a room with another woman several doors down. She did not accept this peacefully. She wants to be with her husband of 62 years, the man to whom she's devoted her life.

Ardene and I chose this temporary respite for my 83-year-old mother while we were trying to keep up with her for only the last few days, discovering how little she understood. I asked the nursing facility if I could place Mom there for "respite care." (For us.) Fortunately, Rocky Glen had room.

The night she stayed with us, the three of us sat together on our sofa looking through old photo albums. Mom exclaimed at pictures she hadn't seen in a long time, but with more fascination than seemed warranted (déjà vu the pumpkin carving last Halloween). We served a nourishing dinner, but every few minutes, regardless of what we spoke about, she asked, "Where is your father?"

"He's in a nursing home, Mom. We'll go visit him tomorrow."

"Oh, yes; that's right," she would reply with fleeting understanding. But then, not long after: "I wonder what's become of your dad?" We go through that again and again. After the albums, we encourage her to take a relaxing bath. Pouring bath salts into warm, but not hot water, we help her in, and she is all smiles. With towels at the ready, we lean in to help her out, but discover she isn't strong enough to stand by herself. Oh, foresight! God help us. We have no business trying to bathe her especially in this partly-enclosed tub. In the narrow opening the glass doors allow, we had no room both to hold and help lift her. We didn't know how to lift her properly in the first place. She was slippery and soft, and we began to laugh. She laughed, too, and we leaned in and lifted, to no avail. Wait. Let me try this. You hold her arm; I'll take her other shoulder...on and on. Eventually, Mom was up, then out, and all three of us were wet. Fortunate that no injury occurred, we won't attempt that again.

In the morning as we ate breakfast she took a number of pills out of her small caddy before we both drove her to Fowler Street in Everett. She said, "I don't think I'll be traveling quite as much after this. It's too hard for me." Ardene and I registered a hard look at each other. When I coasted into their driveway Mom recognized home. We walked to the back door, unlocked and opened it; she stepped inside and called out, "Dad? Carl, are you here?" She broke my heart.

In the last six weeks I have experienced so much life I have run out of days to live it. Life tripled. Events cascading in frequency and urgency so there is hardly time to process one before I move on to the next. In fact, I cannot process much of anything. The prospect of seeking professional help completely left my mind, I was so busy arranging details, moving clothes, doing paperwork, visiting my parents.

Others have envied my retirement from the schools with time to read, write, and study at Seattle University. But I can't remember when I last read anything unless it was *The Christian Century* while on an elliptical trainer at the gym. I can't even read the morning paper…much less to restore my soul. I've taken to listening to podcasts on my phone in the car from Krista Tippett's website *On Being*. Talk about a paradigm shift. I am reeling. The sudden and debilitating losses probably will not lessen. Where is my tidy theology in the midst of this whirlwind?

I had hit a wall. Perhaps, a "dark night of the soul" when all I knew how to do was to keep going on with what I had learned in the past. But I had no skills for what I faced now. And I had no time available to think this through in the tumult. This happens to all of us sooner or later. But after the crisis, and with help, we are designed with a capacity to ponder what problems ask of us and/or to invent new solutions. If we hold our personal experience together with common reasoning, and then with what faith/Scripture teaches, these three sources make a three-step tool that is called theological reflection. I am learning to take the time to weigh what I encounter day to day with Scripture, my values and thinking, lest I run off the rails trying to wrench an episode to fit my beliefs or vice versa, junking reason to apply beliefs to my life. Following the spirit of rigid religious tenets is quite difficult enough. And the more we try to wrench our agenda into a vision of holy peace, the more peace eludes us.

How can I get up early like Jesus does to pray before anyone else is up? Forget the early part. I'm the last one up. Although I tune my car radio to classical music driving to and from town, I go to bed promptly at ten and sleep most of the night, it's not the same as free time. That may be scarce in the next few weeks. I set up color-labeled files in my study for the countless responsibilities: bank accounts, bills, medical insurance, Medicare. I have three new sets of house and car keys, a house and assets I never imagined I would oversee. Chalk it up again to the lack of a discussion with our parents to consider just these responsibilities, not to mention eventualities. I could use some help! And Ardene is doing all she can.

I forget something every day. Since I know this is part of my grief and trauma, I try to let it go. This morning I forgot the cookies I wanted to take to church for the staff. Yesterday it was stopping at the cleaners to pick up my dad's shirts. Sunday it was the organist: I forgot to serve him communion. I am moving so fast a mirror would capture only a blurred image. Although I am surprised I am normal, I am relieved. We both know that losing things comes with grief. Ardene and I have no end of conversations about choices, alternatives, where to go for help with insurance, Medicare, and so on. She has done a lot of this herself, but it was 6 years ago. Things change.

This morning I listened to a church member as he shared a tender story. Quieting myself from my own inner din, several words "spoke" in my head—appeared, really: *Trust me. Just trust me.* I sighed. At least I don't have to rush to catch up with God; God is caught up with me. At such a time, catch-as-catch-can faith is comforting. Such words are rare. But real. If I am listening, I hear more of them. The first time they really surprised me was on the Sunday I first preached. I walked up the two steps of the platform to the large chair next to Pastor Romney and sat down anxiously in a spotlight with him. I asked myself, *Who do you think you are?!* The answer came before I ran out, *You are just where I want you.* I breathed more deeply. In this first crack at standing at the pulpit, attempting to sound like myself as well as to add value to worship, my knees shook, my breath was shallow, and I hardly smiled. This is how I began:

"The choir has just sung, 'This is the new Jerusalem that will not pass away. Jerusalem! Sing for the night is over. Hosanna in the highest; Hosanna forever more!' The narrator in the book of *Revelation to John* proclaims one day God will again rule the world, and there will be no more night, for the glory of God will be our light. Years ago in the Everett First Baptist Church youth choir we sang this anthem at the top of our lungs. It was always a pleasure to have an excuse to make noise.

"We were otherwise obedient in those days; silence was golden—and stifling. We learned that this new world of God was expected—not on earth—but only in Heaven after we got our 'golden shoes.' Here in this veil of tears, we were to pass like quiet and reverent pilgrims. But I didn't have that quite right: the pilgrims I pictured were from New England in broad-brimmed black hats with turkeys gobbling in the underbrush."*

I grieve and know I will grieve more. I feel guilty for my treachery with my mother, but there is no alternative. There is no alternative. Given her forgetfulness and bad heart, Mother *should have been here* a year or two before—or at least in assisted living, alone or with Dad. The nurses offer their professional assessment that Mother is in an advanced stage of congestive heart failure and vascular dementia. I wish I had known how bad it was! I grieve over the sadness of her isolation and her sense of abandonment when she cannot remember that her beloved Carl is just three doors down the hall. And *that* beloved Carl is the one who's been relying on her way too long. Was he neglectful or trying to protect her—or himself? He owed her more than this.

> "…we want our parents to remain decision makers and to
> be omniscient, to regain the sense of normalcy. We're upset
> when we have to take over their roles. We feel guilty about
> the role reversal. We assume moving them into assisted living
> declares loudly and clearly that we can't handle taking care of them."

[www.aplaceformom.com/planning-and-advice/articles/eldercare-decision-and-guilt]

One day in March, even though Mom and Dad are as settled in their separate rooms as they're going to be at Rocky Glen, the phone rings at 6:45 a.m. It's Mom, fiercely.

"I shouldn't be in this place, Cathy, and I want to go back home. Where are the keys to the car? And the house?" She is very angry.

---

* "An Unworldly Peace," inaugural sermon. Fransson. May 1998

"I'm sorry, Mom. Try to be patient; I'll be along in a few hours and we'll talk about everything."

"Where is the car?! If I can't find it, I'll just walk home. I know where I am." She's quite clear what she wants. I should have expected this, although her anger is usually expressed through silence.

The day before, she called to tell me that Dad was in surgery just down the hall. She didn't know when he'd get out. Could I come to sit with her until he did? Panicked, I called both the Providence and Colby hospital campuses as well as the nursing home, all within the city limits of Everett, only to find no one knew anything about a Carl Ramstad except the one who was sleeping soundly in Room 122.

Rocky Glen is not far from their home near a park and stands of evergreens. Mother may know that. But she wouldn't get far outside on foot in this cold weather, not knowing the way or why she was outside alone without any keys.

"Mother, you need to stay where you are, and we'll talk when I visit today."

"If I can't leave, then will you move in with me?"

Argh! If I weren't already trying so hard to make this work, I would simply cry. *I cannot fix this.* Fixing was one of my early vocations. But that is out of the question here. At some level I must let go. Easy to say, hard to do. As we deal with our aging parents, letting go is required. We are not in control of much of our lives, sometimes very little. Practice helps. Learning to let go of small things throughout adulthood begins to add up. In my case I need to trust the universe, God, and other people, whatever it takes. Grief is part and parcel of joy, eventually. It isn't happiness; that's for sure. But it comes to a deep joy—*eventually*, as Lamott might say.

After our conversation calms her a little, I drive to Everett and walk toward the locked doors at my Dad's, and now my parents' residence. I feel such anguish and fatigue that I imagine slipping into an empty room myself, curling up in bed, and welcoming someone bringing lunch. Years ago, Ardene, when beleaguered, used to say, I just want to live alone in a one-bedroom apartment! Now I understand. Stop the world! I want to get off.

When I saw *The Shawshank Redemption*,* I was in such personal tur-moil that I considered living in a locked cell block myself. An escape from the untold decisions and values I weigh—all of us weigh—every day. The presumed safety, the cloistering of it, beckoned to me. But that was a long time ago. I can't remember which trauma prompted the panic. I try to monitor those feelings now. They're a sign of serious self-care deficit. And there is no way prison offers comfort, full stop.

At Dad's care conference he is anxious to know if he could lose the sup-port he has, fearful he'll be released before he's ready to be on his own. He was so eager for help—yet couldn't ask for it. How sad. He's appreciative of everything anyone does for him. He told a care-giver, "I can put on my own socks and shoes, but it is so nice that you do it for me." He is grateful for the juice delivered in the middle of the afternoon. I have never ob-served him so gracious and accepting about conditions altogether outside his control. Where was he hiding *this*?

After visits to several retirement and adult family homes, Ardene and I find one that has both independent and assisted living south of town near Silver Lake. We used to swim there when we were kids when the area was rural. Now the lake is surrounded by housing developments. When I tell Dad I have found a place for Mom—a facility where she will have a room of her own, a bedroom and tiny kitchen with plenty of room for him to move in when he's strong enough—he is wary, remote.

At the same time I am afraid Mother will blow her interview. And instead of thinking she might not be eligible (she can't hold two thoughts together), I worry about her making a good impression. I am so naïve. I don't want to have to keep such close tabs on her. She has been com-pletely dependent on Dad and now can't remember where he is. She assumed they would be sharing a room and wonders why he doesn't come to see her.

Dad doesn't want her near him. He says he can't get any rest that way. And no one knows really how long he has been trying to run interference for her and cover for her, both. When he admits, "I can't have Mom in my room; I wouldn't get any rest," my mother is standing next to me. Her

---

* *The Shawshank Redemption* is a 1994 American drama film written and directed by Frank Darabont, based on the 1982 Stephen King novella

eyes widen with disbelief; she summons reprisal. And then something in her breaks. After her loyalty and support for over 60 years, I don't blame her. I am desolate to see her grief. It has never been clearer that my parents each have their own lives and have to live the core of self alone.

They're not my children. I can't save them from this grief. But were they my own children, I still couldn't save them from their griefs. We cannot rescue others from incurable disease or random acts of violence. Sometimes children, strangers, or even parents can be rescued from burning houses, or car accidents, or from accidentally stepping in front of a bus. Incurable disease like cystic fibrosis or cancer? Deep grief? Fear of dying? The last two, perhaps. If it is a mood disorder, there is a greater chance for a cure or medical intervention. But aging? When do we stop trusting how parents handle their own lives?

For my parents, I can only be present, loving, and prayerful about how they'll get through it. I recall the shock and grief of an elderly couple's final separation in the film, *The Garden of the Finzi-Continis*,* when husband and wife, dressed to the nines, carrying suitcases that were rudely ripped away, were abruptly walked in opposite directions by the Italian secret police. I can't get the scene out of my head. I dwell on the grief without respite.

It would be one thing if an invading army separated all families from their homes and children from their parents in this country as the German Army did in Europe, as border guards are doing to millions of immigrants in Europe and the Mideast today, and Immigration and Customs Enforcers in our own country. But these are my parents struggling to come to terms with how they will face the future when they must separate for absolutely natural reasons—death, which is usually the way it comes. Who knew—definitely not Mother—that Dad would outlive her? That he would be exhausted trying to keep her safe in their home because *she* was so disoriented? That she wore him out. And he needed to rest without her desperately needing his support. She can't understand. And no explanation will suffice.

I weep for my mother.

---

* *The Garden of the Finzi-Continis* (Italian: *Il giardino dei Finzi-Contini*) a 1970 Italian film, directed by Vittorio de Sica

On a spring-like day, I pick Mom up for the interview at the retirement home. She is glad to see me and ready to go. I'm thinking her memory is in her favor now. She's forgotten about Dad. It is sunny but cold, a good day for a drive. And I am filled with hope that this is a wonderful solution to the heartache Mother and I both experience.

Mom rises to the occasion. She is open, pleasant, alert enough to make conversation and pass muster. I'm proud and relieved. Fairly certain we can afford it with both their pensions and Social Security, I write a check for the first month's rent. But as we head back toward the nursing home, Mom struggles to catch her breath. Knowing this as a sign of fluid in her lungs, I drive straight to the Everett Clinic. The doctor who examines her on short notice immediately doubles her diuretic.

She's ready to collapse when I settle her back in her room near Dad, then walk out to my car and return home. It seems the height of carelessness simply to resume with paperwork after seeing my mother in such distress. But I am trying to clear a space in the midst of my parents' bills, my bills, their schedules and mine and I can't help Mother in this condition. She's in good hands where she is.

I take this in stride because I have to, but it's very difficult. I am fortunate I have a loving partner who cries with me and comforts me in the midst of my grief. I am also fortunate I followed two professions requiring growing self-knowledge and developmental maturity. We are no earthly good to others if we cannot take care of our own feelings, losses, and confusion. But even we do not do it alone. It takes companionship, therapy, group support, and ongoing friendships. A therapist who feels so needed that she sees any client who asks whenever he asks, will shortly run out of strength to help. This is unfair to the client. We sometimes have nothing to give.

This is where boundaries come in.* Apathy toward the complaints of others is flat-out lack of interest. A response shockingly like, "So what? Or Who cares?" Or "Look what I had to go through when I was fired!" —drawing energy toward oneself. Empathy sounds something like, "You look a little down. What's going on?" or "You look sad," in words that encourage openness and sharing—if desired. Finally, sympathy is belittling: you feel sorry for others because they can't manage their own bad luck.

---

* From *People Skills* by Robert Bolton

Empathy is *feeling with* the other, and sympathy is *pity*, as if the other needs rescue. My dad was annoyed with my older brother and pitying toward his youngest son. What did he think of me? I really couldn't tell you.

Good boundaries protect us from being absorbed into the moods of other people. Or assuming we can help them significantly. Sometimes, in small ways, we can. In many ways, there is nothing that can help.

It is nearly two weeks since Dad was admitted to the hospital, and one week since both my parents were placed at Rocky Glen. I am reeling—amazed I am still coping, processing the grief of my mother, the peace and relief of my father, and wondering what on earth could happen next.

With a newly-installed lead pastor at the church and my mother destined for an attractive new room with windows looking out on a stand of alder—soon to be joined by Dad as he gets stronger—I hope to regain my balance. There is a vision of something new for them and for me. Or perhaps I am merely adjusting to the unexpected and learning how to roll with the waves. So much change. I envision Mom at Silver Lake enjoying the view and the assistance, imagine Dad moving in for a whole new kind of life when worries are few for them both. I could return to my "real" life, right? But I envision many things. Some of them are not to be.

A few days before her interview, I had taken Mom to get her hair done and then to Anthony's on the Everett waterfront for lunch. Not many people on the roads. Senator Henry "Scoop" Jackson saw to it that Everett was awarded a navy yard that has taken the place of the pulp, paper, and lumber mills—somewhat more scenic. There is a steep bluff between the rail lines along the piers below and homes above; only the homes on the lip of the cliff have views of the Sound. The home I grew up in is almost adjacent to this restaurant, but 100 feet above it and three blocks east. In sixth grade my boyfriend, Jimmy, and I used to walk to the bluff to try to capture the sunset with colored pencils. Mom had a flair for art; I tried, but didn't put in enough time. Eventually I asked myself, do you have to do *everything*?

"Oh, boy!" Elated, Mom said, "We get to have a glass of wine."

With deep pleasure she took in the expanse of sky through the large windows, grey and blue water with low chop, boats rocking erratically at moorage. She loves being outside in the sun, the breeze caressing her hair.

After lunch I drove north along the tracks and industrial buildings with Puget Sound on our left, continuing on West Marine View Drive uphill to Legion Park at the very north end of Everett, encircled by the delta of the Snohomish River. I turned onto Alverson Boulevard where my parent's first home was, the one Dad, his father Elias and brother Art built in 1938. Flanked by the original pyramidalis they planted, the house stands today as it was then, still too small for two, then three children. I wonder whether Dad imagined just the two of them forever in a blissful twosome. Did he never imagine having kids? Once I was born, joining Dave when he was not quite two, we four moved closer to town for schools and bus service. Then Lewis joined us. I can imagine Mom also grieves these old memories (if she can call them forth) of her first days and months with Carl, her two pregnancies, and the realization they needed a bigger home.

As we continued south into town on Colby, passing 1810 where I grew up, Mom asked, "Can we go by and see Dad before we go back?" She was content, both tearful and joyful, but she had completely forgotten where Dad was, and was very weak getting in and out of my car. Fragile. I was happy the afternoon had gone so well and that I had had one more lunch to share with her. Every moment was like a mirage. It was there, and then it wasn't.

Synchronicity appears in the midst of chaos. A Jungian concept my good friend and colleague Gretchen mentions often, it delights me with its surprises and ironies. It snowed, for example, on March 7 just when I needed to stop long enough to take stock of the myriad dynamics loose in my world. In the Northwest snow is an excuse for staying home, regardless. The previous week I poked my fingers into a basket of small pocket stones in Seattle's Episcopal Book Store, fishing around with my nondominant hand, then pinching a partly flat rock and turning it over to find the word "Trust" incised in it.

No surprise. Near a myrtle-wood madonna and child in my study is a caramel-colored rock inscribed with the same word. I have a history with trust—or I should say, no history. I am wary much of the time, cautious. But I discovered in graduate school in both the '70s and the '90s— and in therapy—that the answer to anxiety was not to try to eliminate its causes, but to trust that God was in the midst of them (or, between me and those I asked for help). To live one day at a time, maybe even one hour. That doesn't come naturally. I don't know why it comes to me—but it is a gift. Faith enables me to make the leap between the familiar and the unknown. I can share it, model it for others, teach and preach about it, but I cannot give it away. Faith cannot be bestowed. Everyone must make that leap themselves. It's never certain that what we trust will emerge, *will* emerge. Faith grows as it's relied upon. Practice helps. Experiments work. Surprises appear. But faith itself "steals upon" us unawares.

Dad said he had "tension." An admission that caused all of us to walk on eggshells as if it were our responsibility. That was the thinking of the fifties. "Weakness," Dad would say, was colored by shame. His brother Art, a popular history teacher, had suffered from depression and been hospitalized for shock therapy in the 50s. Dad must have been afraid he would suffer the same fate. How sad that these two brothers (and no doubt their father) suffered from what we now know is a chemical imbalance. I was told by a professional who descended from Norwegians that depression was its "national disease." The hyperbole makes people laugh, but we laugh at our characteristic weaknesses, don't we? And Garrison Keillor made his fortune telling stories about Scandinavian eccentricities. A little counseling, perhaps therapy in serious cases, and medication all come into play here. We needn't suffer as we did in the 50s. We can learn to live with our mental illnesses as we do with our physical ones if we seek support, advice, and treatment.

Life is always a trust walk, as if I am stepping gingerly along a tight-rope unaware of how far I am from the ground. Instead of trying to eliminate uncertainty, I need to learn to live with it. All of us do. There is no way at all we can arrange our lives to avoid the unknown. It's part of what makes life Life. Stability can be reached only by an inner gyroscope that rights itself after a wobble, if we can say what we're experiencing and ask for what we need. That takes time, patience, and guidance.

As a remedy to the chaos, I brought home the dishes from my parents' home. Mom and Dad had no dishwasher, and I can imagine they didn't hand wash dishes thoroughly every day. I pulled on rubber gloves, grabbed the scouring powder and rubbed each dish with a sponge. Making a huge lather, I steamed up the kitchen window. Then I polished the silver and lathered that with lemon-fragranced soap. Finally, I put the whole caboodle into the dishwasher on the antibacterial cycle. An hour later dishes and flatware emerged with a satisfying shine. I had really accomplished something. The Zen saying is, "Chop wood, carry water." This, before enlightenment. And what, the student asks, will I do after I attain enlightenment? "Chop wood and carry water."

"No matter how menial the task may seem, practicing mindfulness and focusing on the present work at hand will help you develop a habit of always doing your best. And once you finally achieve "enlightenment" you still must chop wood and carry water. Do your work, do it well, and when you find success, do it again."

~www.lifehacker.com, four-confusing-zen-quotes-and-what-you-can-learn

Washing dishes made the day worthwhile in a way that meetings, phone calls, and conversations cannot. We never escape the daily tasks of living. Or we escape them at our peril. Jesus' parables are full of the quotidian, objects and natural phenomena that illustrate how God's care radiates throughout all that is, the miracle and the mundane. Somehow this lightens all work.

And then there is the time-honored memory of having to wash dishes after dinner at home on Colby when we were kids. That fell to Dave and me. Dishes came before we ran to the red plush chair by the Stromberg-Carlson floor radio. I hated to wash without rubber gloves; there were slimy, evil things in the water. But the one who finished first always got the seat immediately next to the radio, and the lagger squeezed in next where it was harder to hear "Sergeant Preston of the Royal Canadian Mounted Police." Washing became permanent for me eventually since I was the female. Dave and Lew got out of the kitchen by mowing the lawn or sweeping the garage, but I was forever inside with Mom. It was a tribute to her for me to do this purifying washing for her new apartment at Silver Lake.

It was curious, I thought, as I dried and stacked four of everything, that the very chore I detested in childhood I chose to do. I took on the tasks of parenting my parents, thinking of them as children who needed help dressing, cleaning their clothes, straightening their sheets and blankets. This comes, eventually, to all of us.

My challenge is to trust that God is close so that whatever I encounter, whatever experience I enter, dishes or errands, God is there, hidden in plain sight. If I look with the eyes of faith, I may see God. I don't always. I can't maintain a perfect sense of peace even with the greatest faith. To judge by hymns and favorite scriptures, this is true for all of us. Jesus spoke of this two millennia ago: "Which of you by worrying can add a moment to your lifespan….Enough of worrying about tomorrow! Let tomorrow take care of itself. Today has troubles enough of its own."*

I finished the arrangements at Silver Lake. Secured a mover for the furniture that will leave their home of 37 years. Friday the furniture; Saturday, Mom. Dad will join her when he's able. Feeling very pleased with myself, I have had two days without trips to Everett, so I'm two round-trips ahead of the routine.

Except for this: Dad does not want to move. Even though I've told him Mom will move on Saturday, and he can follow when he's stronger, he's clear he wants to stay put. The social worker, Thelma (we're on a first-name basis now), explains that he has been released from the rehabilitation routine, but apparently is going to stay at the nursing home from now on. What did I miss? Dad's physical therapist has not given him a clean bill of health. He released him because he is no longer making adequate progress. Progress? At 97, how much progress does he have to make?

Dad is not robust. I've misjudged his readiness. I thought he was Okayed even with the Foley catheter, but now I'm not sure. On Friday, I drive up just to drop in and confirm that Mom is going to be ready to move, meeting Nurse Practitioner Brenda for the first time. She invites me into an empty room and asks me to sit down across from her at a small table. Oh, oh.

"Your mother's heart is in bad shape, Cathy. The doctor recommends changing her diuretic to reduce damage to her kidneys." I know so little about diuretics and side effects. I mention how short of breath Mom was when I took her to the new assisted living facility for the interview. Brenda nods gravely and explains they've reevaluated her condition. It's worse.

Mother may not be moving. Dad clearly doesn't want to go. Are they both just where they need to be? And just in time? I feel as if I've stepped onto the porch of a house that has collapsed behind me, plaster dust and debris swirling over my head. *Only I have escaped to tell thee.** In a dream

---

* *Matt. 6:27, 34*

I saw myself on the porch of Dorothy's house just as it landed after whirling around in the tornado.

I wrote "…in all of the opportunities we encounter, we are invited to grow in our definition of love. The call is in the invitation. To accept it daily is to grow. That can happen only if our hearts are open, not just our heads. Heads demand answers. Hearts can live into the questions. We know we do not know enough. We keep offering ourselves to God, to the Cosmos, in whatever way seems most fruitful at the moment. To write, to sing, to walk, to sit…to choose a way to respond is what is required. To engage in life, to be open to the stranger, to accept the darkness, to persevere."

"It's not so much about behavior. It's about attitude."

~Fransson, *Spirit Stones*, Dec. 11, 2001. V. 2 No. 43

To try to come to some normalcy around my parents' new home in this facility, Ardene and I plan to celebrate their anniversary. This Sunday is the 17th of March, St. Patrick's Day—the date when they were married in Mother's home on Lombard Avenue in Everett in 1939. It's sunny and bright outside today but very cold. Sun enhances the day room where we're hanging green crepe paper. At their home, we found dress clothes: slacks, suspenders and a dark green cardigan for Dad; Mom's black sweater and slacks under her camel blazer. We brought them green carnation corsages. You can't tell by looking at them what is going on behind the scenes. They make a handsome couple still.

My brother Dave and some of our small family come to enjoy cake, punch and ice cream. The green balloons at the door match the napkins. We take pictures, knowing this 63rd anniversary may be their last. (I remember my friend Ann telling me this is the time of a thousand good-byes.) I am warmed to see a number of my parents' friends come from their church, Our Savior's Lutheran, just a few blocks away, where most of us had worshiped at 10:30 that morning. Mom and Dad were the official greeters—a wonderful ritual.

"I still keep up my own house, and buy our groceries," I overhear Mother saying to a close friend of similar age who nod. How well Mom carries it off! Dad, unable to hear anyone, pauses on his way back to his

---

* *The book of Job*, Hebrew Scriptures

room to peel off a strip of frosting from their cake with his index finger and poke it in his mouth.

The night before I had talked with a friend who is also a nurse. At the words "congestive heart failure," she just shook her head.

"They can go at any time," she said.

I had no idea the condition was so delicate. Today, after everyone leaves and Mother gets into more comfortable clothes for the evening, I see her fatigue. I imagine she is just too tired to adjust to yet another room in a whole different place.

That evening I write, "I don't want Mom or Dad to enter unhappily into the limbo of nursing home life. I would rather see their lives end. I am sure that if one of them goes, the other will quickly follow. That is fitting and reflective of their great dependence on each other. They gaze at each other quite fondly now because, of course they must know, each glimpse could be their last. Or do they?" Now I wonder whether they're as aware as I think they might be. If they were, they might have been more prepared to move from their home a few years earlier.

The nursing home staff tells me my mother has diabetes. Upset because of my woeful ignorance about what happens in the end of life, I realize it behooves us sandwich-generation children to inform ourselves about the stages of aging and dying. If we knew how to define where our parent is from year to year, we could be more helpful and supportive in practical ways. Or we would know when to ask for help. Do parents have to give their permission for us to find these things out?

Diabetes is simply part of the process. Several of Mom's systems are failing. I doubt she knows how ill she is. That is some comfort. My goal for her, and for Dad, is to be at peace. To sleep all night, to enjoy their meals, or refuse them, to have what they need. I was beginning to understand why Dad wanted to stay where he was. Moving to another new place with Mom no doubt reminded him of the trouble he had trying to keep up with her before.

Whatever the first signs of memory loss, behavioral lapses where there used to be responsiveness, lack of interest in daily life, forgetting to make appointments or refusing to go, all signal aging that might, indeed, be the beginning of a real and practical need for assistance. I wish I had had a check-list of what is important at this stage of their lives. Perhaps

Dad is without symptoms besides great age, but Mom is rife with them. I'd like to have known how heart failure progresses beyond how fragile she is. Her nurses are very kind to her and sometimes Dave and I gather around the recliner Mom rests in as she sleeps. Dad teases her and asks her to sing for him. But she wakes briefly to respond, eyes flashing, "You can't have what you want now, can you?!"

Nurse Practitioner Brenda concludes: my mother has a "very, very weak heart." She is going no place but into her room. Well, finally. I reel at the realization that Mom and Dad's daily routine in their home completely masked their poor health. My weekly lunches rarely caught them unawares or in situations they couldn't appear to handle until just weeks ago. Mother could prattle on about the weather, the groceries, how convenient their lives were, without my being the wiser that she could not remember anything but those familiar routines. She could no longer go to the grocery store on her own. She got lost on her way home or couldn't find her car. I learn these things only after the fact. And hear from friends that parents often are at their best when others, especially their children, visit. They pull the wool over our eyes so we can't see their vulnerability. This is where "putting your best foot forward" isn't entirely honest.

How much more important it is for a family to have some sort of sharing of information, a conference—several, to discuss their parents' alternatives at the end of their lives. It is unrealistic and unfair to expect them to lead us through this stage of their lives, of course. But it is also unrealistic for them to expect we would know what to do. An excellent resource for this conversation was created by Trudy James, MRE, a chaplain who worked for years with AIDS patients and now focuses on seniors and their families dealing with aging and death.* My parents hadn't thought about what was required. Was it the lack of true intimacy in our home that led to this outcome? We weren't a family that could level with each other. If we couldn't as teens with middle-aged parents, we certainly couldn't as seniors with elderly parents.

When I next see Mom, she smiles, and says, "Hello, Darling," in her warm lyrical voice. I choose a new, clean sweater for her to put on. We sit together and talk of nothing. And when I leave, I tell her I love her, kiss her, and know each time I go, it could be the last time. She is fading so

---

* Heartwork film, *Speaking of Dying,* www.speakingofdying/trudy-james

quickly it is hard to take in. I see now there was no way she could have handled the assisted living facility. I will have to move the furnishings I had arranged back to their garage. I had even made their bed, turning down the covers in welcome. The thought makes me weep.

In the last week of March 2002 forecasters say we have the coldest day in 35 years. The passes between Western and Eastern Washington, normally open by now, are closed. There is enough snow for snowmen. But it is dry today. I read my last batch of the final Pastoral Communications Skills papers from SU, and then head north.

Dad is flat out asleep on his bed, fully dressed, of course, so I walk down to Mother's room, where she stares out her window from a wheelchair. How sad it is that they cannot comfort each other now. When she tells me she needs to go to the bathroom, I maneuver her wheelchair there, and then realize she is too weak to stand again by herself. I can't lift her. I call for help to get her back in the chair. I feel foolish even offering to assist. Once an aide comes and she's settled, I roll her down the hall to see Dad. Since he is awake, the three of us perambulate the other way up the corridor to the lobby.

Mom lives in a completely different reality, thinking she is in the reception area of the Everett School District office.

"I remember this place," she says brightly, "it's the District office." She's wearing a nylon knee-high on one foot, and nothing on the other. At least the shoes match.

"It sure looks like it, doesn't it?" I respond.

"Am I dead?" Stunned, I look at her, take her arm, and say,

"No, Mom, you aren't dead." I lean over and kiss her on the cheek. She smiles.

"Is Dad dead?" Wow. He can't hear her of course. How far apart can they be emotionally? Perhaps for her, Dad is as good as dead, as of the day he said he couldn't thrive with her in his room. Now I realize how much trouble she would have been to him, and how much she had already caused him in their home.

"No, Mom, he's right here, over on my left." …but he's not listening. He is also not helpful. He presumes to control what ought to be in

Mother's room and has forbidden her a telephone and radio. He's treating her as he must have treated us when we were kids.

"She doesn't know her own mind," he says, barely disguising his irritation, hating weakness in himself and others, especially hers. She's been walking into other rooms and going through the residents' things.

When I walk out on the concrete porch into the sun, I drive to Silver Lake to get the clothes I put away for Dad in what was to be their new apartment. The new beginning that was not to be. Everything will go back—and not for long—to the garage at their home, because now that the two of them are in this facility permanently, I have to sell their home to pay for their care.

This morning I open my door and am delighted by the size of a package on our front porch. It's smaller and heavier than I expected—an addition to my home office from my favorite office supplies catalog, unassembled. With the glee of total distraction from what's on my mind, I unpack, styrofoam flying, propping the parts against the walls until I discover the neatly packed directions, a little box of casters and a tiny set of tools.

In the vein of "Chop wood, carry water," I like nothing better: putting together a compact file cabinet on casters whose tag says "Jeeves," with a leather top that doubles as a seat or lap desk. It is a wintry spring evening when the mere fragrance of alder fire and a cherry-stained three-dimensional project capture my zeal to create something that actually works, that is handsome and useful when put together.

This project is a blessed alternative to endless lists, discussions about my parents' care, the need to keep my whole family apprised of their health, and the expectation my own work continue as if life were normal. Normal? We do ourselves a disservice to expect such a thing or measure our lives by it. How on earth do those who live thousands of miles—even just hundreds—from their families, offer this care?

Put six lock-bolts into the right side and six lock-nuts into the back "as shown." Nope. I must have it backward. Switch the two sides...ah, this is it. Now I am ready to attach one side to the back. Why isn't life more like this? Some people find it easier to live by such rules. But that puts God out of the equation. Why did God give us brains if God expected we would want operating instructions for every step of living?

Anne Lamott writes that it is so difficult to keep "my sticky little fingers off the controls of this spaceship, especially when I get scared...." She would prefer God "be more like Jeeves, streaming into rooms like sunlight with all that I need to feel comfortable—God as cosmic butler."* Wouldn't we all? In fact it is those of us who believe God *should* be a "cosmic butler" who get so angry at what we can't control that we *blame* God.

Lock-bolt A into lock-nut A. Simple. Yet we grow into a lot more of who we were created to be if we relegate lock-bolts and nuts to stained-cherry file cabinets and bookcases, allowing the Mystery of the Cosmos simply to be, trusting the instructions will appear just at the time we need them. Lamott masters her own wrestling with faith, letting God do it, without it being magical or so Bible-bound it can never become metaphor. I have problems with the Bible. Especially if its pages are taken literally as if written last year. The promise of its books and verses, stories and characters, is that if you let them simmer on a back burner, you might discover that the behavior described is true of human nature. Those Hebrew Scripture myths are so familiar to me. I love the old stories. But I rarely can apply them directly to my life today. I can apply their meanings (multiple), their suggestions, their humor, and the ways they remind me of people I know—including myself.

The next day Dad is napping in an institutional wing chair when I walk into the familiar lobby. He says, "I'd like to have a room of my own." Classic. His roommate has moved out and he's relieved to have the place to himself, no longer sequestering himself behind the rose curtain. He's asking for chocolate, and today he's having some strawberry yogurt. His appetite has improved. He's getting better.

Mother is not. She's angry. She has investigated her roommate's clothes more than once, perhaps looking for her familiar items, and was told to leave. She is bored and unhappy when she's feeling well, but oblivious when she is not—which is more often the case.

In a day, even hours, my mother reverts to something close to comatose. Comatose is more comfortable; she doesn't have to know where she is. Frankly, she's much worse. At the recent care conference, I learn that not only does she have what I know, she has a urinary tract infection, kidney failure, and remnants of pneumonia, part and parcel of the body

---

* Lamott, *Op.cit.* p 112

shutting down organ by organ as it comes to its natural end. She is on her way on her own timing. And so death comes to us all, more or less out of our control, a mix of many factors.

With a sigh I picture the delightful small apartment at Silver Lake overlooking the alder where I created her "new home," and know with sickening dismay that it is empty now, and ready for other residents. Before I left the place, I poured a small glass of wine and drank to the concept I was abandoning—my mother's luxury retirement apartment. The place for her last years where her meals would be prepared, her room cleaned, and she would meet and enjoy new friends. And I wept; I am such a romantic.

"When your Dad is gone," Mom had always said, "I'll travel more, I'll have friends in, and I'll move to a retirement home, and do all the things that were too hard for your dad."

It was not to be. What if it never is as we think it will be? What if we continue to plan ahead, thinking once circumstances change (and how would they if we didn't take some action?) we will do thus and so, something we've always wanted to do once the impediment is out of the way (a partner, enough money, a last child married or through school, etc.). I need to do the things I want to do when I want to do them. Why am I putting off seeing the whales in Cabo, or cruising down the Rhone, or…. I had not helped my parents plan for the ends of their lives. I would have run into a brick wall. Their plan was to stay put until one of them was rolled out on a gurney. And that's what happened.

I was beginning to accept the problems of being the "only one," despite the willingness of my brother and sister-in-law to help. When I am tackling a new challenge as big is this is, I tend to get into it all by myself in order to learn from the beginning everything about it, and how to progress through it step by step. Then I can share it with others. I approached teaching this way, I remember. I could never use anyone else's notes.

How do only-children do it? How do people without resources do it? Or those who cannot leave jobs that are their sole livelihood? Ardene had her hands full with her ninety-two-year-old mother. She was working full time and so she hired a generous friend who took Esther out to lunch often and to have her hair done every couple of weeks. But she spent her days alone and had, by necessity and then choice, for years. Then there needed to be a bath aide, but her mother wouldn't allow the "stranger" in the front door. And somewhere along Ardene realized her mother needed more care than she could provide.

One of our friends used to say we would all end up in a single bed in a room with a television. Fortunately, that friend died at home in a double bed with a view, no TV, and in the care of a dear friend. I have visited enough nursing homes to know good from bad, better from best. But my father's experience at Rocky Glen was outstanding. He made it so. He was in such good humor without my mother to look after, he befriended the staff, walked to the cart to get his own meds twice a day, and welcomed relationships with the aides.

Meanwhile, I've begun to prepare 4715 Fowler so it can go on the market. I removed the rugs in the bedrooms to reveal not a bad-looking oak floor. I had the living room carpet cleaned. My eldest niece's wallboard company repaired the ceiling cracks in the living room, bath, and bedrooms.

My younger brother Lew (who died in 1996) had begun his antique business in the basement. There have been stain, varnish, verathane, glue, and finish-remover on the floor for years. I arrange to have the linoleum scraped, bleached, and repolished, leaving an indescribable motley finish. Clean, nevertheless.

When I brought some of their home furnishings to Rocky Glen Mother was pleased to have the straight-back padded wooden armchair in her room. I was able to hang small pictures on her walls, set a figurine on her dresser, and place two stuffed animals on her bed. Her room seems more homey. If this is where we will be for the duration, it will be as familiar and comfortable as I can make it. When I arrive with everything, she says, "You are doing so much work," not commenting at all about what I bring.

Sometimes I just cannot drive those 18 miles north. It's as if I lose a bit of stuffing on each mile. My resolve leaks out. What have I forgotten? How will I find my folks? If Mother is worse, what do I do to comfort her? If Dad is angry or frustrated, how will I mollify him? What will we talk about this time? It is so difficult to be with them as they are. But once I arrive, they are not as they once were.

Mother doesn't have anything lucid to say. She doesn't know what day or time it is. She's polite about "all my work" but unable to enjoy it.

In fact, she's packing up the things I put on her bureau: family pictures, small vases, ribbons, a tiny teddy bear. She's rolled them up in her underwear and stuffed them in a drawer, preparing to go home. I sit in a cloud of despair for a moment, and then pull each thing out and hang it back up, ending with the bear on my lap. I "talk" for the bear, and Mom smiles. There being no parting word to leave by, I stand and embrace her, tell her I love her, and turn to leave.

Life Surprises us even in the Midst of Loss

Most faiths have some sort of dark time to endure: Ramadan, Yom Kippur, Lent. Can the "Nones" (those who declare no religious affiliation) revel to their heart's delight with no cause for alarm, no sense of guilt, no voice-over warning them that excess is dangerous? Or after partying, there is some price to be paid? I doubt it.

Something tells me even so-called Nones live with fear and levels of dread, core to the human condition. People live with "faith" by many names even when they reject God. When I first read M. Scott Peck's 1978 book, *The Road Less Traveled,** I was enormously relieved to find I was not the only one to find life difficult. Everyone suffers with anxiety. Freud clarified in his work that the task of therapy was to urge a person to move from neurotic pain to the "normal" pain of our lives. Anxiety is normal. I wish my parents had known that when I was 12 and 13. Disappointment and grief abound. Perhaps then, rising to meet these constant challenges is, itself, success? "Live with creativity amid the vicissitudes of life," my Systematics Theology professor used to urge.

When events cascade upon us at the speed they are cascading upon me these days, there is hardly time to worry. Wakeful nights leave me no energy to deal with the next day's emergencies. Worry ruins what otherwise might be a good day. I am forced to respond in the moment to encounter a widening spiral of circumstances no one can adequately prepare for, which is why I write this book. Caring for my parents is teaching me to stop trying to wrench my agenda into a vision of holy peace. Perhaps someone will read it who still has elderly parents she or he

---

*   Touchstone NY 1978

can help better than I did. I try to respond with my own sense of peace within, and bring it with me, the proverbial doing the best I can with what I know. Nevertheless it is easy to despair at the lack of resolutions to my parents' circumstances, except for the ones they are living. I am reminded of what a favorite theologian of mine wrote,

> *I want a God who will cut my losses and cushion my failures,*
> *a God who will grant me a life free from pain.... what I... have*
> *instead is a God who resurrects us from the dead, putting an end to it by*
> *working through it instead of around it—creating life in the midst of grief,*
> *creating love in the midst of loss, creating faith in the*
> *midst of despair—resurrecting us from our big and*
> *little deaths, showing us by his own example that*
> *the only road to Easter morning runs smack through Good Friday.*

~Barbara Brown Taylor, "Can These Bones Live?" *The Christian Century*, March 13, 1996

Taylor's observations help me accept a very messy view of life, everything all mixed up. We need "Jeeves," indeed. Legos to assemble. A celebration followed by grief. Mourning followed by a renewal of life. Events come in three's? It isn't unusual to lose a matriarch and soon after welcome a great-grandchild or accompany one's husband to his own unique end. Life perpetuates itself, just not in the ways we like.

I am confirming something I knew, but not to the depth I know it now: I cannot make trouble vanish. I can neither save anyone from grief, including my dad, nor assure a friend she will survive her cancer. What I can do is preach that life emerges in the midst of that grief, love surfaces in the midst of that loss. Faith actually can grow when life gets tough, and often does. I know, even so, that, almost as often, faith is lost.

Witness the hundreds of helpers and millions of contributions that support the survivors and families of the lost at 9/11, Hurricane Katrina, the Oso landslide, the Las Vegas shooting, Marjorie Stoneman Douglas High. See the first responders who run towards disaster rather than away from it. Trust, that in the face of tragedy, others carry us through and put us back together, like Anne Lamott's "pit crew" swabbing her off, putting air in her tires, gassing her up for another round.*

Good Friday is important to me for the same reasons Anne Lamott enlists her pit crew. I need to know its grief year after year, because month after month, I recognize that grief in myself, in the world, and in my congregation. We do not celebrate a man passively giving in to death. We celebrate the courage of one who dared to challenge the powers of his day whose story survives antiquity. Jesus died, certainly. We all do. And lives are resurrected in the families who survive the loss of the twin towers, the blasts in Boston, Paris, and Syria, the concert killings in Las Vegas, the responders who continue to risk their own lives saving others, and all who support their recoveries. God and new life resurrect us from our big and little deaths because it's true: the only road to Easter runs smack through Good Friday. Or in another way, our "way through" a frightening challenge is to accept its pain and hardship, and come out the other side sadder, but with knowledge and truth, holding someone's hand.

We can walk away from the gathering, the bread and wine we share, renewed for the next days of our lives. Specifically, the *one* next day. Knowing the worst, we can more readily live life fully, whatever comes, given enough pluck, medical care, support, and therapy.

It is a beautiful April day, almost balmy. I meet with a painter at my parents' place for an estimate on the newly repaired ceiling, and then grab a shovel and set about scraping the moss off the driveway in back. I unlock the Dodge Dad was so proud of, start it, and leave it running for a while. It is no worse for disuse. I'm waiting for my friend Sue to arrive to see what she'd like to choose as keepsakes. Expressing her own grief at this necessity, she's reluctant to choose anything. The previous Saturday I invited my three nieces and my brother to choose the things they might want to keep. What was brought back from my parents' place in Silver Lake is in the garage: sofa, chairs, bed, end tables, lamps, Dad's homemade stereo cabinet, bookcases. But there are still books, tea cups and china in the dining room cupboards, vases, prints on the walls, wall-hangings, a roll-top desk my brother chooses to ship to his son. My eldest niece chose the Chevy wagon, the younger one chooses all the teacups. Each leaves with something to remember her grandparents by. The empty shelves speak for themselves.

---

* Lamott, *Op.cit.* p 12

After time cherishing all the events inside and out on the patio at this home, I head over to Rocky Glen for one of my regular two-or-three-times-a-week visits. Mom's pleased to see me for once. I smile broadly.

"I'm ready to go home anytime, Dear," she announces as I walk into her room.

"This *is* your home, Mom," I said.

"Do I have a room here?" she asks. I tell her yes, gesturing around the space as we set off for Dad's room down the hall. "And Dad lives over here."

I realize now how strange this must have seemed. "Where you lived," or where "Dad lived," is at 4715 Fowler. Not in this place that feels like an office or a hospital. I keep expecting her to respond as if she understands, but what have I been observing these past months? She doesn't know where she or Dad is unless I tell her, or unless she's at "home." My spirits sink. Even as I walk her to Dad's room, I am afraid he won't want to see her, or will brush her off somehow, and not welcome her with the hug I hope for.

Where to, next? She wonders. Relieved, I see Dad sliding his walker up to meet us. And then I walk them both to dine where, at assigned places, they will eat their dinners together—and yet apart.

I now discover when I can't help at all. I grew up as mother's little helper. There was no end of things I could do and could never escape that were helpful to her—and woe to me if any were left undone. I was both honored and constrained by this early calling.

My father occasionally called to ask me, "Can you come up? Your mother needs you." I would dutifully hop in the car to travel to sit by her side. She and I had a pact that should she ever be hospitalized, I would arrive before anyone else and see that she was fit to be seen: makeup in place, hair arranged, modestly dressed. I loved this supporting role I played to her "celebrity." Yet now I see that I was fundamentally limited by it. It has taken me years to untangle the threads.

My father called me two weeks ago from his room and said, "Your mother needs you." His alarm wasn't an emergency, so I waited until my next trip. Then I responded and offered what I could to someone whose life is ebbing and who is no longer able to account for what is lost. I finally had the perspective to know Mother had to go through these last stages of her life herself, and should, no doubt, have relied on me less when I was young. She did me no favors when she presumed I could prop her up in the places she felt weak, and alternately discipline me when I was out of line. I was confused by the role reversal.

. Helping is a false calling. It has tremendous and legitimate limits. This may surprise you—especially if you've grown up in a family or community where you were taught always to put others first. We end up propping up others and feeling righteous (and sometimes subtly angry) while giving ourselves short shrift. One of the best illustrations of how this works—it doesn't—is in Norman Maclean's *A River Runs Through It*, a semi-autobiographical account of Maclean's relationship with his brother Paul and their upbringing in an early 20th-century family. Robert Redford directed a film of the novella in 1992 starring Brad Pitt.*

Each of us has the resources within to see ourselves through the sticky wickets of our lives. Others can only guess—and only from their own perspective—what, exactly, is needed to help another person walk through their conundrum. They may or may not succeed, but failure may be what helps them learn. Putting ourselves in a position of knowing more than others do, we risk taking responsibility for their lives, and they may one day rue the day they did what we advised.

We make too many assumptions; we assume we have the answers. But how much of our wisdom can we give away? Only those trained to listen therapeutically can be helpful to those seeking support. Or partners in an AA group who learn how to listen effectively and follow a time-worn and highly respected practice. We need to be cautious distinguishing between what a good friend may offer, and what we need to figure out by ourselves, or with the help of someone who knows what they're doing.

I discovered that Mother had again taken down pictures and the teddy bear, putting them all in her drawer. She said, "Tell your father we need to go home now, dear. We've been on this boat too long." She gazes out the window. "We need to get our things together and head back to open up the house." I am speechless. It isn't that I am dismayed she is in a fantasy world because that surely saves her from the painful reality she is living. I'm sad to say I've told others what she said and laughed—so I

---

* Maclean, *A River Runs Through It*, Univ. of Chicago Press 1976

won't cry. But it's not at all funny. I kiss her and we share a hug and then I head out to find my dad.

"I don't want those pictures you brought," he announces as I walk in. "You can take them home." Well, we're at 100% here. Neither parent is happy with my decorating. Sad at his choice, but accepting his preference, too, I say merely, "Okay." I leave him, take the pictures, and wave at Mom who is now in the lobby as I walk out the door.

With the age my parents are now, almost 84 and 98, another limit I realize is that what I hoped is no longer recovery. What is recovery with persons their ages? In my mother's case I hope she will experience less pain while she travels slowly to her death. With Dad, as he grows stronger and stronger, it is no doubt good enough health in the year or years he has left. He cannot return home. He cannot live independently, and I hope only that he remain comfortable, content, and can accept the assistance he is given with grace.

On Sunday I skip church. It's the first Sunday I've missed in nearly two years since Rod Romney, the former pastor, retired. Ardene and I fix eggs, toast, bacon and fruit, then sit down to enjoy a leisurely conversation, a rare gift these days. I am too tired even to make small talk, and as I try, then stumble to a stop, I give up and cry. Ardene embraces me and lets me grieve.

Through my tears I manage to say how I miss Mom's laughter and ebullience. I just miss Mom. The weekly lunches, the occasional lunches out, dinners here when we drove up to get them, brought them down for the evening, and then chauffeured them home later. I can't even call them on the phone. Maybe my dad for a few months longer, but those days are fleeting.

Ardene tells me softly, "You're being a very good daughter," and continues to hold me as I try to pull myself together and realize I haven't accepted the thought. I keep thinking of what I haven't done or cannot do.

A few nights later there is a lovely shift. I make an evening visit and find Dad in great spirits. "I have so much time now, I'm even watching baseball," he says, and laughs. I've never known him to watch baseball. Laughs were rare. Still, Mom initiates less and less. She thinks today is some sort of occasion and wonders why there aren't flowers on the receptionist's desk in the lobby. Turning to me as confidant, she whispers miserably,

"Your father watches everything I do." I commiserate and wonder, although that might have been normal in their home, how could it be possible here? But the attendants affirm just this. Once this week Dad was so angry, he lifted and slammed his walker down to emphasize his point. The attendants separated them.

God only knows when this might happen at home, but they each had other parts of the house to escape to, before silently (with some resolution, I hope) curling up in a double-bed to sleep. It's clear Mom forgets that her husband is also here, nor does she know where "here" is. They are a rare couple at 83 and 97 years old, sixty-three years together. Many more couples divorce before this, or one of them dies. My folks have had to make adjustments in their lives for their own parents' loss, and more recently, and certainly more troubling, the loss of their 48-year-old son. But not a partner. I sustained myself through the relationships I had, the losses and new beginnings. Come to think of it, how did they come to terms with Ardene after they had so loved my former partner? Those are discussions I will never have.

I'll also never find "closure," a misleading word if there ever was one. It is nigh impossible to understand our parents fully, to accept their decisions, especially the ones we think cut us off at the knees. Our relationships with them go on beyond their deaths. We continue—I continue, anyway—to keep conversations going with both Mom and Dad. And occasionally, I see more of what they struggled with themselves. Little by little, I see some of what limited or disappointed them. What they resigned themselves to, or grieved, for years. Even as I write these memories, I have insight. I have a better glimpse of an argument I walked in on, a silence that persisted, or genuine laughter they could not hold back, conversations they might have had with me, or with my brothers. I understand them better. But I will never know completely how they adjusted to the emptiness or fulfillments of life (outside of "sex and the church"). I can only hazard a guess.

On a rare day without an agenda, a warm patch of sun draws me just as it draws my cat...an excuse to breathe. I have shifted down. Sunshine intensifies my desire to paddle off the main stream into a small eddy where the frenzied issues, dilemmas, and decisions of the last three months float, sort, or settle to the bottom.

Hurrying was something I learned at my parents' knee at the same time as doing things *right*. Not only right but fast. "Someone might be waiting!" I remember going out to dinner (not to church) perhaps for the first time when I was quite young to a nondescript cafeteria on Hewitt Avenue in the center of town. Nothing "special." Simply eating out was extraordinary. We got in line. When it was my turn, I was so awed at the number of dishes and kinds of food that I had no way of making up my mind. Behind me, Dad said, "Hurry up! People are waiting!" I just grew more anxious.

CHAPTER 8

Facing Loss

❦

Rocky Glen calls. "She fell again today, sat hard on her bottom, but she's all right." They attached an alarm to Mother's bed.

What bones! How many times has Mother fallen, and never—yet—broken anything. There was the time when she was working in the yard on Colby and walked toward the iron tine rake leaning against the house. She stepped on the tines and the rake handle slammed hard onto her nose. It did not break! Her face was black and blue for several days, but no fracture.

Mother never moved slowly and rarely paced herself. Just a few years ago, she walked a wet, mossy sidewalk too quickly toward her dentist's office and slipped. She bruised her face, broke her glasses, she said, then went calmly inside, had her teeth cleaned, and came home. I assume they daubed her face with gauze and alcohol, but for the hour she was there, she told me she insisted she was "fine." I wondered if the dentist was paying attention, or whether he had been assured by her own confidence.

The Ramstad drill: when something happens, go on as if nothing has. Poise, it's called. At six when my large doll was playing "Moses" in a church pageant, I was Miriam, rocking him so vigorously (while absorbed in the song Mother taught me) he rolled out onto the floor. Without missing a note, I walked over, picked him up, and rolled him back in his blanket in the crib. Originally this drill was known as the McGhee shuffle. Paired with the Ramstad influence, it is a recipe for self-control at all times in all circumstances. Never let anyone know you're not in control.

The new lead pastor at church offers directions and clear expectations. But alongside this clarity is the specter of my folks, dependent, staring into space or napping much of the day in their separate rooms. I've been bringing Mom's clothes home to launder and iron. After at least two forgotten tissues decomposed in the washer and spread fibers over everything, I learn to go through every pocket. It's something I can finally do. I take Dad's shirts to the cleaners, but Rocky Glen is doing his other clothes. They look terrible, but he's content. He's trying to save me the time and effort. I feel much better seeing him in fresh, ironed clothes. It makes me feel competent.

This time when the sun creates another pattern on the back deck, I sit in shorts, barefoot and hopeful, but not for long. The cedars and a fir loom above me, vigilant, soon creating shadow. Yet it is related tall sentinels my dad prizes in his own backyard and now, only in his memory. He sat on their patio looking south, watching the firs respond gently to winds he could not feel at ground level. It was this view he refused to give up when considering moving out of his home. The power of trees!

Dad majored in forestry for three years at the University of Washington in the late 1920s, quit when he ran out of money—and possibly, out of vision—and never went back. He'd also driven open-roofed touring cars at Glacier (in Montana) and Mt. Rainier National Parks, no doubt regaling his fares with tales of the trees sheltering others that thrived near them, and the fires that threatened them. He told us those same stories when he took us to the mountains on summer vacations. He was happy, engaged, and enthusiastic about the forest.

He worked in canneries in S.E. Alaska and eventually helped build a pulp mill on Everett's waterfront where he then worked. The dissonance: driving awestruck through the ancient cathedral of trees, then stewing wood chips into the mash that produces paper. At this stage of his life (if he is actually processing it as he broods through the days and nights) he must bring these old and hopeful memories back, reviewing his life. The joy of falling in love, late at 34, building a home for June and himself, welcoming one, two and then three children, whom he worked to support.

Ultimately his intense accountability at Scott Paper Co. scuttled his ability to risk the hazards for his work crew. He was too anxious. He moved then from instruments to packaging, taking a large pay cut. I wonder if this subsequent position salved the wounds, "bandaging" the trees he had so admired. I realize as well that a $500 pay cut (annually $6000) could easily move him to choose a local junior college for his daughter as the most affordable choice.

When Dad retired, he opened Custom Picture Frames on Hewitt Avenue. People in Everett still remember him and his shop with fondness. He was friendly, fair, and artistic—a Carl I knew little. Since I have become his legal representative, however, I have met countless admirers: the hearing aid specialist and his receptionist, the personnel at his doctor's office, his dentist and assistants, the lawn man, his banker and podiatrist. All greet him with enthusiasm.

This is a father I did not know. I knew best the man who sat in the far corner of the living room behind the newspaper, a potentate I was never supposed to interrupt, disturb, or distract. The man who legislated judgment without allowing debate. Rather, his children were to respond politely to the questions he posed at dinner. This was a man whose attention I both feared to attract and died to have. And here we are on the other side of the garden gate. Now he is a man grateful for help and gracious to his helpers, one of whom I have become. How have I now passed muster? Or is it he who has changed?

I am doing my own life review as I help my dad in his aging—my own life with Carl, a man I couldn't read, a man I feared. I can talk more about what we did as a family than the feelings it engendered, which is to omit loneliness and sadness. As I ponder my memories, I can see beyond his distance to the enthusiasm he had for our getting as close as we could to his love of the forest. The homemade trailer he built, and when once discarded, the large green umbrella tent we camped in.

Even as we sit together now, he's telling me stories I have never heard. Laughing at some of his mistakes, his adventures with his brother Art. He trusts me. Is that because I am the responsible woman in his life, as Mother was, or is it because he truly sees me as an equal, admired for my own talents and work teaching and helping others?

This is a stage of my own aging. Coming to terms with my parents. Something I had little time to do with my mom, but also something she avoided when we were together by telling me versions of her unhappiness rather than facing her own lack of vision or courage. I listened sympathetically. Her dementia prevents us from reviewing her life now, and certainly hers with Dad. Every time I see her, she is worse. So, my presence doesn't engender more than my love for her, that could easily be forgiveness, which is all that can be expressed.

On a Monday in mid-May, the warmest day of the year to date, I water the yard, gauging the reach and spread of the sprinkler to mimic the rain. Setting the sprinkler on a freshly cut lawn has long signaled peace for me: waning sun, rainbows in the yard, time to sit and admire the work. Especially on Camano Island where a large sloping lawn led to a view west across Saratoga Passage to Whidbey Island. Water blesses the landscape and gives us a way of participating in the force of creation that continues to bring forth life of every imaginable kind. Yet in the midst of such life, "I am in death," *The Book of Common Prayer*, asserts.* This is a penitential anthem in the old form of burial. Although I would not use it, and find other sections of it unacceptable, I do think reminding myself that I am mortal is not a bad thing. On Ash Wednesday many of us, whether in a liturgical or "free" church, go to accept ashes to remind us of that mortality. *"Remember that you are dust, and to dust you shall return."*

Surely all of us are dying. My mother manifests it openly. There is no telling when, but now I am beginning to know how. I am left to ponder the dreams I coveted for her that remain only dreams. The illusions I conjured that we both used to share cannot save her now. All those years of our singing Sigmund Romberg duets, me at the keyboard. Her solos in church and at Purdy and Walters or Solie memorial services with Helen Stiles at the organ. The hours I spent reading to her—once, *Ring of Bright Water*—while she rolled the family sheets through a mangle. She bought it second-hand and found it superior to her iron for sheets and pillow cases. But soon, she could press Dad's shirts, too. The laundry came out beautifully, a sign of how seriously she took her role.

I want to blame the nursing home. Or her doctor who never told me this is how it would be. But she has plenty of medical reasons for her descent. I have to accept what is happening, though I often disparage its closing in on me. I am too surprised to accept it just yet. No longer is Mother on the phone on Sunday night, saying musically, "Hello, Dar-

---

* The Episcopal Church, 1979. Burial Rite I. p 484

ling." No longer Mom and I sharing a juice glass of wine at lunch or walking arm-in-arm out to shop. Her quick, warm smile.

I have these lovely memories of my mother, a star in my younger years, now leaving before we have a chance really to level with one another. Maybe she couldn't ever have done that, and exits as she wishes in a cloud of illusion. Life encourages illusions. How much I wish otherwise.

Privileged to share some of the more intimate details of the lives of my congregation, I continue to learn how people cope with their own pain and/or try to lighten the pain of those they love. Norman Maclean's evocative novel reveals the helplessness of helpers. Yet there is another level than what Maclean evokes, the spiritual level of sharing the sacred space of another—with their permission—to walk alongside them in times of challenge and loss. We cannot "fix" the pain, we cannot change it, we cannot change the response. We can merely share the space, calling on grace to sanctify it, praying that we choose behaviors that will comfort and calm others as we companion them until they can again take hold of themselves.

I struggle with the pain in people's lives. Pain I cannot ease. Blessed with an uncommon empathy, I hurt when others hurt. I learned this at my mother's knee. Although the skills themselves are valuable, what I had not grasped until much later was how to set a boundary so I did not become an accomplice in her life. I needed to let her handle her own challenges. This important skill enhances my ability to walk alongside others and let them live their own lives as well. It's not easy to do. But it's the only way to be truly helpful.

While watching the classic film *Come Back, Little Sheba*,* a number of years ago, I was moved to tears. Shirley Booth makes elaborate preparations for a dinner party to include her specialty, twice-baked potatoes, but her husband fails to appear. The party is spoiled, and the potatoes grow cold. I did not have the insight to realize she might have chosen another behavior or have actually been able to handle her disappointment differently. But, of course—Hollywood! That would have ruined the film.

---

* *Come Back, Little Sheba* is a 1952 American drama film produced by Paramount Pictures

The challenge of accepting disillusionment comes to us all. It's not a bad thing to learn to be more realistic about our illusions when they don't serve us. Disillusion can be a healthy thing, such as in Jane Kenyon's striking poetry.

> *I got out of bed*
> *on two strong legs*
> *It might have beeen*
> *otherwise...*
> *But one day, I know,*
> *it will be otherwise.*

~Jane Kenyon, *Otherwise.*

The sprinkler on my lawn is a false promise. I can mow and weed, prune and water, savor a moment's perfection. But by the next morning new leaves will have sprouted, weeds will have sprung up, mushrooms emerged. Perfection yields to chaos. It is the yielding of the illusion of perfection that wounds. The guest who fails to arrive. The belief that I can grasp what is or wish the pain of others away. I savor the touch of my mother's hand and let my palm linger on her fragile thin shoulder because I know, one day soon, it will be otherwise. Yet chaos itself is where the mystery of God moved in the beginning of Scripture, evoking a whole world into being. Chaos is the matrix for creativity.

A "pray-er" as a kid, I read my Bible under the covers with a flash-light. It seemed a subversive activity. A holy practice. I read Genesis over and over thinking I could remember its thousand details, or it would lead somehow clearly to Exodus. Wasn't happening. But my need to spend time pondering Scripture and praying with others, looking for answers, persisted. As a kid I went to a church conference and a breakout group on prayer, delighted to find prayer *a thing in itself,* something to do, something to stay up late doing. Prayer need not be sanctified or sanctioned by churches, mosques or synagogues. It's not limited to denominations or sects. Prayer may be shared in front of an icon, a candle, a deity or Bible. It may simply be hopeful thoughts offered to the cosmos when we're in a contemplative mood. Many of us gather to pray at the bed of an elder, a dying parent, a seriously ill child. We don't have to be a member of anything but the human race to offer our hopes silently or aloud, alone or in company.

Did I have to tell God what I needed? Will God know who needs help? Does the Spirit really intercede with "sighs too deep for words?" By now I have resolved the questions into one conviction: the mere intention to talk with God—with Mystery— is all that God requires. Mystery looms between rain drops, or in a strip of cloud; it is we "who have gone out for a walk," said 14th century Meister Eckhart. Every time we do connect with ourselves or others or the beyond, it is more than booting up the computer to tap into the worldwide web. If that were one millionth of one percent of what the mystery/God is, we cannot imagine the scope of the forces that spawns the expanding cosmos. Lest I limit others even here by mentioning "God" too much, omit the word. If it doesn't capture what you see/believe or intuitively know, create your own word for the power in the chaos that generated the world. From the random events that brought Mom and Dad together, spawning Dave, me, and Lew, a family was born and is now leaving memories and likenesses, habits or avoidance of habits. These relationships, stories, coincidences, and intentions that brought us to our assisting in the ends of their lives, never really end. They generate stories in all the lives who knew ours, and are passed on through the human story.

Love in the Midst of Loss

Having emptied and blessed all the corners, cupboards, closets (including the laundry chute) and rooms of the house, home to Carl and June for 38 years, I sit on the patio steps. I carried a fragrant candle in one hand and a wineglass in the other (not cheap wine this time) as I blessed each room and every memory that made this empty house our home.

Blessing the space around us sanctifies what has been, and what may be. From John O'Donohue, Irish teacher and poet, I learned blessings for every possible human situation. He writes, "We enter the world as strangers who all at once become heirs to a harvest of memory, spirit, and dream that has long preceded us and will now enfold, nourish, and sustain us. The gift of the world is our first blessing."*

My first spiritual director, Alexandra, suggested blessing my home when I moved from my apartment in downtown Seattle to commit my life to Ardene as my partner. I did. I burned old letters in the fireplace, took a candle through every room giving thanks for the experiences the space held for me, and the freedom I had gained to commit myself to a new life.

Baptists, secure in "soul freedom" and justice, seem not to have the temperament for spiritual direction or soul companionship. I am more contemplative than many. When I was an Episcopalian, I liked to touch base with my Episcopal priest from time to time. I thrived with his spiritual encouragement. I also luxuriated in the liturgy through that time when I had no words. When students entered the School of Theology and Ministry, we encouraged them to find a spiritual guide as well, someone to help them adjust to challenges. We also recommended they see someone therapeutically if we thought it wise. Spiritual mentors are not therapists, though some can be. Credentialed counselors in the schools and the church are priceless, especially in congregations.

At the end of my ritual in my parents' home, I go to the back patio and listen. Robins sing. A neighbor's curious gray tabby walks by, eyeing me warily with his yellow eyes and cutting a wide swath around me. I now gift this home, ready for another family, who is signing papers at this moment.

I have been the matron for three months. To have and to let go as, in the course of Mother and Dad's disabilities, everyday loss occurs. And yet I am not sad. I am grateful they have been so content here. This place has nurtured them and their growing family of grandchildren, new spouses and great grandchildren. They've been safe here beyond my knowing: The Fourths of July when the grandkids put Dad in a yard cart and rolled him around the yard, all of them laughing out loud. The picnics on the back patio with croquet on the lawn. I marveled how Dad played with my nieces and my nephew. I had no memories of his playing with me. "You just don't remember," Mother told me with a tone of caution.

Mother's end is near, but unpredictable. Although Dad appears healthy, he is frail; still, he has moved to a single room and is enjoying

---

* John O'Donohue, *To Bless the Space Between Us*

his privacy. No one can predict his end either. I had better look for a new black suit. As I walk to the car, a young eagle flies south to the fir chased by two angry crows. I take this as a good sign, an omen of life's constancy. In spite of loss, there is always new life.

"Look! I am doing something new!...Can't you see it?" (Isaiah 43:19)

I try.

When Dad and I found our seats in the Rocky Glen conference room with Mother's nurse, Dad announced, "Cathy is the CEO of the family." I was dumb-struck. An achievement not sought, and the first time I had heard him say this. There was a time, yes, when I wanted acceptance, affirmation, approval that I was who I was. There was a time I needed to have the stamp. Especially from my dad.

While at seminary I read a copy of theologian Paul Tillich's sermon ("You Are Accepted") slowly, meditatively, until I could sense the grace I heard about but hadn't known how to embrace. And then I began to repeat to myself: "I am *accepted*. There is nothing *I need* to do, nothing I need *to do*, and nothing to answer for, accept to say *yes*." That helped. My need for approval shrank another size. In spite of being baptized at the age of 8, I had adopted "faith by works"—not faith itself. I thought of God as someone like Santa Claus or a parent, rewarding me for being good, punishing me for what I forgot or the mistakes I made. I was learning my parents demanded that obedience, but it needn't have been God. My image of God was being revolutionized by my seminary courses and the exceptional teaching of Seattle U. professors. God was growing bigger, more mysterious, less intrusive, and even closer.

Our faithful and fiercely territorial tabby Tully comes in with sticky rhododendron blossom covers stuck to her paws, flower dust on her ears. She deposits some on my desk where my parents' lives lie in layers: copies of powers of attorney, unpaid bills, health insurance forms, Medicare instructions, and sticky notes tracking utilities, telephone, and house chores.

As for the bills and the unknowns, I direct frustration with my parents' decline at their bank, their insurers, and all those who must have my authority verified, certified, and guaranteed. Mark Twain said requiring a birth certificate was senseless when quite obviously, if one walked into a room, one certainly gave ample evidence of having been born. As a life ends, documents certify every stage.

I disconnect the telephone, the number going back over 60 years. When I was small, Mom had asked me to call her mother, Kittie Mc-Ghee, on the wall phone in the den. She called her every night after dinner as if it were a sacrament. Anna Catherine Stilwell McGhee was my maternal namesake. She was Kittie to her friends. On that particular day Mom was in the kitchen, and I was standing on a stool to reach the wall phone in the den. I didn't hear her say the number clearly enough to tell the operator. I asked her to repeat it so many times, ultimately the operator heard *my mom* and put the call through to Bayview 1079. We were Bayview 3008. In the early sixties that became Alpine 2-3008 and eventually 425-252-3008. Names for exchanges seemed so much easier to remember than a string of numbers. But I can't place a call to my parents at this number now. No one will answer. Home has vanished, as if in that dream where I had stepped onto the porch as all of it, furnishings, glass, plaster and lath, roof, had collapsed just a moment before. Stunning. No more comfort-calls home. I am on my own.

Tears well in my eyes and roll down my cheeks. Once back home I go out to the garden and find Tully lounging under a bright pink azalea, disturb her with the hose, then spend the next half hour sprinkling new plants and yet unplanted annuals. Rain threatens but doesn't come, so I am glad to make puddles in the mulch. I peer at the foliage, sun peering through hemlock, dappling huge old cedar and fir. Nevertheless, things come apart a little at a time. I water the rest of the bedding plants, nuzzle the cat who's come in for a snack, and watch the sun weave its way through our cedar, then restore my soul beside tidal waters at Edmonds beach. Books cannot do this work. It takes friends, sun, nearly-blooming iris and tide flowing over the driftwood to break through the grief of losing both my parents' home, and soon, them.

A week later, I drive past Edmonds Memorial Cemetery on my way to Everett. We live just behind it. I maneuver carefully around cars parked hastily on the shoulder as groups of people walk to the ceremony there. It's the first Memorial Day since the overwhelming losses of 9/11. Grief gathers and hangs in the fir and cedar like clouds lingering to deliver rain.

Mom is not good. She fell on Friday. Even though they have put her bed on the floor, she managed to get up, although I am sure once she gets her feet under her, she will move impulsively and could easily fall again. They're trying.

I visit with Dad a few moments, giving him the red azalea I brought. He's delighted. Such a lover of these plants (doubtful the ostentatious ones) he and Mom frequented nurseries that specialize in azalea and brought new ones home every spring. He also moved the azaleas and rhodies he already had so he could see them at newer angles from his window views inside. I set this one on the bureau next to the small television set as I leave, and spot a Hershey's dark chocolate bar with almonds next to the TV. There's one bite missing; a sign he's regained his sweet tooth. I smile.

I wish I could just sit with Mom. But were she in my home I would have to be elsewhere in the house, as she was when I was small. We cannot sit in each other's presence and adequately honor being together. The fleeting moments we have done that and do it now have to add up to enough. Columnist George Will once wrote in one of his *Time* Magazine backpage editorials, "God moves in mysterious ways. Indirection, doubt, and one's own daily death." I know that valley of shadow. It is there, unnamed, more than we realize. Sometimes it's our daily grief we're trying to elude when we rush into a frenzy. I pray our closeness was enough for Mother and that she is ready to let go and move on.

I cannot control the time in my own schedule because of unexpected phone calls, sudden deaths or long-anticipated ones, people who need to talk with a pastor. And I cannot enter the time my parents occupy—their aging, and movement toward death. I shuttle back and forth as if accompanying travelers only a few yards at a time. Not a guide, certainly, hopefully a companion.

Mom and Dad have always been out of reach—at least with what is true intimacy. That's hard to achieve between parents and kids, or it was in the middle of the last century. Our times of real connection were few but rich. When I lived alone, they drove down to Seattle on weekends, either to accompany me to the church I was attending or playing for, to walk in the U. of Washington Arboretum or Discovery Park, or to see an opera or symphony. When I sang in the Seattle Chorale, they came to the performances at the old Opera House on Mercer. I bought them tickets for symphony and opera for their anniversary and birthdays and have had more in common with them than either of my brothers. We enjoyed music and walks as well as church engagement. But of course I was the one free to spend time with our parents alone and listen to their stories. My brothers were busy with growing families.

In these last three months, our visits have changed dramatically. Dad does listen to me, although he misses a lot due to the imperfection of hearing aides. But he also checks up to see whether I am making the small (to me) monthly donations to nearly 15 charities and nonprofits (Housing Hope, Bethany of the Northwest, the Volunteers of America). He names several more. I nod and don't quibble.

There is no way we can afford to give away even that kind of money now, given the costs of their care here. Think of what I'm paying! Some $12,000 a month for the two of them. I study the numbers and estimate when the money is going to run out. As Dad feels more and more himself, he emphasizes to me the importance of these old commitments he's made, and I know how recent and perhaps still fragile is my position—in spite of being the "CEO." I change the subject.

Meanwhile, in Edmonds, there are two new households in the yard. One showed up a week ago when a pair of chickadees began to feed a hungry brood high up in a pine birdhouse tacked to a cedar in the backyard. The parents flew as a tag team feeding their growing family whose insistent and high-pitched chirping attracted the neighbor cats. And then another pair set up housekeeping in a smaller white birdhouse nearer my study, hard at work with dried grass, bits of dryer lint, hair, and twigs. New beginnings. This scant evidence of homebuilding could as easily end up tossed into the brink as thrive. I was on the verge of so much loss, I needed to believe the birds would thrive.

Today Mom smiles, eats a little, and says with apparent good humor, "I am not getting any younger." "No," I say, feeding her a tuna sandwich one section at a time, and pea soup spoon by spoon. At age 83, she has survived a weekend when she reacted to morphine and sank to a low point.

"I am not ready to see you step over that threshold," I continue, brushing her hair off her forehead.

I invest this time of good-byes, never knowing which is the last, with a tender farewell. I focus fully on my mother's fading life, as is true when I pray for invalids approaching death, whether conscious or not. I am blessed that it is my mother's journey I minister to. I have every hope that she is in good hands, hands beyond the ones I bring, hands that link to those beyond my own. She is at heart a deeply faithful woman. Such a comfort to me. Life is fragile, but her faith is strong.

In Wilder's *Our Town,** Emily cries, "Oh Mama, just look at me one minute as though you really saw me." She eventually understands: "It goes so fast. We don't have time to look at one another." Emily tells the Stage Manager, "I didn't realize. So all *that* was going on and we never noticed."

We can, but we rarely notice the value of each moment. We can't stop in the middle of the grocery store and completely value the bananas, the kiwi. The lights reflecting from the shower that crisps the vegetables makes vegetables shine. When we pay attention, we can presciently see a transitory truth appear and disappear in displays, people, traffic, and while standing in line. Life goes on and so do we. A certain amount of taking-for-granted is required. Wilder's Stage Manager, speculating, says, "this [world] is straining away, straining away all the time to make something of itself. The strain's so great that every sixteen hours everybody lies down and gets a rest."

Jesus said, "Look at the birds. Consider the lilies ... and do not worry." (*Matthew 6.25-31*) Really? How can we stop worrying? There are so many choices, so much danger.

Does our busy-ness distract us from life, or does life distract us from being in the moment? Whichever, isn't it marvelous that we can lie down and get some rest? Sadly, that doesn't help us look into each other's eyes. I can only hope the times I have done that with Mom over the years register somewhere, add up to something, and count for the love I feel. There is no way to guarantee it, certify it, make it real. It is clearer and clearer to me now that we must "live every day as if it were going to be [our] last; for one day [we're] sure to be right."

---

* Thornton Wilder, *Our Town*. 1938.

Nearing the threshold of her death frightens me. What will life be without her? In Hebrew Scripture God says, "I have set before you life and death… Choose life." (*Deut. 30:19*).

It isn't that simple. We can want desperately to live *and yet* escape the circumstances we meet: brutality, war, abuse, famine, terrorism, and of course, life-sucking illness. Death is becoming a more acceptable choice in some tragic cases. "Planned" death creates fierce debate, especially among people of faith who believe that nothing human should impinge upon the life force. But even for those of faith, there is a season to be born and a season to die (*Ecclesiastes 3.1…*). I have and will continue to pray for a peaceful death for those who have no hope of a meaningful life to come, who have lived fully and deserve a good death. It is the *choosing* that is the rub.

On the first day of June, Mother's birth month, I pick up the escrow check for the house sale and toss my one remaining house key away. Cancel the insurance. Done. With Dad's two cars delivered to my nieces, and the house in the hands of new owners, I expect things to remain calm for a while, even though I am frequently despondent. Sadness alternates with resentment at the fact that my mother is dying, and my dad will soon follow. Why now?! All of a sudden. I turn my anger toward paperwork, toward what I cannot do for my parents, and what I have to figure out for myself.

At church that next Sunday I sit naively in the back of the sanctuary, rapt, yet unsuspecting as the church pianist plays the Shostakovich Second Piano Concerto with a small orchestra. I was looking for musical respite, my *ground*. Music goes directly to the heart, generating feelings I am not always able to express.

So, not surprisingly, in the first movement, I lose it. It didn't even take the familiar and haunting second movement I so love. I walk out to the foyer weeping, lost in grief. I think of Mom and her love of music, how we shared it from beginning to end, rehearsal to performance, year after year. I haven't thought of all these memories in a long time. The ways we were together in wordless sync when a subtle glance or gesture would prompt me to respond with exactly the right tempo or smile. Mother taught me everything about music, what to listen for, how to breathe between phrases, how best to memorize lyrics, how to retain composure performing, how to enjoy. Where would I be without being able to share music with her? I'm fortunate that Mom has lived this long, and though she will live far less long than my dad, I am grateful to be with her now.

I'm glad no one else is out here in the narthex. I compose myself and return to the music, but the spontaneous weeping was good for my soul. Good lament. We have many social rules about when tears are appropriate, but we've already written new rubrics that attest to the fact that men who can weep aren't afraid to show their vulnerability. Research is not definitive about the causes or the benefits of tears. My tears of sadness have intensified my expression of grief, bringing relief, and also feelings of joy. If I lament when I feel in sympathy with a tragedy, for example, I am even more joyful when I'm celebrating. Tears come with both emotions.

I am painfully slow in accepting that Mother will be free only in death. She could not free herself from her perceived obedience to my dad in this life. She really is leaving us both. In some ways she's already gone and there is no way to be with her. Every time I visit, she is worse. Everything I prepare is too late.

How does anyone "prepare" for death? We don't, unless we schedule it and have the state's permission to take the necessary pharmaceuticals, or if others will allow it, stop eating and drinking. There are certain latitudes of choice with those who are in coma, or so injured they will not survive. The rest of us have to take it as it comes. In Washington state there is voluntary stopping eating and drinking or VSED. We have already discovered that some thoughtful adults simply decide they are ready to die (often terminally diagnosed, sometimes already on hospice) and stop eating. Perhaps this was how, years ago, healthy people whose hearts were "broken" made their way to death when they were not physically ill. Who can separate grief from illness, though? My nurse colleague and friend Ann told me some time ago that those who stop ingesting liquid or solid food slowly become euphoric, and eventually fall into a peaceful coma. *Guide us waking, O Lord, and guard us sleeping; that awake we may watch with Christ, and asleep we may rest in peace.*

Having arranged to have my brother look in on the folks, Ardene and I manage to get away for a few days. We drive across the Canadian border north about two hours to visit Dad's birth place in Annieville, now Delta, B.C., south of Vancouver on the Fraser River.

In Annieville's Trinity Church we ask to see the record of Dad's birth on July 2, 1904, and of his christening on the thirty-first of that month. Baptism dates in Annieville were painstakingly handwritten in ink on fragile yellowed pages in a large record book. In a 100-year-old newspaper article of this early era in their church history, his mother, Joakima, is noted as a leading member of the Ladies Aid. How I wished I had known her when I was small. A pioneer, a courageous, vital woman, and mother of three children (one who died in infancy). She might have been a wonderful grandma and my role model among Ramstads in the Northwest.

Ardene and I enjoyed walking the boardwalk and a sunny beach at White Rock B.C. where we stayed. We watched eagles and people, catching up with ourselves, snuggling without any alarm or phone call to summon us. Then we head back home. Once we are in cell phone range, I receive a voice message that Mother is not doing well—I should come right away. Within two hours we stop at Rocky Glen. Mother is breathing very slowly, lying still in her nightie with covers pulled up to her collar bones. She is nearly comatose. Although she doesn't stir, we sit with her for an hour.

The next day, June 14, I sit again at her side as her shallow breaths come more and more slowly. I hold her hand, stroke her hair, murmur to her. Soon she will see my first piano teacher and Mom's best friend, Bernice, I tell her, who died when I was 12. And her own dad, Joe, and mom, Kittie. I can't help myself but comfort her with these projections even though I hardly believe "heaven" exists as I imagine it, and there are no promises that we will be reunited with family. Hearing is the last sense to go. So I say the most comforting things I can. "I love you, Mom. We were the perfect mother-daughter pair." As her breaths come less and less often, slowly they end.

June Minnie McGhee went home today, sleeping herself peacefully into eternity with me on the bed by her side.

Death comes in the last bloom of age and the flush of youth. I try to shift the image of Mom now to her walking jubilantly years ago with us three kids and Dad across the uncomfortably hot dunes at Honeyman State Park on the Oregon coast, or frying bacon in an iron skillet on a Coleman stove in the woods clad in Dad's black-and-white-checked wool shirt in early morning chill. I remember our tossing a flaming potholder out the back door onto the rainy, wet porch at our home on Colby while she and I prepared a big holiday dinner together (when at least one pot holder caught fire on the oven elements.) Nevertheless, we were experts at working together in the kitchen, silently in sync. And similar to our performing, an arched eyebrow, a certain look, and I leapt into action.

There are so many stories. Laughter amid shopping trips when we stopped at a candy store on Colby to pick up a quarter pound of warm cashews from a lighted circling platter, and another quarter pound of chocolate truffles. We ate them all. There were too many singing gigs, and there was the looming silence, when she could not accept my questions, or chose to disapprove of what I was asking. There is silence with Dad, too. Life as I have come to know it exceeded their understanding. All conversations with them come at some point to silence.

How do I reconcile the joy and love—adoration, really—with the silence? How do I go on with Dad without Mom?

Dad appears to have put Mom's death out of mind. He spent most of Mother's last days alone in his room, unable, I think, to see her again. I can imagine in some way he was relieved for her to have ended her own confusion and come to peace. Yet he never visited her at the last. Despondent? Distracting himself? He talked to me about his Dodge. The one I gave to a niece. He is hurt I gave it away. Such dissonance with the dear life passing so near us! Is he distracting himself on purpose?

"That was a wonderful car," he said. "With very few miles on it, it was worth a lot of money." Clearly he meant to get a little money back if I had sold it. "I haven't gotten a thank you note; wouldn't you think I would?"

Oh, Lord, of course. But I suppose my niece thought it was I who gave it away, and not Dad. She did thank me. It would take a fairly prescient grandchild to realize her grandfather actually released the car through my hands and should also be thanked. My fault I didn't clarify that.

The Norwegians in my family outlived the Scots/Germans. I am about to bury my mother, a McGhee, having just turned 84 years of age. No youngster, she nevertheless was a junior to my father, a Norwegian who was naturalized a citizen along with his father in Everett, Washington, in 1910. He will turn 98 in less than a month. The McGhees and

Stilwells, whose history reaches back to the Hessian mercenaries in the Revolutionary War (fighting for the British) called him a foreigner. Her mother was so unhappy with her marriage that she did not speak to her for a year afterward.

When my mother began to fail, I couldn't speak. All the comfort I found for myself and others flew away. Scriptures I knew and phrases I offered in memorials seemed rote, shallow. The dreams of her future without my father vanished as did some of my own, accompanying her in the new freedom she had always anticipated. Since it appeared she could not be herself with him while she lived, she died too soon to enjoy living in the freedom his death would allow. Now I am picking up the pieces, discovering who I am in a world newly empty of color and song.

When I sold my parents' home, I expected to feel bereft. Instead, I went back to that empty house feeling grateful for the years they (and we) enjoyed there, the memories, the life that spilled from the doorways into the yard and beds of rhododendron. I dug up iris from my mother's small garden, a blissful bounty of eclectic plants so unlike the straight rows of my father's gardens, and planted them in my own yard next to the fern Dad gave me the year before, the one that was too ungainly for his taste. I treasure the family 300-day clock that now anchors my mantel. The 108-year-old copper luster pitcher, a wedding gift to my paternal grandparents in 1894, is in the oak and gracefully curved-glass china cabinet from Grandma McGhee, one Mom offered me a year or more ago, and I brought to Edmonds reluctantly, not wanting to impoverish their home. I then passed the pitcher on to my brother's widow who treasured antiques. What lack of foresight that I couldn't help my parents begin to hand some of their art and china to their children and grandchildren. Some watercolors and prints from Fowler Street now hanging on our walls make our home *more* like home. Dishes and cups speak more of familiarity than value. What I expected to be dark has become a different quality of light.

But even more than these are the musical lines of my mother's solos. When I was just a toddler, she sang while hanging up the laundry on lines Dad strung from the joists in the basement. I learned the melodies and the words—I inhaled them. "Beside still waters."‡ and "The Lord is my light, and my salvation; whom shall I fear?...."¶

I treasure the warmth of her voice when she sang, "How lovely are Thy dwellings."* Despite the language, which has aged, the message is clear. Mom believed it. Her singing brought it home in a way nothing will ever diminish, and often made Dad—and me—weep.

I sing and say psalms to myself while falling asleep, remembering the words and even the tunes because so many are set to the music my mother sang. I hear them as if she is singing to me. Picking up such pieces is an exercise in recovery, not loss. I am rich in the gifts of a mother who now sings with the angels and still in my own heart. I will never forget her song.

---

‡   Bernard Hamblen, composer
¶   Mary Frances Allitsen
*   Samuel Liddle, composer, 1908

CHAPTER 9

Breaking Trail

❦

Every time I write the month of "June" it becomes Mom's—
the whole month takes on her color.

I am flooded with memories that are both funny and outrageous: the time Mom thought it wiser to paint a closet in the nude because we wouldn't get any paint on our clothes; the times we looked at a circumstance the same way and laughed out loud or stifled ourselves because we were waiting to perform at an Eastern Star installation or a memorial service and couldn't possibly laugh. She brought flair and humor even to somber occasions.

That is one side. There is also her silence, the arched eyebrow, her withholding and monopolizing Dad. I am feeling freer of her earthly manifestations and ready for her whole spiritual self. I am exhausted. I cannot take in the swing of emotion from loss to fullness...so dramatic it causes whiplash.

"Now I have to keep up with the enemy," I lament. Mother created and shared the song in my life. My father had no such opportunity. Fearful of his judgment, I dread dealing with him.

Now my mother, in spirit? will be my companion as I break trail across a far-flung, unfamiliar swinging bridge with a father with whom I know only challenges. I am amazed at the hold our original crucible of family has on us. I am now freer of it than ever, but my! Does it show up when I am angry or upset and can't find the words to express myself. At this point in my life, following Mother's death, I have had virtually no contact with my father except in the last six months after he made me power of attorney. There was business to transact which made it easier, but now, when the business is laid to rest, what do I say to him? How to begin? I defer to him without thinking. I wait for him to take the lead. I serve, as if I were ten years old. So, I begin by treating him as I would a parishioner, with prayerful respect.

Dad is reading when I walk in and sit in the chair on the other side of the institutional corner table, bringing a list of his assets and liabilities in order to assure him that we can continue to afford his single room. He hasn't said so, but I know he's feeling vulnerable, wondering how this will all work out. His life has changed yet again. How does one recover from the loss of a beloved who shared 63 years of his life?

He's ready for me. In a three-by-five-inch spiral notebook he uses for his meager shopping list, he's written Oreo cookies, hearing aid batteries, Chap Stick (he calls it lipstick), his slatted table. I know the new home owners haven't yet rid themselves of all that was stored in the garage. He wants his hand-made end table and the lamp that were by his recliner at home. They will fit well into the corner of his new room, as will the chair that was in Mother's room at Rocky Glen.

I grew so fond of this slatted table in the next years, I couldn't let go of it, and moved it to my church office after he was gone. He went through periods of shop projects: routed lap trays, slatted benches and tables. One memorable evening not long after he had begun to use the ShopSmith, he shouted, running upstairs from the basement, "I've cut my leg! I've cut my leg!" waving a table-leg, and laughing at Mom's stricken face, before she saw he was only kidding.

At Rocky Glen, I check to see that he has a supply of dark chocolate. When we get through his list, comparing notes, I do what seems natural: I stand, he stands, we embrace, and say we love each other as if we've always done it this way. I never would have thought it possible, as if he has returned from a long trip. Perhaps this is true. I haven't ever been with him. There always was Mom. And for him, too? Always his wife who rushed first to hug me before he had time to gather himself.

When we used to walk on sunny Sunday afternoons as a threesome, we formed a couple, with one following. First Mother with me, Dad following. Then Dad with me, Mom following. Each had a different conversation with me. As soon as the other stepped up, the third would drop back as if it were a rule that only one of them could talk with me at a time.

I revel in the diversions I find at home to lighten the heaviness I feel. A war is going on in the backyard. Tully, the tabby, is stalking the robins that are warming three bright blue eggs in a nest woven on a diagonal brace under the deck. Whenever the cat goes out from the dining room slider, an immediate alarm sounds: two robin parents take defensive action by flying in different directions to the railing and up into the cedars, shouting threats. Tully makes a beeline to the margin between the decking to eye the nest below. She scans warily overhead; crouching low when one robin swoops to ward her off. She squints and skulks to find cover under the barbecue where she can watch where she thinks she can't be seen.

My cat creates a ruckus simply by being herself. She is clueless why the birds are upset. It doesn't seem fair for her to be vilified for this natural tendency. I can't fault her even when I watch her toss a field mouse in the air, even when I try to distract her so I can free the prey. These diversions sidetrack me from pervasive concern for my father after Mother's death. Dad needs time to absorb his new realities. So do I. Tully offers respite.

She models tranquility, absorbs my anxiety, and distracts me by her sleeping and eating habits, lobbying for snacks and treats all day long. There is always one more mouth and heart to pay attention to in our house. Her presence lightens the realities of our imaginations and fears.

Today I water the shaded yard under a mature cedar whose branches block the plants underneath from rain, water the tree hasn't already drawn into its extravagant height. Even plants prevent one another from thriving. I mow the lawn. Rake the clippings. Wash windows near enough to the ground to be reached with a sponge and squeegee. Then the sun emerges for good from under the clouds blowing swiftly across the high sky, warming the deck long enough for a nap. Contentment.

In a world of rivalries, animal and human, there is strife we have no responsibility for. There is a natural order we cannot disrupt. There are things we can only struggle to accept. But, I am a pastor. Yes? Can loss possibly be a gift? At least this, we have first to accept and possess our grief, holding it, learning its dimensions, before we can let it go. Mary Anne Radmacher wrote, "Those who see eternity in the sea, know there is no loss, only difficult gifts."*

---

* *Simply an Inspired Life,* by Mary Anne Radmacher and Jonathan Lockwood Huie

After Mother's death, I do not feel orphaned. I am aware of her as she appeared to me in the past when she worked for the school district and walked to and from her office at lunch time, and when the dining room table was covered with needles, thread, designs, and scissors, brocade and silk destined to become liturgical banners for Our Savior's Lutheran Church. That very name I confess I ridiculed in the family fashion years ago, "Your church thinks they have a monopoly?"

Today I think these are not old memories. This is not the past. It is essence: June as God created her. June returned to spirit. This is the real thing, her spirit loosed into the cosmos, free, and more whole in my heart than she ever could be in the world. In a civilization where we count death as loss, I resolve to let her go, to thank God, to celebrate her gifts, and to trust her gifts continue to abound. This is a loss that already has become a gift that will grow over time.

We celebrate Dad's 98th birthday on a sunny Fourth of July when Dad seems to enjoy himself, walker in hand, in and out of my low car, relieved, perhaps, of a burden. He and I sit on the back deck warmed by the sun as he talks with several of his grandchildren.

He's more aware now and free to talk about some of the matters I've been handling for six months since his first hospitalization. He wants his driver's license back, though he hasn't driven since Christmas. He needs ID? I am frantic trying to remember where I put it.

"I wish I knew how the property was distributed to the kids," he says. I wonder how to tell him, feeling responsible and quickly guilty. And then he adds, "I suppose you had your hands full." In spades! I think, but say nothing. I should give him a list of what went to whom. Even with legal authority to manage his affairs, I stand back in respectful distance. He is my father, after all. And all I feel I have done is pay him respect throughout my life. He trusts me now, clearly. So I learn day by day to speak to him as an equal as if I were his pastor or friend.

We have a number of issues to resolve, beginning with a Social Security Administration telephone conference to verify his eligibility to receive Mother's benefits. He can use a phone in a private room off the lobby and in fact, he's made calls there already. I'm impressed how he's rising to these new occasions.

"I'd like to check into getting a new hearing aid for my right ear," he tells me. The last purchase was one for his left ear, costing $2000. Who can afford hearing aids? He's worn them for at least 50 years. They're fallible, requiring constant tinkering.

The title of one of our hymns is, "God of the Sparrow."* I adopted the phrase for my prayers. The Creator seems so immense to me, yet so tender, that nothing—no creature, nor any of us—is beyond the reach of Mystery or its grasp on us. It is we who turn away. This is not everyone's view, of course. But I certainly prefer not to imagine this great mystery as a bearded elder on a cloud.

Today, one day for myself, I am content with the morning quiet, sipping coffee on the deck while reading the newspaper. The call of chickadee, junco, robin, crow, and Northern Flicker articulate the silence. Once I am absorbed in my day I forget to listen. So at the beginning, it is a gentle way to waken.

My past tells me the cosmos offers a hand when I don't know what to look for or how to look or listen. A discovery or sudden insight I often miss altogether—an unseen presence that speaks in the reflections of fir on a still, mountain lake, the veiled cloud-framed setting sun, the rings a stone makes when tossed into a pond. When I see a weasel, raccoon, or seagull on the side of the road injured from a collision, I sigh and give thanks at my hope that such as these are also gathered into the fold at the end.

Last year, I tore out the fence that separated our front yard from the yard to the south. Now we have a wonderful mélange of theirs and ours, the border indistinct. We joke about whose weeds we ought to pull. I am surprised that even there in the view of neighbors through the foliage, I can scoot along on the ground trimming the edge of the grass feeling alone in the world. The cosmos writ small in my own plot of ground, I feel a part of it all. I place a small basin in front near the forsythia to reflect the sky. Tully stops there now to have a drink as she scouts the perimeter.

---

* Tune, Roeder, Lyrics, Jaroslav Vajda. *The New Century Hymnal*, Pilgrim Press, p 32.

In the stack of my mother's music was an old song titled, "My God and I,"* The companionable words sing again in my heart as I remember how far back my own journey began and how faithful God has been "through the years," "in the fields," wherever I was. I didn't always think so. And even when I draw into that comfort alone, there is the danger of exclusivity, of imagining only me and Jesus together without acknowledging, including, and honoring the myriad others with whom we share our lives on this fragile planet.

While I relish those old words and images, I use the strength I find there to reach out of my solitude to others, to engage in difficult encounters, to risk ventures without predictable results. Even as Jesus relied on intimate communion with the one he calls his father, he chose to spend time with 12 or more named men and a few women, and a host of unnamed female and male companions, teaching them what he knew. He engaged in relationships that certainly must have tried his patience. But those fellow journeyers, as flawed, as human as we, carried on the message.

How do I translate my own blessed communion to the world? By tearing down fences and learning which weeds to pull, which branches to prune between me and my neighbors.

Dad and I are beginning to adjust to decision making. We're getting better at it. I also experience a softer side of Dad than I've ever known. As a kid I saw both the negative side—absent: remote and disengaged—and the punitive side. In my adult years he was always glad to see me when I drove up for lunch, and stayed long enough with Mom and me at their kitchen table to be polite, but he left for his nap soon after. Our conversation has always been awkward.

"Cathy?" It's Dad on the phone.

"Hi, Dad."

"How are you?" Hear this gracious inquiry now.

"I'm fine; I'm doing fine," I assure him, surprised he asks.

"That's good. Listen, I'm wondering if, when you come up, you could bring some new socks, and some hearing aid batteries. I'm almost out."

---

*   Lyrics and tune by Austria Wihtol, aka I. B. Sergei, 1915

"Sure, Dad. I'll be coming Saturday."

"That would be great. Thanks a lot, Honey. I love you."

Astonishing!

"I love you, Dad."

When Mom was around, she used those words of love and Dad didn't have to. Now, if he doesn't or I don't, they aren't expressed. What surprises me is that he does it. Could it mean he also believes it? It has to. It rings true. I am glad to respond, even in my disbelief. I am delighted. I have years of love to make up, and now is the time.

We never know when mercy or grace will appear. How fortunate we are that we can accept it when we recognize it and return it in kind. His affection thaws the ice in me.

In the film *The Natural,** Robert Redford's character is told, "There's the life you learn with, and then there's the life you live with after that." I've been bogged down, disappointed with myself in the trials and errors of learning how to live in healthy relationships. But the errors were how I learned. If I didn't feel God calling me forward through the mistakes to push the boundaries, to persist through the obscure valleys, I probably would not have come this far. Something drew me forward. Something sustained me. This is hope. Spirit energy. Belief in what I can imagine. The examples of others. The easiest way to see the hand of Mystery is in the past, like the wake of a small boat on a quiet, still lake. But sometimes it is luminous in our eyes.

As I learn to know my Dad, I'm sad that I'm only beginning to see him whole. How many wasted years! But that diminishes both him and me. They weren't wasted, really. I developed other strengths I might not have while I adjusted—or tried to adjust—to his emotional absence and intrusive judgment. How I have wanted a father like this one! And I am nearly 60. That in itself is amazing, and since he is 38 years older than I, it is nothing short of a miracle.

I am trying to practice being a silent presence, offering deep listening, and a witness to the Spirit who hovers among and between us. The people I pray for circulate in my head; I see them as clear as day. I can't do anything tangible for most of them. But *doing* is not what is needed.

---

*   1984 American sports film based on Bernard Malamud's 1952 novel

To balance our lives, to grow, to heal, what we need are periods of *being*. Maybe only when day shifts to night, when there's nothing to be done but sleep—or pray—will our concerns come to rest. I don't know. Everyone has to find her own way. I don't think I can bring peace to others as if it were a gift. But maybe in forming my own prayer, sharing it, and letting it go, I can leave others a sense of presence that they can ponder, and perhaps embrace and extend.

Since I have spent most of the last five years in the still point of retirement, seminary, and very part time work, I am learning again to adjust to the whirlwind of a church calendar. There is lag time between my thinking and feeling. It's often only some time after interacting with others that I discover an image or example that might be helpful, if not to them, at least to me. A way to hold them. Maybe I have a slow integration ratio between being and doing. Will the ratio shorten with time and practice? A busy weekend at church leads to a quiet Sunday night. On such a typical Sunday evening, the work of the day laid to rest, I used to call Mom.

"Oh, hello, Darling!" she'd say in her expressive voice, pleasure shimmering. "I was just thinking about calling you."

Now, I hold my sadness close. I pause, breathe thanks, and call forth a consoling memory. I like to think she's nearby, flying in low. She thought flying saucers were angels; why not she an angel now, checking in to see how we're doing? She was tired. But when the handwriting was on the wall, she fought back. Angry, she didn't go gently.

I recall her frustration: "Which is my car in the parking lot?! Give me the keys, or I'll just walk home! I know where it is."

Is she happy now? Able to be who she wanted to be? I weep. How can she not be at peace in ways the image of "heaven" as a place spoke to her? I use these images at memorials myself. Some of the phrases are tongue-in-cheek, familiar lines of old hymns, spirituals about "golden shoes." Others are Scripture: *Don't let your hearts be troubled. You have faith in God; have faith in me as well. In God's house there are many dwelling places; otherwise, how could I have told you I go to prepare a place for you? (John 14.2)*

I call a nurse to check in on Dad. She tells me he's in his room with the door closed watching television. "He said to tell you he's doing okay, and gave me a big smile," she says. I smile, too.

Loving the Enemy

The lesson of aging is not mastery but letting go.
When things reach maturity, they decay of themselves.

~Lao-Tzu

Recovering from seven months of frenzy, I spent those months trying to react to, then to anticipate, and finally simply to accept my father's and mother's conditions. How fortunate we are to have medical personnel who know what to do. But it stopped my heart when they said, "We don't really know; we can't tell." And then I had to accept there were circumstances beyond anyone's doing anything at all, similar to my little brother's experience with a double kidney/pancreas transplant, one of the first at the University of Washington Medical Center in Seattle.

As I'd approached his room, I saw a group of doctors in white coats standing near his door, talking together very quietly. I began to realize even they didn't know for sure what to do for him. Now, life as I knew it has moved inexorably toward my mother's end as I continue beyond hers (beyond my brother's) and into a reality without them both.

William Bridges, a master of the process of transition from one phase of life to another, urges us to make way for the new. If we don't, we complain that things aren't going our way—the way we want them to go. We're trying to push the river rather than letting it flow, regardless the way it naturally flows. Of course this is murderously difficult in the face of death, break-ups, loss of job, and so forth.*

I have not always been a gardener, and still am not. Ardene loves to care for our yard, with my help. I love the trees, and our yard emerging with new perspectives as the seasons change. It is one of the ways I get my mind off myself.

Bridges counsels we give ourselves over to the way of transition. Let go when life presents us with a time of ending, abandon ourselves to what seems like a plateau when that is where we find ourselves, seize the opportunity to make a new beginning when that moment presents itself. I love this quip I overheard on campus one afternoon: "I know when one door closes, another one opens. But it's *hell* in the hallway!"

---

* Bridges, William. *The Way of Transition.* Perseus Publishing, 2001

It's time to watch the neighbors garden. I want to simply be and stay put.

Six years ago I could not have said where my entering the School of Theology at Seattle University would lead. Today I cannot say where my role as one of four pastors at an historic American Baptist Church will lead. Spiritual quest is not about charts; it is about readiness. It is not about our gifts alone, but about what we make of those gifts. God does not call the equipped, an old saying goes; God equips those God calls.

After Dad and I spend an hour on the will made when he and Mom were so sick, I feel dragged into the past trying to bring up-to-date a reality he apparently does not see. Although this is a formality only, it reveals his parsimony of the past and makes me sad. I get through it as fast as I respectfully can. Then I drive home and nuzzle my cat on the back deck.

Even I am not who I was 10 years ago, 5 years ago? Five minutes ago? My searching has attracted other seekers and we sit, knee to knee, parsing out the grammar of a God whose ways we don't understand. But my experience of that God cannot inform anyone who does not undertake her or his own journey. I can describe mine, but all of us must try to see the mind, the design perhaps, or its lack within my and their own worlds, even to describing who that God is for them.

Some of us experience a God we cannot name. Others begin with the name, cannot find that God, lament or rage that anyone with the name ought not allow the condition of the world, and walk away. But Benedictine Joan Chittister advises we explore the difference between "what the authorities say about God and what the heart knows about God."* God is a matter of experience, first, and doctrine, second.

I review the accounts, make out calendars, try to predict how long the money will last. The likelihood that Dad will deplete his funds is remote. I am annoyed he stayed in "his" home until Mom was exhausted. They could easily have arranged to move to a retirement home and she, no doubt, would have qualified for assistance. This nursing center costs upwards of $6000 a month, including prescriptions and incidentals. The first few times I wrote such large checks I hyperventilated, staggered by the cost. Now I have adjusted, and the costs are a bit lower. But it's still an amazing amount of money. When could we ever have held a conference to

---

* Chittister, Joan. Op.cit. p 102

question the decisions they were making in their lives, and how might they have been more comfortable without doing everything for themselves?

"I'd like to see the invoices from the nursing home and the pharmacy, Cathy," he told me on the phone this morning. Fine. Complete the loop. He's still in charge. He is never settled, never done. Always something on his mind. I am there at least twice a week. In between, I believe he needs to adjust to his situation.

The phone rings, and as usual, Ardene answers. And Dad asks, "June?"

"No, it's me, Ardene," she tells him.

Dad laughs, realizing what he's done. Still catching his own mistakes at his age. He's thinking about paying me for the time and trouble I take to support him. About time! But he's not clear about a rate. His bias to support others who need "charity" takes top tier.

He begins many statements and never finishes them. Can't he pursue his thought to the end? He begins, then pauses until I find myself completing them. Did Mom do that for him? First I think this is an inability to prepare, but I wonder if it's an inability to say what he wants. He has always done that about some issues, of course, like buying a new car, or notoriously, a lawn mower. His were state of the art. But those were surprises to the family. The worst of his spontaneous "good buys" was a used Nash Rambler that we soon discovered, hanging on as it swayed when we turned corners or hit a bump, the headliner powdered us with red dust. Unbeknownst to him and no doubt a coup for his salesman, the car had clearly been driven somewhere in a desert. We complained ceaselessly about that car. He didn't keep it long, but soon had another. When he finally decides, he acts unilaterally; but when he's deliberating something, he trails off in wonder.

I dreamt Dad had moved home! I couldn't fathom how he had gotten out or who had allowed it, but here he was, big as life. Not good. And then my dream shifts to a church meeting where I sit with a stack of lavender pages printed so faintly I can't read them. Shades of the old ditto machine.

Someone once complimented me on how demure I am. Demure, *schemure*. Frank and truthful would be a big improvement. I am trying to step more firmly into my own sense of authority. When I'm "in charge," such as in the classroom or at an event, it's not a problem. But in interactions with peers sometimes, or with superiors much of the time, I defer far too often. It's an old habit encouraged by my parents' interpretation of Scripture, "Value others over yourselves, each of you thinking of the interest of others before your own."*

I still am afraid something I don't know or haven't done will sabotage me and some grand opportunity. As I write this now, I'm sad at the many years I spent being fearful. When I was in elementary school, I used to worry that when I got to school on the first day in the fall I would be told to repeat the prior grade. Added to that fear, I used to pray for friends. I was lonely and clueless why I felt so distant from others. I identified with Theodore Roethke's 1950s poem about his care of a bedraggled geranium—his anger when a maid threw it out. Like Tully with the angry robins, I've lived my life ducking—not from real—but from metaphorical blows.

Dad told me a few weeks ago, "Your mother and I always made our decisions together. We never disagreed." My jaw dropped. No kidding! He remembers his rich life, and he misses her deeply. But he clearly never knew what she told me behind his back, or how often she blamed him for the things she couldn't do and wasn't strong enough to lobby for. I would have hoped what she told me was her rehearsal, and then she would tell Dad what she thought. Apparently not.

For his part, I'm realizing Dad has rarely planned ahead to forecast his mood while taking the wishes of others into account. He can't multitask. Maybe he could once. But not now. Can he visualize? I wonder how it was possible that he was such a creative craftsman and picture framer. Why did he stay so long in their home without thinking his wife could use more support and time off? On the other hand, I stayed at Roosevelt High 25 years myself, in four different roles: At Tune-Inn, as off-campus alternative-school manager, English teacher and annual advisor, counselor, and finally lead counselor. One school, different positions. Eventually I see what I learned in that crucible of family sixty years ago is still at work—in Dad and in me. I have to let go of a dimension of my criticism.

There was the summer our family of five "decided" (he chose) to go to Banff, Alberta on the spur of the moment (he'd been there as a youth). We threw sleeping bags, canned goods, camping equipment, the

---

* *Philippians 2.3*

tent, camera and clothes into the car that evening and headed out the next morning. What Dad failed to anticipate was that even in summer, mountain nights are very cold. We didn't have a single woolen blanket; our sleeping bags were cotton flannel. We nearly froze. Getting ready for sleep, we took off our clothes, put on our pajamas, and then put all our clothes back on including coats before climbing into the bags. It was a beautiful, exotic trip (Mounties, the tram to Sulphur Mountain, elk, deer), except for the freezing nights in our dark green umbrella tent. A counterpoint to this were the huge fires Dad built at campsites after dinner. Roasting marshmallows for S'mores and being toasty warm under the fir and cedar of the campground were restorative. I felt at peace in those camps. When I went to church camp near Burton, Washington, I loved the Madrona trees that studded the site and carpeted the trails to the beach, the great cedar and fir that lined our walk to the "Green Cathedral" for worship. After that quiet time, my friends and I charged with anticipation down the trail to the bonfire on the graveled beach where we enjoyed the blazing fire while we sang together at twilight: "Tell Me Why," "Do Lord," "Viva L'amour," "Spirit of the Living God, fall afresh on me."

It might have been hard for Dad to negotiate with Mom, but impossible with three other egos. He could never have met our initiatives with any rational rebuttal. I think he must have had a hard time finding the words for his decisions; he said no—or sometimes yes—and stopped short of explanations or rationale. To this day, in spite of my deepening experience, I am still just as disconcerted by Dad's control as my brothers were.

When I walk in one morning in late August, Dad looks sad. Bored, perhaps, and a little depressed. He has not enough to do, but also no inclination to do much of anything. He has another infection, but with treatment I think he will bounce back as he has before. He's also probably come to the realization that this is what his life is now. It will not change. It seems natural to me that he will not maintain his mood any differently than he did at home. Any transition, even one as stark as this, eventually merges into sameness, and no matter how peaceful or comforting, will promise little. Perhaps my own anticipation and anxiety are settling into routine as well. How can he not continue to be who he is, content or anxious, confident or fearful, from day to day?

As September opens, the nights and mornings colder, Dad is slowly rediscovering how to entertain himself. On a cool but brilliantly sunny day, he finishes trimming the leaves of the Dracaena that's flourishing under his care on his corner table.

He must wonder why he doesn't hear more from his grandchildren, some grown with kids of their own. Visits are few and great grandchildren arrive only with their parents. But didn't he spawn the distance, emotional and otherwise? I know his silence in my past, so austere. How else could I have returned to him anything but silence? Oh, I have tried. Believe me, I am still trying. How can others, even his own grandchildren, who have forgotten the rides in the yard cart, respond to him but to return the silence? Or perhaps he's just far too old, and too deaf, and they're far too busy to make the time to have an awkward conversation. Grandchildren in many of the families I know tend not to visit their grandparents on their own either.

It's a severe judgment that when we sow the wind we reap the whirlwind. Didn't Dad do just that? Sow detachment and judgment within his family, without grace, without forgiveness? Now he is reaping a desert void of feeling, especially with his eldest son. It seems a given. But he can't see it. No doubt it was the way he was parented, to the extent he was at all. The generations of immigrants had many challenges to face. This makes me sad. But it's real. I wonder if we'll ever talk about any of it? Thankfully, the gospel doesn't end there. Scripture also says "Those who sow in tears, will reap in songs of joy." None of us is competent to predict or judge how the future will unfold—certainly not beyond the grave. I have seen Dad deep in conversation with one grandson, and I know he and Mom spent time with my eldest niece when she was in high school. He must not be able to remember these nurturing dialogues now.

Nevertheless, it is incredible to sit knee to knee with him and have a conversation, he in the so-called "wedding" chair with his weathered and fragile hands on the wooden arms, me on the bed with my notepad, reviewing the details he is weighing. When I return home later that afternoon, he has left me a message; he feels good about our talk. We have done something together successfully!

It is a chilly and clear afternoon, maybe we could go out for a walk? My longtime Camano friend, Sue, has given Dad a notebook, colored pencils, and a bag to stow it all, so he can explain and illustrate the process he used to frame pictures step-by-step. What a good idea! But she doesn't know him well enough either.

He laughs, shaking his head. "I don't know what I'm going to do until I start to do it," he said.

So he appears capricious because he simply does not know what he thinks until it comes out in words or action. He never took the time to learn who he was, of course; doing that was not the call of his generation. He grew up in the teens and '20s. Conversation by conversation, I am getting steadily closer to understanding how he thinks and what he can and cannot do. These revelations reveal a new dimension to his personality, distinct from patriarch. Softening at each new expression, I see his humanity, his flaws, and vulnerabilities he once wouldn't reveal and that might lead to apology. I'm grateful, more empathetic.

A week later I arrive home to a message explaining Dad has yet another urinary tract infection. I could lose him at any time. Our time together, so long sought, may well end before I am ready. And who is ever "ready" for endings? Life is dangerous. I am surrounded by people with illness: lungs, eyes (macular degeneration), cancer, hearts, Alzheimer's, Parkinson's, MS. It's as if I'm waking up in the nick of time to be a player for the last act. God, I hope there's more than one act left.

I spent some time with the poetry of Mary Oliver. Her poem about wild geese illumines our own calendar. Northwest geese are circling overhead, regrouping to fly south. The waxing harvest moon floats as if it's a ghost planet in the darkening sky. Ardene and I have felt the chill in the morning and put on the heavier comforter, readying for winter. We spot two, then three such migratory circlings organizing themselves. The clear blue sky persists, deepening contrast with the russets, reds and golds of early-turning maples. We are in the midst of God, as God is in our midst: constant, creative, and unseen.

Good thing. Without a reference point, we risk thinking ourselves the center. The spiritual life calls us deeper and deeper into a sort of wandering. Yet not wandering—grounding in the present. Once we weary of our culture's itinerant touch stones, we become accustomed to the dance of the seasons, the sun and moon rise, the constant stars. One of the trips Ardene and I love to take is north to the delta of the Skagit River in La

Conner. It's smack in the middle of the Pacific Flyway for birds migrating north: chiefly, Snow Geese and Trumpeter Swan. They're wary of people and thus highways, so we pull off and find a muddy trail to get close enough to a damp pasture where they flock together to eat, flying over each other to get to the front of the group and fresh grass.

Snow Geese fly hundreds at a time. And Trumpeter Swan are gorgeous flying machines, resembling the silhouette of a Boeing 747 when aloft. The weather is still hot midday and late afternoon, but chilly at night. There are cozy inns in the valley and at La Conner on the Swinomish Channel between Saratoga Passage and Bellingham Bay, very busy with autumn boaters.

The darker side of the world also registers with us. Life seems unprecedented in its eclipse of constants: terrorists appear on our own soil using our technology; trusted spiritual mentors take advantage of innocent charges and their bishops move them like pawns to conceal them, idols of corporate success feather only their own nests. What icon can be left unsullied?

I have taken the time to account for the hours, errands, purchases and mileage of the last six months, before and after my parents' move to the nursing home. Going over my calendar and the bills, I come close to a reasonable estimate. I am also able finally to resolve a lingering conundrum about health insurance for bills dated last January. It took nine months for the hospital and the insurance company to agree. The insurer did not account for what I paid them, or my check is applied to the wrong account, or the hospital bills the wrong insurance company, etc. The representatives on the phone are consistently gracious, thank heavens, and eventually things work as they should. The paperwork takes at least a day a week.

It's only fair that the agreement between my father and me remain on the table. He's the one who asked me to account for my time. The result is that we have a reasonable financial agreement, and I feel less put upon than I might. When I was young many of my activities with Mom were unacknowledged and to her, a gift—yet not always with my gracious regard. As much as I enjoyed the pleasure of accompanying her, I put in hours that were far beyond what I felt like giving. Now I will pay myself only for time if it's a consultation with Dad's attorney or his doctor. Mileage only, to Everett and back, period.

This morning the congregation officially affirmed my three colleagues and me as a pastoral team. The church affirmed the search committee's choice of the new lead pastor to follow Dr. Romney, and in addition, my two colleagues and me as the pastoral staff. Church members laid hands on us as we prayed together. A tear rolled down my cheek, marking the culmination of four years of hope and patience. In spite of the opposition of the American Baptist Churches of the Northwest Region to ordain to the ministry a gay woman married to her partner, the struggle of Seattle First Baptist Church to find itself after Dr. Romney's departure, and my own doubt, now I am an integral part of this pastoral team. I am in my fourth year of part-time ministry, and the first woman pastor in this church's history whose tenure exceeds three years. We are an historic "First Church"—one very like the one in Everett in which I grew up. When I first walked into Seattle First Baptist in 1993, I was so delighted with the familiarly designed sanctuary, although far grander than the old Everett church, that it and the warm welcome from strangers felt like just returning "home." In a year or more, I truly felt at home, and here was the place I felt called to the ministry. I have truly returned to the place I began and am beginning to know it for the first time.

While most Protestant churches have been wrestling with the ethics of accepting sexual minorities, ours chose to accept the LGBTQ community without question in every dimension. We were not the first. The United Church of Christ preceded us all in 1969. But one of our pastors celebrated the marriage (then, not legal in itself) of two women in 1979. We have continued that practice since, legal or not. We worked for Marriage Equality in Washington State, and when equal marriage passed, we were the first church in Seattle to marry 12 couples who made vows to each other while three pastors shared the liturgy. The church was packed.

CHAPTER 10

On Being with My Father

❧❧❧

When I walk into Room 106 in early October, Dad is asleep, his eyes closed, his mouth gaping, hands folded across his chest. It takes more than a few minutes to rouse him. How will it be when his sleep is eternal? I am rehearsing for his death. I watch him for a few minutes since what I see in him is entirely different from what I used to see. He is completely vulnerable, not likely to waken angry that he's been disturbed.

He sits up, organizes himself to stand, keeping his walker nearby, and settles in his favorite chair which grows dingier by the week. He's felt weak because of antibiotics, he explains, but it's clear he finds being here comfortable and calming. So recently settled and on his own, he hates to change the routine. He's not looking forward to our trip to have his eye pressure and hearing aids checked.

"It's hard to leave," he offers. "…too much trouble."

I agree, silently wondering how long he'll be here, how long I'll be delivering him to doctors and hearing aid specialists. How does one follow a father of such an age that any day could be his last? What can we talk about that is not always the last things? He had been married for 63 years. The last time he lived alone was winter of 1939. When we were kids, he made only two business trips for Scott Paper Company that I know of, one to Chicago and one to Philadelphia where he took a host of slides to show his children the beginnings of our nation, Betsy Ross' flag, the Liberty Bell, the whole nine yards. From Chicago he brought me a menu from *Chez Paris* where Helen Traubel sang pop songs. He admired her, once thought one of the best American Wagnerian Sopranos.

We're ready for three appointments today. Dressed in his blue-and-white-striped shirt buttoned up to his chin under a dark blue cardigan, my father walks into the medical office with a big smile as person after person greets him with warmth. It is months since he's been out, and seeing Dad cheers them. Being here is cheering him. He is remarkable at 98: walking jauntily, not leaning on his walker, but swinging it over the cracks in the sidewalk and curbs without missing a step.

He is as pleasant now as he was harsh in my past. I quailed when I accepted the responsibility of caring for him directly without Mother as go-between, but as I watch him face his limitations and hear him think out loud, I begin to understand my past. I see why he held himself so taut and others to such a high standard, scorning those who appeared weak— even pitying his younger son because of his illness rather than encouraging Lew to be the strong, creative person he was. He also overprotected me, and left me with the impression I needed to be protected. This is not unusual for a first generation of immigrants. They'd rather their kids lived at home until someone else—a spouse, of course—assumed "responsibility" for them. Then they could relax. This legacy led one therapist to tell me I had learned "helplessness" rather than self-assurance. I am still trying to eliminate it. Part of Dad died when he lost his mother at six. Without adequate grieving or compassionate parenting, he passed that death on to us.

As I help him in and out of the car, I am beginning to know that he is just a man who did the best he could with what he had. It may not have been what I wished, but as I more fully understand his wounds and how he learned to cope, I am starting to accept all of him, daring to bring more of my own life into his closely-held space. Now that Dad actually depends on me, we are developing a relationship in real time.

As I grow into my ministry I also need time away from it as I accompany my father and seek respite, which is part of the fabric. Recovery must be observed as seriously as the events I attend, the people I see, the worship we plan. Worship itself is renewal. And respite is as integral to reaching out as stretching is to exercise, quiet to conversation.

I have kept a journal ever since my Aunt Evelyn gave me a diary in 1953 when I was in fifth grade. Much later I read that a writer recommended we stop writing when there is still a little water in the well—

drops that will flow together in the night, leaving plenty for the morning. I write out of the overflow—out of the overflowing cup. I try to live out of it. The mystery is that we can experience abundance simply by recognizing and naming the full half of the glass. It is all in our perspective. We need to respect the welling up of abundance as we rest.

I grew up with a sense of scarcity, a constant fear of never having enough money, safety, or love. All was jealously guarded lest we run out. The irony was that we had enough. We rarely went without. Sure, my first bike was used. I painted it blue with silver trim (and the next year chartreuse). But my shoes fit, I took piano lessons, and Mom annually made me new skirts and jackets. We spent hours searching for fabric in Seattle, from Frederick and Nelson to the Bon Marché, Penney's and Rhodes Department Store. This was to match the sweaters we bought so I could wear matching colors like my friends—who bought Jantzen outfits already matched. It took us hours, relieved by lunch at the Green Onion café across Fifth from Fredericks.

When I went in search of the abundant life in earnest, I was surprised to find in the places I searched, an opportunity to give. Abundance was not exactly where I expected to find it. I was learning to seek, to ask, and to knock. Plenty was hidden in plain sight. Unless we are part of the great population of underserved and underrepresented people without adequate work and shelter, abundance can be as simple as a shift in perspective.

My father laughed at himself this afternoon, sitting on the blue chair, his walker at his left. "Sometimes I spit when I talk!" And then, "I misread my clock and got up at 1:00 a.m. last night, thinking it was morning." He laughs (laughs!) and adds, "They love me in this red sweater." A beautiful soft wool given him at a Christmas long past.

Smiling, I concur. "Yes, you look great."

"That's what they say," he replies, grinning back. "They must think I'm a character," his smile broadens. He *is* a character. He is 98, with a sound mind, delighted with the new phone I brought him, not hesitating to call whomever he likes—even though he can hardly hear them. Slowly he refeathers his nest.

Where was *this* man for the last 60 years? Has his separation from his long-loved wife freed him to the simple pleasures of bachelorhood?

Or has he chosen to settle for what is, and be content? Why has he relinquished the harsh judgment that met all of us at the door? I am sad that only now I seem to be on par with him: he asks me questions and even listens to me. I wish it had not taken 60 years. On the other hand, what if now I am merely the only woman in his life like Mother was? Surely he talked with her like this. I grieve that his softness has come so late when my brothers and I knew only rigidity.

David withdrew, I excelled, and Lew dared to improvise, not caring about rubrics. Now ignorant of his effects on his children (as far as I can tell) my father wonders where his remaining son and his grandchildren are. In his disappointment, he sits alone, seeming to grieve not seeing more of his family. But it's difficult for him to picture the growing families of great grandchildren whose parents are not far away, but much too involved in their lives to visit.

On a cold November Saturday Ardene and I turn TV to football; for a while I love the crowd roaring, the band, the hoopla. And then I am done. It is as satisfying to turn it off as it was to turn it on. Or, find a quieter place downstairs in my study. Silence is my respite. I remember an early recognition of silence during a prayer in a home where Mother had been asked to sing. The silence that complemented my organ practice in our cold, empty church when I was 14. The silence between the words in worship, the rests in the music emphasizing the phrasing of the line, the awesome pause at the immediate end of a symphony—until the conductor lowers his arms. I stop breathing.

Silence also surprised me on sunny afternoons when I drove west to the home of my best high school friend, Ann. I coasted up the sloping driveway to her place on the bluff above the Mukilteo beach, put on the brake, turned off the key, and stepped out. Utter peace. I could just hear the lapping of waves on the pebbled Edgewater beach below. Something inside loosened. I felt free enough to breathe, and drew deeply of the salty air.

Ever since, I seek the absence of sound to balance the noise of the city. Silence allows me to hear the soft click of Dad's cherished 300-day clock, now on my mantel whirling its gold orbs to the end of their cycle and reversing. The refrigerator clunking to a stop. The furnace, finally at temperature. Silence. I wish I could hold it in my hands or capture it in a box to open at will. Lift the lid and let out vastness of space to absorb the clamor of our lives, leaving a whisper of vacuum behind. Silence. Cathedrals beckon me where thick, tall doors and stone walls shelter the soul. Forests where ancient trees create sanctuary. We need to preserve places like this in the midst of our world, insist on keeping places like "One square inch" of silence in the Olympic National Forest on the Olympic Peninsula, and seeing that we set aside others. Gordon Hempton records environmental sound from many of these natural locations.*

On my next visit to Rocky Glen decorations are being hung for Christmas. Dad talks for 45 minutes nonstop, then wants to nap before dinner.

"I sleep a lot in the daytime because I don't sleep at night," he explains. "I don't sleep at all. I just watch the clock." Sleeping pills, antidepressants, nothing seems to work. Or does he sleep without realizing it? Today I understand that what he is saying may not actually be his reality. It is his impression of being awake he remembers, perhaps a dream; to the observer he is sound asleep.

It is helpful for me to see him in this place, experiencing his final months. Year? Because I can imagine how it may be for me one day. I have accompanied no one to death as closely as he now, particularly as aware as he is. But even his keen awareness is skewed by the fugues of his napping and waking, conversations and baseball games. What is real for him? What does he imagine and remember?

Aging adults, even with sound minds, spend much of their time reminiscing, dreaming, reviewing old stories and people in their past. Dad still reads the news, so he often has some comment about the administration. Even so, some of his stories are from his twenties, and in a couple of years, they will be of his childhood.

I discover that no one visited Dad for Thanksgiving when Ardene and I were on a break. Even my brother hadn't been by; but I suspect Dad is just as comfortable without him. They took adversarial stances when Dave was just a child. He never approved of Dave's interest in cars and model planes, thought them beneath him in spite of his skill, winning eighth place in a national contest for building a model car from a kit

---

* www.soundtracker.com/about-gordon-hempton

and then redesigning the model. His name and picture appeared in the Everett Herald. Did Dad expect a son who would excel in the subjects Dad hadn't? Forestry, I suppose, or engineering? (Dad left college without a degree). And Dave couldn't imagine who that would be besides who he was while working so hard to meet his father's expectations. After all these years, nothing can be done. I grieve for my brother's pain. My nephew and his wife live across the country with their two sons; my nieces are absorbed with their young children. I wonder if no one but me, the so-called "maiden aunt," imagines there is a "whole family." But, I ask myself, what family did I think I was attending to all these years?

Who were those four persons whose lives I balanced? I joked when things were too serious, I made sarcastic remarks when I thought I was funny, changed the subject, explained motivations when any two of them were at odds. Was this a natural invention? I was the middle child, trying to steady the tensions. It was constant. My awareness, unceasing.

The more we try to wrench our agenda into a vision of holy peace, the more we must learn to let in the peace we know we have—or that, with practice, blooms from within. The easier it is then to see the one in front of us, the one person whose eyes meet ours, whose life stops long enough for us to tease out the fragile, inexplicable common ground between us. We are surrounded by crowds, canned music, and the cold blast of air from ever-opening doors. But we behold an unfolding that is not unlike communion. This day, this person, this bread, this wine. The things of eternity are simple. They don't need embellishment.

Our noble fir is propped against the fence at home, its butt in a bucket. The crèche is still in its box. Little by little, the greening will grow as December progresses and we put Christmas together, one piece at a time.

But I don't feel behind. So many meaningful relationships! Conversation with a woman who recently moved to Seattle and suspends her fragile life to cope with the holidays. Another at lunch with an elderly friend who will spend his first Christmas in a home for those living with Alzheimer's. Then a telephone conversation with a young man whose advancing symptoms of AIDS threaten his life. How does he hold onto the life he has in the midst of its ending? Each moment shared with one person stops time and becomes my ministry—presence alone. Companionship and listening are ministry from all of us if we offer them authentically, open to the sacred space between us, the mysteries of spirit and humanity.

Everyone who opens to me is like a book with its own language, imagery, dark places and light; introduction, foreword, footnotes, end notes, annotations, dog-eared pages. Tales worn with retelling. These encounters have become my Advent, the four weeks Christendom spends preparing for Christmas.

"Not a creature was stirring—not even a mouse," is also what we're living at home. The field mouse Tully brought in last July is still here, just not very robust. He or she wakes us with tiny claws scrabbling inside the cupboards, amplified by the night. We spent weeks with appliances askew, elaborate arrangements of netting, cheese, and plastic bags. Then there were the weeks of peanut-butter-baited spring traps and two humane traps that would have captured the little guy, so I could set him loose in the backyard from whence he came.

But too much chaos: it's nearly Christmas! Time to put everything back and accept the fact that he lives under the floor. His scratching was not access to the kitchen, but mere clandestine meandering where eyes and hands cannot reach. Apparently, even he cannot get out. I drilled several holes in the wall behind the refrigerator, hoping the critter would venture out into the open, gobble up the peanut butter to become a peanut butter sandwich. No such luck. Now I have holes to patch and a barny odor drifting out of the drawers. Cartoons depict articulate mice holding conversations behind tiny arches in the base shoe molding, maddeningly out of reach. Someone said mice can live a long time eating only the slivers inside fir cabinets.

Dad reads my latest sermon. I opened with Rilke's poem, *God speaks to us as he makes us, then walks with us silently out of the night...* *

then walks with us silently out of the night....which suggested to me that we might as well forget trying to escape from mystery. Even our blessings are mixed with challenge, I thought. There is persistent unknowing that cloaks our awareness. I wrote, "we have to ask of everything, is this something God has visited upon me? Or something I need

---

* *Love Poems to God*. Riverhead Books, 1996. Barrows and Macy translations

to work through to find God on the other side? Is my feeling of dis-ease intended to get me moving, or get me to give in? Or perhaps, simply to accept."

I said, "We have asked these hard questions as far back as the camp-fires in the Sinai desert. And let me tell you these people in the nativity stories asked them too. There is no escape from mystery. If we're fortunate, Mystery is a constant companion, however enigmatic. To discern meaning we tell these stories, listening for clues to find our way.

"Rilke says God speaks to us as God creates us, and then walks with us silently out of that night. We can only dimly recall God's words: something like ...*go to the limits of your longing. Embody me. Make big shadows I can move in.*"

Dad then says, "I think you are only beginning to find your faith." Shocked, I pause, but then I agree, although I feel chastened. But he's lived more life than I have and no doubt read more Scripture. I wait. There is more.

"It was Gabriel who stood in the presence of God, not God, who announced Mary's pregnancy," he explains. Okayyy, I think silently.

Why justify that I spoke of God as God appeared *through* the angel Gabriel? The God who raises a hand (through Moses) to make waters part? A God who speaks Word into flesh? Things deteriorate with ex-planation. Instead, I nod. I listen. And Dad goes on to explain Gabriel's first appearances in the Book of Daniel (chapters 8 and 9, in case the reader has forgotten). Things must be precise. Literal? Of my eulogy of my mother, Dad said: "You used 'I' too much." These picky comments are what sank my ego when I was young. Now I can take them in stride. One of the students I advised when I was at Roosevelt told me that her mother said the same thing to her. "Why is it, 'I, I, I?'"

Used to self-effacement, or the pride that often conceals it, Dad is worried someone might think he plays his radio too loud. So he won't turn it up enough even to hear. I am self-effacing, but not necessarily to a fault as I once was. His legacy, no doubt. Day by day, a few sentences at a time, he grows more real to me; he's no longer merely the authority who defined the parameters of far too many years of my life. I listen, nod, and a whole life takes shape I have never known, the life of someone who certainly knows what a mouse sounds like traveling between the joists under the flooring.

Since it is Christmas and the celebration of my 60th year to boot, Ardene and I splurge on a weekend flight to San Francisco. We sit in chilly Grace Cathedral on Nob Hill to hear *Messiah* sung by the Bach Soloists. Halfway through we also hear rains hammering on the cathedral roof, splattering on the entry plaza outside. People smile in the common pleasure of escaping the flood. It is dry again when we step outside at 10:30 p.m.

We enjoy high tea and champagne at the Top of the Mark, celebrating because we have survived this year which has been a trial by ordeal. I feel strong and competent. Perhaps, for the first time, I feel it in my heart where it counts.

On my return to Seattle frustrations resume when I get on the road too late to see both Dad's closest business friend, Frank, and also my brother who made his Christmas visit at 2:00 p.m. We aren't late, but Dad is tired. He declines to open our gifts. We share the slice of pumpkin pie we brought and head back home.

There is no "family" Christmas, Ramstad or otherwise. It was just last year Ardene and I brought Mom and Dad to our home for Christmas dinner. And now, without the family home to draw us together, I am distraught. This is our first Christmas without Mom. June. (Her granddaughter called her "June the prune;" it rhymed and we laughed). I feel lost. Last year Ardene and I realized how difficult it was to engage both of my parents; we saw their frailty. But they were so well defended there was no way we could intervene. Their frailty soon made intervention necessary, and now we are on the second round of accompanying a parent as far as he can go.

On Christmas morning I read the Seattle Times accompanied by a Merry Christmas Bloody Mary. The phone rings.

"Cathy? It's your Daa..aaad," he drawls, singing the vowels in a cascade from tenor to baritone.

"Merry Christmas, Dad!" I shout cheerfully and loud.

"Thank you for the two shirts! Good color," he says. I hope so. Born so close to the Fourth of July, somehow he's a red, white and blue guy. So are his shirts.

"This is the best Christmas I've ever had!" he exclaims, telling me about gifts from the staff. A navy blue cotton blanket, handkerchiefs, even pajamas. "We wouldn't have been able to do what we needed to this year without your help, Honey," he continues. With a bit of awe, I think, me? He's thanking me for what I've helped to make possible this year?

"I am still not sleeping through the night," he adds, repeating for the nth time. Before I speak, he adds, "When will you be coming back?"

This is the first time he's asked me that. He's lonesome for my company.

Therefore we will not fear, though the earth should change,
though the mountains shake in the heart of the sea;
though its waters roar and foam,
though the mountains tremble with its tumult.

~Psalm 46

Surely the earth has changed this year and is changing today. Surely the mountains do shake in the heart of the sea, its waters roar and foam; mountains tremble at its tumult. These things do happen.

Yet, "God is our refuge and our strength." In the midst of the loss of my mother and new responsibility for my father, I wouldn't be who I am without the assurance of faith. I sometimes find solace in Scripture. This is not something I impose on others, though I respect it in all faiths and all those who find solace in ancient texts. Scripture for me is one source of peace, a place where anxieties can be laid to rest, troubled waters calmed. I find peace even more quickly in music.

I don't know if I ever would have pulled the trigger, or sat in an idling, garaged car long enough, but there were times I was miserable enough to pull the plug. The first time in fact, I had no other thought at all. I had tried everything I knew. I was just 22 and had no clue what to do in my calamitous marriage. Since there was a .22 pistol in our apartment, I took it off the top shelf and sat on the bed with it in my lap, brooding. Were I not to end my own life, it had to be the marriage that should end, but that felt worse. How could I go on? I had never faced anything quite so daunting. I felt powerless.

I don't know how long I sat there, afraid to raise the pistol any higher, and then something drew me forward. Nothing tangible. I don't call it courage unless the definition of courage is hope in mystery in the face of the impossible, the whole creation moving toward some hoped for completion. I didn't have a new solution. I rejected death. There had to be something more in the universe. Now my ministry calls my bluff. It challenges me to act as if I have a channel to God, as if I have answers—even if the answer is, I don't know. I've taped a Chinese fortune to my computer that seems apt: "Courage and optimism are your best traits." I think, *I just don't want to miss anything.*

Faith is the great gift. Not doctrine. That comes after belief, before and after, actually. The understanding, perhaps, of one's encounters with the inexplicable, the daunting, the alarming. After the engagement with Mystery come the attempts to demystify, to explain, to prepare, to arrange an architecture of belief that can be studied and learned and lived with. Each of us has the privilege to do this ourselves. American Baptists call it *soul freedom.*

In the face of life itself, of people who inexplicably withdraw beyond our reach, who relentlessly try to intrude, or who struggle with addiction and break our hearts, my only solace is the mystery of a God whose presence broods over the chaos with me, helping me work out my own salvation.

On a January Saturday in the new year, Dad and I begin to catch up with each other. Since he has received a picture frame for Christmas, he asks me again to bring snapshots. He smiles, laughs and points at one of the photos I've brought him, "I weighed much more then than I do now." It's true—he's thinner now.

"Do you want this one of you and Mom in the backyard?"

"No," he says, his face a mask. He is thinking.

"How about this one?" An old portrait for the church directory.

"No. It's from too long ago."

He chooses nothing. No family pictures to hang on his walls or stand on his bureau. After looking at pictures of Mom, he says, "When it comes down to it, nothing captures how I remember her."

Taking a break from pastoral calling, I throw myself into another fall project: hauling five bags of orange cedar and yard debris out to the curb. That should be the last of it. Even evergreen cedar litter the yard with their fall fronds and seed pods. It takes from November to the end of the year to rake the backyard back to its parklike state. Sidewalks in town seem swept clean, waiting with the emptiness of trees for buds to burst into bloom. It feels like spring. The redwing blackbirds have returned to the Edmonds marsh, their taxi-flute whistle singing out in the chill air as I pack out of the car with my bag and head toward the gym.

But it's still winter. Going coatless chills hands and feet. Without rain clouds, dreary mists and downpours, the illusion of spring is hard to deny. I feel out of sync and miss the excuse to stay indoors by the fire with my nose in a book. In fact, I take great comfort in the variety of calm, storm, cloud, and rain that constitute the Northwest climate.

The yard waste having dealt with the pungent cedar, Ardene and I sweep off the driveway, hoping it's the last bushel of fronds and leaves. Front and back prospects are now clear across the moss, flagstone and bark paths.

The next Sunday when we come home from church and change, I find myself heading for the phone to call Mom. Peculiar. Prescient. This is the week everything fell apart last year. Tonight is the night Mom first stayed at the nursing home, the first anniversary of the beginning of the end.

Dad is not well—tired, and still unable to feel rested. I went to Evergreen Memorial Cemetery to pick up a sketch of the new headstone I had prepared for Mom and Dad together. As he gazed at it, I couldn't discern his feelings. His face was a mask. The social worker told me later she thought he seemed depressed. But what would I think if someone brought me a picture of my own grave marker? I was aghast. I tried to change the mood as I walked him down to the dining room and said goodbye till next week. He was as flat as he was when I came in. Damn!

My dad is one of the many faithful men of his generation who could not evidence love except through deed. Many of those deeds I was not aware of, and others were not apparent they were intended for me. The children of midcentury European immigrants seem similarly to withhold their feelings, and the men and women who have been through war, fleeing persecution all through Europe and Asia. Trauma in the lives of our grandparents and great grandparents is handed down through generations. Dad quoted Scripture, drove us back and forth from church whenever it was open, planned vacations, yet spoke harshly of our shortcomings, ridiculed my older brother, and withheld overt affection. He was unforgiving, trying to exhort rather than to invite us into his faith by goading us to read the Bible every morning as he did, then undoing that very example with his criticism and rigid expectations. Such a man now sits boyishly in his room, reading. (He's always looked years younger than his age.) Defended against all dialogue because he can't hear well enough to answer anyone but staff, and then only sporadically, he is turning my world upside down.

It is nothing short of revelation to experience my father so open in ways I've never experienced. I hardly know what he'll say when he opens his mouth. He surprises me all the time. He can simply talk, because he can't hear me despite his two expensive hearing aids. Lately he asks me how his voice sounds; apparently it doesn't sound right to him anymore, either.

Maternal grandmother. Anna Catherine Stilwell McGhee

Paternal Grandmother. Joakima Severinson Ramstad

Dad at Scott Paper Co., 1952 when they bought Soundview Pulp Co.

Mom waiting for her cue as I accompanied her at our piano in the dining room.
Photo by the Everett Herald

Annual Easter snapshots of Lewis, David & Cathy at 1810 Colby

Dad and I in a rare cozy mood in the late forties

Sibling harmony in our living room, 1950s

Cathy often looked after Lewie after school when they were both older. This scene is posed for Dad's camera.

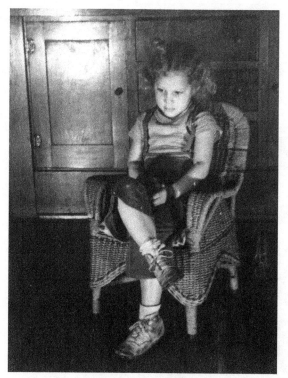

A thoughtful moment sitting pensively in the dining room when 1810 was new to me.

Cathy sitting for one of many portraits the family was often taking.

Mom and I dressed for a wedding when I was a flower girl.

1952

June and Carl in the 70s after moving to Fowler Street

A formal photo of Cathy in her Head Counselor role
at Roosevelt High, Seattle. Photo by Phyllis Dukes

Striped tabby Tully lounging in front of pictures
of herself, Carl, and Cathy, 2002

The territorial Tully in a solemn pose.

Tully looking for action. In the downstairs study.

*One pastor in a four pastor team at Seattle First
Baptist Church, 2003. Photo by Phyllis Dukes*

*In full preacher mode during a sermon, 2012,
at Seattle First Baptist Church. Photo by Jim Segaar*

Carl Abner Ramstad turns 95 in 1995.
Backyard birthday party.

Dad turns 100 on July 2, 2004,
while at Rocky Glen Nursing Facility

My big brother Dave, Dad at 100, and Cathy
celebrating with cake, balloons, and family.

Chapter 11

Dad Sees Catherine

"We never do enough for our parents, and our timing
is off at critical times. But isn't sitting with them part of
the caring we must do?—to be in touch with our place
in the family, to be attentive to the pain and mortality that
are part of being alive, to tell stories about who we are in
relationship to the people and places we love, and sometimes,
to sit quietly in the dark and cry."

~Kathleen Dean Moore. Pine Island Paradox.

I was eight when my parents took me to see La Bohéme *at Everett Civic* Auditorium. The sets were minimal. Mimi's bed looked like a big box with a sheet thrown over it. I didn't know how she could sit on it, much less lie down. But when she did die there, one arm falling limply off the bed, I burst into loud sobs. A row of devotées turned to me with smiles of sympathy. I was a little too young to appreciate the story.

Today, as I tune in to the Saturday broadcasts of the Metropolitan Opera, I think back to our Colby home where Mom and I vacuumed on Saturdays with the opera at full volume. We stopped, perching on the arms of a chair or sofa for the arias. Since Mom studied some of the same arias when I was very young, she breathed as if she were actually singing, fully concentrating. When the aria ended we resumed our work. Music dramatically voiced emotion that our family never expressed. Sharing it while listening side by side with Mom was as close as we came to naming the longing and loss in our lives. She shared her longing with me, and I strained to comfort her. At least that's what I thought in my thirties when I began to untangle our relationship.

Dad spoke of Mom last week. Their 64th anniversary approaches with St. Patrick's Day. He said, "She is always with me." No wonder he didn't want an old portrait. He could see her better in his memory. Her spirit is enough. I suspect he carries on conversations in his mind; I should ask him that.

Yesterday, I finally got to the end of last year's to-do list by ordering the grave marker. I was stunned when I visited the spot at the cemetery and found nothing at all where her remains had been laid and covered over just a year before. Smooth grass without a seam blanketed the small crevice. How rapidly nature covers what we do.

When I told him I had visited Mom, Dad showed little interest. Is he looking forward to the green streamers and shamrocks of St. Patrick's Day? Maybe he is marking the days of this time last year, when Mom's dementia was so apparent. Or more likely, he is calling forth memories far before this when she was in her prime, or when they were newlyweds. It may have been a relief to him when she finally surrendered to her confusion.

The year's distance gives me freedom to grieve, time to see again what I saw then and could hardly take in. I ask myself how Mom may have felt. What she knew. How do I hold her? Honor her spirit? Or hold a sunset, a poem, an aria? With deep gratitude. And tears. I think of Mom now, as I embrace my dad, knowing we walk the same path.

The familiar rain has returned. How I love it pouring through the day and pounding the roof at night. I can't say I much enjoy sloshing about in boots, but I like to watch water cascade off roofs, into gardens, sluicing down gutter and culvert. Rain tips the winter scale from dry to wet. An excuse to stay in and read. It tempts even me to clean house.

But the ornamental trees are not daunted. They're standing everywhere among the fir, cedar and pine with pink, mauve, red and white blossom, a startling incandescence amid the faithful evergreens.

On Friday, I wash my car with sponge, suds, and hose, toweling it off to a shine. I know it will rain and spoil the job, but I enjoy the time with sunlight blinking on and off through the sailing clouds borne on a fresh wind, with robins hopping under the rhodies and a squirrel digging up nuts cached last fall.

Come to think of it, while I was polishing, I didn't think about the threat of impending war with Iraq. I am grateful for home, Ardene, Tully, and time to enjoy them. And what if, as spring blooms in the Northern Hemisphere, we have begun to count the ways earth itself and its people need care, and the myriad ways we contribute to its health rather than its frailty? Our consciousness cannot hurt. Our consciousness is growing. Mary Oliver mused about the spring that beckons her away from her desk into the yard: thinking paying attention is the basic task, the world being simply, a poem.

Dad is awake, still resting on his bed when I walk into Room 106 at eleven one morning. It takes him a few minutes to gather energy to rise from his supine position and shuffle into the chair next to his bed. His words are slow and labored. How difficult it is to put words to his thoughts. He's not had even one conversation before I arrive. I sit on his bed and take the small erasable white board I am now using to write my responses and questions; it's easier for him to discern what I'm talking about. He reminisces and smiles a little, asking me how I am and how things are going. He is subdued. I wonder how long he can hang on like this.

He apologizes twice about old opinions he's offered, including a comment he remembers making about my mentor's last book (I gave him Dr. Romney's *Wilderness Spirituality* for Christmas two years ago). Dad tells me he's been dipping into it again and finding it a comfort. He reviews his memories, assessing. I wonder how he finds himself when weighed in the balance he has used to assess everyone else. Alone so much, and so passive now, often he has only his memory for company. It is more his companion than life itself. Perhaps even he wishes there were no interruptions in his reverie. I hope to God he is not punishing himself for his lapses.

A pall settles over my emotional landscape as the invasion of Iraq becomes reality. None of the people and places I frequent is pleased. It's not only the horror of war. It is the moral horror of attacking a country that, as far as current intelligence reveals, has done nothing.

Though he doesn't talk about it much, except for occasional disgust at the current administration, my father is depressed by both national and global states of affairs. He watched *The MacNeil/Lehrer Report* (now *The News Hour* on PBS) for years and is rarely without an opinion. He can't follow that now, can't hear the television news, and won't use the closed captioning. Nevertheless, he ventures an opinion from his reading from time to time.

When I was coming of age during the civil rights struggle, I planned to cast my first presidential ballot for John Kennedy's second term. The assassinations of the sixties added to my deep unhappiness with our country. In 1968 when the Seattle Schools hired me, I asked to be assigned to Garfield High in the center of old Seattle, known for its ethnic and racial diversity and widely considered the most conflicted high school in the city. I worked very hard to make a difference. The political climate affected students directly, and their parents may have had serious disagreements with their teens' opinions. The local catalyst was the new bar of flashing lights affixed to the tops of police cars. When the cars raced down neighborhood streets at night students felt they were being invaded.

While we are discussing the virtually sudden loss of my mother (three months from her admission to the nursing home to her death) and my anxiety at getting along with my father, a wise friend suggests everything is perfect as it is.

That's ridiculous! How could I possibly see this circumstance as the right thing? I do see that knowing the difference between the things I can change and those I cannot is a key to my peace of mind. I am still learning to discern my own power. But I am a distance away from accepting the current circumstances as good for me. Maybe he meant perfect as whole, or simply the facts that are.

I seem suddenly to be meeting myself in my father. He tells me, "I can't ever relax." Hell. I know that—I can't either! One day ahead I will be able to see my relationship with Dad growing beyond where I ever expected it could.

I have tackled several worlds of challenge he may have never assailed. He had serious challenges of his own. We all do. But as I grow my newfound voice, I declare, I know how to do this! I was born for such a time as this. I know I am on the cusp of a new calling. I am more awake than I ever have been. Forge ahead, I urge myself. I used to think launching from youth into maturity occurred in the early twenties—once and for all. I had missed the sailing. But at 50 and 60? It happens then, too. Life is a continual emancipation out of formula to the freedom of one's own heart. Dad must be doing this still.

I try to take time to keep up with the day's events, to cope with the darkness of war. Routine won't do. Ardene and I choose good books on any topic other than war, looting, and death; trips to the gym, and me—occasional naps. "I try to take one day at a time, but sometimes several days attack me at once."* It happens.

Few people were aware of the deleterious effects of stress in the 50s. Dad explained that he suffered from "tension," not what caused it, but a condition he called tension itself. Our lives are constantly more and more vulnerable to developments we have no control of. I have worked for years to adjust to my anxieties, and once a friend suggested, "Don't go to the Symphony if you're anxious in crowds!" In spite of agoraphobia in my thirties I loved music so much, I had to go. I managed to work it out. All of us are tense about something, but we never will have our world under control. Control is an illusion. That becomes the point.

One of the less helpful tenets of the so-called "prosperity gospel" is that if we are good little girls and boys, God will reward us. We will not have illness or death in our lives. Rather, we will succeed beyond our wildest dreams. This makes God little more than Santa Claus and the art of living mere good behavior, or capitalist acquisitiveness. We have no control over our lives, really. Some, yes. But as our wisdom grows, we begin to know that life is dangerous, that decisions have real consequences, and unanticipated disease and accident occur in everyone's life. Accepting this reality is no little thing. But the realization that today may be the last day of our lives moves me more and more to choose carefully what I think and do. Life is precious and fragile.

Our lives offer many reasons for anxiety and pain. The rhythm of light and dark in worship helps me prepare for the darkness I meet in my own life. As we approach Holy Week, circumstances move quickly from triumph to betrayal and torture. Jesus' faithfulness in the face of rejection, ridicule, and isolation is not unique. The same circumstances repeat themselves every day somewhere in the world. We cannot escape them. To know that Jesus suffered may be of some comfort. He—and others—have been there before us.

---

* Ashleigh Brilliant

"The suffering of Jesus may be the one proof we have that Jesus was really human and that humanity, whatever its pain, can transcend the burden of it," writes Joan Chittister. Quoting John Donne, she concludes, "'Affliction is a treasure, and scarce any man hath enough of it.' Suffering erases our illusions. Then there is nothing between us and God."*

I journey back to Everett to find Dad reading. When I greet him he looks up, smiles, and asks me how I am. And then he adds,

"You have changed so much in your adult life, it's unbelievable."

I am stunned. Is he really seeing me for the first time in months of routine? Why now? He reads our church newsletter and sermons sent out monthly—some of them mine—so he knows the classes I teach and the activities I lead. But I can't think of anything to say.

"Thank you," I offer, sitting as I reach to pick up the whiteboard. I held my tongue and did not say, "Finally!"

"What does it mean, 'all that jazz,' in that class you taught at the church?"

"Oh, it's a common phrase that means 'everything else,' all the stuff you expect and more. In this case it also meant that creativity in any form has a lot in common with jazz."

"Oh, I don't suppose I would like it," he remarks. He was creative in a number of disciplines, but he's right; he wouldn't like jazz, music so unstructured and unpredictable. The one time he, Mother and I went to hear Sarah Vaughan open for Bill Cosby at Key Arena at the Seattle Center, he was annoyed by the way she "slurred" her words and notes. He had no appreciation for those who ventured outside the lines. Imagine—Sarah Vaughan!

Dad is beginning to see *me* rather than who he required me to be. I've stepped out of the bounds of dutiful daughter. Beyond obedience, even beyond one profession to another, a person beyond his expectations, beyond the narrow proscriptions he and Mom laid down years ago and followed themselves. Is he amazed I show up every week and bring him what he needs without fail, sometimes unbidden, but always when he asks? He must have read something I wrote that made sense to him.

---

* Chittister. Op.cit., p 102

Something that gave him a new insight. He had to change his perception to accept it. We're getting somewhere.

I have never before had the opportunity to do anything for him. Not a gift like time or attention. Since he commanded both, I couldn't give them. All duty. As I experience this painstakingly slow turn-around of a relationship that wasn't, I am well aware that I never expected to see this. I couldn't have anticipated it. I had given it up. I had no idea how I was going to carry on with my father as he was when Mother was alive. What I did was keep putting one foot in front of the other as tasks grew around settling him into this nursing home while I saw my mother declining unto death. Grieving her loss, I dreaded being with him. I had no idea what to expect.

His presence has been an absence to me all my life. Rare are the moments I have seen him smile at something I've done, compliment me, or ask my opinion. So I have arrived at Rocky Glen to do the things that need doing, slowly, methodically, trying to anticipate his needs, maintaining a high level of awareness of his mood, my own state of mind, and how much energy I have to spend on a project that ended up in the deficit column all the time.

So as we contemplate Lent and anticipate the betrayals, the losses, the grief of Holy Week, I face once again the darkness in our lives, and wonder if new life will truly come out of this time with my dad.

The darkness in Scripture *then* illuminates the darkness *now*. I find solace and solidarity in witnessing wounds, mine and others, in deep community. I want to sit in a candlelit room in silence and know I am not the first person there, nor the only one who feels deeply the pain in the world (much which we continue to cause). In view of the new war, is now the Orwellian time when peace is war? When safety is destruction?

It is not healthy to dwell in the realm of darkness days on end. But it is no more healthy to rise unthinkingly above it, as if darkness were a figment of our minds. The rising comes from the sinking. Darkness is transformed only by our presence in it, our awareness, and an acknowledgment of our complicity. Singing the blues, whether ours or the world's, mourns our humanity, our falling short, and moves us to humility and awe that might lead us to do something—even together—to overcome it.

The Blues are cathartic. They move us together in solidarity through the hard times to the creativity beyond them.

With so many of our institutions revealed for their moral bankruptcy, there seems nowhere to turn for solace. Wall Street, corporations, school districts, public television, clergy across all creeds come under scrutiny and are found wanting. And in spite of papal encyclicals celebrating ecumenism—especially this week, when Christians of all stripes have so much to share—the Vatican reminds Catholics not to "dilute their vows" by taking communion outside their faith. What parochial bigotry.

In William Walton's cantata *Belshazzar's Feast*, a finger writes as a sepulchral voice intones, "You have been weighed in the balance and found wanting." That very night, Belshazzar is "SLAIN!" the chorus shouts. The trouble is, since Jesus and Jung, we know the line between darkness and light runs through the center of us all. Contemplating our own shortcomings stifles our pleasure in pointing fingers at others. Our faults keep us busy enough.

Dad's cold is better, but his cough lingers. His words come slowly as he tells me a story from my year as Miss Everett of 1962. "We drove to pick you up from Vancouver, Washington, on the Columbia River after the Miss Washington Pageant, remember?"

Mother and I had driven down early with Dad's signs posted on both car doors announcing my title. He and my 14-year-old brother Lew drove down later. I was pleased he was that proud.

"When we were touring the capital on our way home," he continues, "because we hadn't seen it for a number of years and Lewie was with us," he looks up to see if I am following him, I nod, "I ran into a couple from church who asked how you did in the pageant, and I told them, 'She sank without a trace!'" He laughs. I wince.

Was this just a cliché or an obscure reference of some sort? We both laugh because it was true. I had emotionally withdrawn from the pageant. I couldn't say another "pretend word." This was all for show; I was bored. Nevertheless, back then on my way home, I sat on the Capitol steps in tears, believing I had let Everett down.

Later in the week Rocky Glen calls to inform me Dad has a lung infection—not pneumonia. I sigh and listen carefully.

"He's coughing, and he's tired, but then, he reminded us, 'I'm getting old.'"

As I hang up the phone I wonder, Do you think at 98, pushing 99, he accepts that he's getting old?

On Mother's Day, in worship I pray for mothers, aunts, and grandmothers, as well as for fathers who mother their children. I ask forgiveness for what I did not understand about my mother. I ask forgiveness for her for what she did not know. Mother's Day is a sweet memory and another letting go.

Within a week, though, Ardene and I quickly drive to Everett General Hospital at the north end of the city to meet Dad in the ER after an apparent seizure. It's his first, with no brain damage apparent. After further consultation the doctor surmises the seizure was caused by yet another urinary tract infection. He decides to send Dad back to Rocky Glen with antibiotics.

"I thought I might be going to join your mom," he tells me afterward, a happy thought. He's not been himself lately, though that's hard to determine in a man of few facial expressions and so few words. He's not as spunky and he's a little more obtuse, no doubt due to the infection and lingering cough.

"I think about exercising," he goes on, "and the spirit is willing, but the flesh is weak." I surely agree with that myself.

Brenda, the nurse practitioner at Rocky Glen, believes the infection caused the seizure so will adjust his medications. As these life-threatening system failures persist, Dad is beginning to feel a burden. Not an encumbrance, but increased watchfulness. He's on my mind day and night, and I know where this will end.

My lunch date cancels, so I clean out my closet, winnow the old from the new, tossing out wire hangers, t-shirts, and things worn to fraying. I am fortunate to be able to choose. I put several of Mom's shirts in the recycle pile. I will never give away her handkerchiefs, nor my Aunt Effie's. I have handkerchiefs from them both and use them regularly. I hate to use tissue. The ones from my Mom are great fun, some boldly printed with green, blue, and purple flowers. She is on my mind as we approach the anniversary of her death. Of the things of hers that I saved last summer, I wore only a few, but it was comforting to have them in the closet—another way of being close to her, of cherishing her scent and the color that was one joy of her life among us. I often wear a bright yellow outdoor jacket. When others compliment me on it, I always tell them, "It was my mother's."

I talk with seniors who share wisdom my parents seemed to lack. There is a whole group of people who parented me collectively from a distance through the years both at church and in the schools. Sitting beside a senior at Bessie Burton Nursing Home helps. One woman is still negotiating the challenges of an implacable table companion, having to respond to schedules when summoned. Accountability never ends.

Yesterday my friend Ann, the parish nurse, and I prayed with a recent widow. At the end of our prayers, Laurel held her pose with her eyes tight shut, a tear sliding down her cheek, firmly grasping our hands for several minutes, until she recited Paul's words from Romans 8:38—"For I am persuaded, that neither death, nor life, nor angels, nor principalities, nor powers, nor things present, nor things to come, Nor height, nor depth, nor any other creature, shall be able to separate us from the love of God, which is in Christ Jesus our Lord" [KJV]. What a testimony. My father can also recite Scripture word for word. He reads from a Bible well-worn but without a single mark. Is this such a reverence for the text that he cannot bring himself to mar it?

In spite of his infection and bad cough, he left me a phone message to thank me after I delivered a new sweater. Since his call was interrupted by a cough, he hung up. But when I called him back and he recognized my voice, he laughed out loud. Such delight from a man whose laughter was caught in his throat most of my life! I love his spontaneous laugh. And I cherish his gratefulness. As obligations do not end, perhaps opportunities don't either. Life continues to beckon us into a wholeness we can never imagine.

Next time I'm at Dad's, I take time to empty and clean out the cookie crumbs from his top bureau drawer. He has arranged several small empty boxes fitted together with paperclips to hold not only cookies but his hearing aid batteries, Rolaids, gum, cuticle scissors, nail clippers, and old hearing aids—all in separate compartments. There is also a larger box for the crumbling Oreos and vanilla wafers which get into everything.

The day after that, he is on the phone apologizing. "I am not properly grateful for everything you're doing for me. Are you upset with me?"

"Of course not, Dad. Why are you saying that?" Had he been unkind, or cranky yesterday? I wasn't listening since I was determined to clean it. He must have reflected on his attitude and felt guilty. He *is* concerned about my feelings.

Dad has resumed his four subscriptions, some daily, some weekly: the *Seattle Post Intelligencer*, the *Everett Herald*, *Newsweek*, and the *The Wilson Quarterly*. But there is never a stack of magazines lying around. He reads them, sorts them, and tosses them, I guess. He could pass them on to a caregiver? Rarely, there's a *WQ* I get to take home before it disappears. His room is never messy. He's always dressed, sitting in his chair napping, and only rarely on the bed fast asleep.

"I can't see the television captions from my chair," he explains of the set on top of his bureau but, as I quickly offer to get a larger one, he stops me. "No, no. I don't want a bigger one," he insists. But it isn't the last time he brings up how hard it is to see and understand what's going on. Apparently it is just one more factor he has accepted. He's not complaining when he shares these things, he's reporting. There is nothing I need do. Does he view the circumstances as temporary? Tolerable? Or is he simply done with allowing other people to do things for him? Maybe in his silences at home he was just as content, and I couldn't read it on his face.

Though I spend consistent time with my father, I worry. A given of my existence. I leave messages with the nurse practitioner and the head nurse to keep in touch through the weeks. It's important that I know what they know, so we can collaborate on the care he receives. He is worried about not being able to eat as he's used to, and to get up with energy in the morning. These concerns do make him sick—and thus unable to eat or to get up some days.

In the kitchen today I liberated a ladybug hiding in a fresh head of romaine. As I was peeling off the outer leaves preparing a salad, I found that many of them were already eaten—and finally, there was the cause, a ladybug drowned in the dark, moist leaves. I laid her out carefully on the window sill above the sink and threw out most of her work. But when I looked up, she was climbing wetly toward the ceiling. After dinner she was still at the top of the window, stretching one wing and then the other from under her red and black polka-dot cloak. She was there the next morning too, so I invited her onto my hand and took her outside to a plump stalk of thyme. The cat has nine lives. How many lives does a ladybug have? Now she has one more. Resurrection? Tenacity. Instinct. Will to live. I was inspired, but no doubt the lady didn't need my help. It was her death and resurrection after all. I could not live it for her. And Dad wants to do his own thing in his way, without my interference, even my help.

Resurrection surrounds us. It's everywhere. But it's not easy to detect in the literalism of our lives. And it's so hard for us to let it happen: to let things be, to allow the pain of events taking their slow and sometimes transformational course. Do all of us rush to fix what hurts? Do those who appear uncaring, walking away, agonize over *us*? Sometimes I wish they would.

Empathy is a wonderful gift, but it has a price. At its extreme I find myself living other people's lives rather than my own. Carefully monitored, it allows me to help others bear their pain (with their permission) and walk alongside in solidarity so that, emboldened, they can face their own terrors.

The foliage and spring blossom surprise me, but maybe I've been looking down too much. Was it this rich last year? My mother remarked about it—each year—"I've never seen the rhododendron so glorious!" Do we forget? Or does creation get better and better? I love the way plants left alone, like Salal and Oregon Grape, cover the back yard under the cedar. They take over everything in reach and beyond, just as the rhodies mature, enlarge, and spread. It wouldn't take long for nature to overwhelm even all this civilization in time. I find it heartening that life will persist regardless of our mucking it up. We may not survive on the planet this time around, but the planet will.

Dad has earned his time in the sun. God knows he had a tough enough beginning, grief, abandonment, loss of guidance. To the extent this is a respite, a time for his own reverie, I'm grateful.

Today he sat on the edge of his bed and refused to walk to the dining room for dinner. As I commiserated, he said, "I am disgusted with myself." Since his will cannot overcome his fatigue, how will he forgive himself? Through the winter he loved returning to his room to lie down for a nap. Yet when he cannot make himself rise to the occasions he expects, he condemns himself. How will he let go of his life? At some level it is a decision he must—or could?—make. Rather than my silence on his own death, shouldn't I be talking to him about it, or trying to?

If we never learn to let ourselves off the hook, or cut ourselves slack, we drive ourselves into corners from which there is no escape. We forever weigh ourselves in the balance and find ourselves wanting, incomplete, unacceptable. Some think this commitment to baseness is the root of the faithful life. I take exception. If we think ill of ourselves, we reject the love the Creator offers to everyone, even "strangers" and criminals. "I called you by name; you are mine. I am your God. You are honored, and I love you."* Who are we to think our opinion of ourselves is more accurate than God's, or that we can reject God's offer of unconditional love! This is hubris, not humility. Dad may feel he has not yet measured up to the standards he set for others. Hasn't his devotion to faith given him confidence in grace?

Paul Tillich writes in his great sermon, "You Are Accepted," that grace is that thing that startles us unawares, saying, You are accepted. Full stop. Yet Dad still holds himself as well as everyone else to an impossible standard. For a man who has orchestrated everything in his life, dying is going to come as an extraordinary challenge.

At his next care conference he says he's disappointed in himself. Though the nurse promises to check him for anemia, it's more likely he is still recovering from the seizure and infection. Both take a serious toll on someone his age. I keep forgetting how old he is since he functions so well, remembers so much, and seems so with it. When he is asked, as he is routinely, whether he should be resuscitated if they find him not breathing, he responds enthusiastically, "Of course." He's not contemplating his mortality at all.

A series of short reflections I've written, titled *Spirit Stones*, needs editing. I began to write them each week in the spring of 2000 because I hadn't found any published, daily spiritual writing that was eclectic, progressive, or open-ended enough to satisfy me. Many such pieces offered fixed answers. I liked to work through the Scriptures myself, discerning my own understanding. On a whim, I began to write these out every few

---

* *Isaiah 43:1-4, excerpted, rephrased*

days, interpreting, modifying. I learned something every time I wrote and then shared them with friends. Lo and behold, eventually there were some 200 readers. Some pieces are tucked away in this book.

I had no idea where this practice would take me, but the reflections continued to help me process what was going on with my parents. I have discovered over these years that my interpretations of Scripture change. Spiritual growth is like that: once you think you have a solution, it changes. Once you find a comfortable path that leads to peace and fruitfulness, you'll discover that changes, too. Our ways of expressing faith, choosing church denominations, and styles of worship are in this mix. That's the point. We're listening for the Spirit in the wind, the breath lingering in the heart. We're drawn toward another understanding, a broader—or new—perspective. The Spirit continues to draw us into our larger, highest selves. If we're paying attention we never arrive at a place where we can remain long without change.

Writing grounds me and reveals what I feel before I can voice it— especially in the journals I write by hand. Thoughts come better at that pace. The words I type sometimes are all vacant verbiage. I have to go back, delete, reword, and begin again. Somehow, when I reread something I've created, I see more clearly; the words I choose actually make a concept more real to me.

I used to think this a character defect. But it isn't. It's a way of being, of making sense of my life. Once I learned I was a natural introvert, that it was a preference of mine and the best way to recharge my batteries, I stopped feeling self-conscious about sitting in a meeting a long time before I offered an opinion. All of us prefer one set of behaviors to another. The ideal is eventually to find balance among them. We need to learn about and then accept our style and not spit in the eye of our gifts. The call remains to reach beyond our natural preferences and continue to grow more whole.

So many of us wait too long to experiment with the long-forgotten passions in our youth. The demands of work force us to forgo early longings with the need to fit in and support ourselves. If we're lucky, if we persist or live long enough, we can continue to rediscover those early delights—studded among the dark times—and gather them in again as we age.

Once again I meet with my wondrous group of very old women at Bessie Burton Sullivan. One of them was a former "Rosey the Riveter." She tells us of working at Todd Shipyard on the deck of a huge carrier, focused on a pattern of rivets, when a pair of shiny shoes appeared near her that broke her concentration. When she looked up she recognized Admiral Rickover. We enjoyed the moment, too. Sharing stories, and remembering the two recently lost in their group, one of them explains, "Death is the last great adventure." The challenges of life do not end with great age; they increase. Just as we think we're arriving, we must begin to let go.

Scott Peck wrote in *The Road Less Traveled* that life was not easy; it was hard.* I've got it, finally. I was a slow learner, or too long lost in the school of following the book, thinking then things would be easier. Now I work on detachment, less dependence on outcome, more being-in-relationship, and differentiated from others, since I have experienced fusion as a loss of identity. It was a long road for me to learn relationship requires two "solitudes," as Rilke captured in one of his letters to a younger poet.

> To a disciple who was always at his prayers
> The Master said, "When will you stop leaning
> On God and stand on your own two feet?"
> The disciple was astonished. "But you are the
> One who taught us to look on God as Father!"
> "When will you learn that a father isn't someone
> you can lean on but someone who rids you of your
> tendency to lean?"
>
> ~Anthony de Mello, SJ. *One Minute Wisdom*

My father is telling me something.

"I want to do what I want to do when I want to do it." When I suggest when I might visit next, he says, "I might be napping," inviting me not to come. I felt dismissed. But on second thought, he wanted freedom to do his own thing. He didn't want to be obligated to my time schedule.

---

* M. Scott Peck. *The Road Less Traveled.* 1978

He needs solitude now and he still doesn't want to put me out. Many people his age want solitude and less company. They need time to reflect.

Jesus didn't want his disciples to follow every word of his teaching literally either. He was inviting them to study, speculate, pray and live his teaching as they/we discover it without looking over our shoulder, without always sitting at someone's feet. When Jesus said, "If you continue in my word, you are truly my disciples; and you will know the truth, and the truth will make you free," (*John* 8:31) he meant we should grow independent from following our mentors in lock-step—instead, trusting our faith in the Spirit. After I outgrew following the people who told me what the truth was supposed to be, the truths I then discovered were far more powerful and liberating than anything I had ever been taught. Never mind the harrowing moments it took for me to take a step all by myself.

Maybe the true liberation is to think for ourselves and ask for what we need without the infrastructure of codependence, projection, and reading other people's minds. Probably it isn't our minds we need so to rely on, but our hearts. Light radiates from the heart, not the head.

Mother has been gone a year. In her wake I have an entirely new relationship with my dad. When I show up at Rocky Glen after a week's vacation, Dad assures me, "I'm holding my own. This place is meeting my needs." He's just had his hair trimmed and his twice-weekly shower; he looks rosy-cheeked and content.

"He's lucky he still has me around after all the years of egotism and control," I think, before I catch myself. Do I wish I could tell him of my pain in the prior 60 years? Of course. But somehow, months of an entirely new connection between us obliterate the past which, Carl Sandburg wrote, is a bucket of ashes. Literally, yes, when the fire has burned itself out, only cold ashes are left. But there is always life to be valued in the past, lessons to be learned and kept safe, love to be celebrated, joy to be recalled. Collectively, is the world's history a bucket of ashes? Is the future the only thing we live for? I hope not. Lest we repeat and repeat the endless tropes of poverty, bigotry, and war.

On a trip to northeast Oregon and southeast Washington, I remembered discovering pioneer Dr. Marcus Whitman and his wife Narcissa in biographies in my junior high library. Only 14, I was inspired by their mission and grieved at their fate at the hands of the Cayuse and Umatilla Natives in the Whitman Massacre of 1847. That was a self full of deep passion, unrecognized repression, and a lack of confidence masked by an ability to do more than others asked, usually for others. The combination led to emotional starvation and a conundrum: Why was I so blessed and so miserable at the same time? That I identified with missionaries who died in their work was an unnecessarily tragic ideal.

After Ardene and I rested as we vacationed in Joseph, Oregon, I left for another week's retreat at the Jesuit center on the Little Nestucca River in Oregon. Lulled by the slow growl of ocean surf, walking in the woods on the rocky promontory overlooking the river, I caught up with my need for silence.

On my return to Rocky Glen I find Dad much more like himself—finally, at 99, as if I can guess who he might have been.

"Oh, Cathy! Good of you to come," he says, formally, as if I were some dignitary. He stands by his chair behind his ever-present walker, leaning forward to be kissed.

He settles himself and announces, "I like eating in my room. It's no trouble for them, and since I can't hear what anyone else is saying to me in the dining room, which is embarrassing, this works much better."

"You choose for yourself, Dad," I respond, sitting to share his dinner, occasionally picking up a small spoonful of soup or forkful of potatoes. At the hour's end he walks me to the door.

"When will I see you again?"

"In a few days, same time."

"Okay, Honey. Take care." He waves me out.

I wasn't always comfortable in medical environments; it took me a while to adjust. Remembered trauma from an early tonsillectomy, I was told. Now I learned something from everyone I visited in nursing homes, convalescent centers, and hospitals. I spent time in prayer while they were sleeping that I didn't always make time for otherwise. A young gay man with few resources, one of our church members, lay propped up in a hospital bed at Bailey-Boushay House on the Madison Street hill east of Pill Hill, which opened in 1992 as the nation's first skilled nursing facility designed to meet the needs of people living with HIV/AIDS. He said, "I'll be moving as soon as I can to a place more like home. There's no room in these closets for all my clothes!" This week already he is gone. I knew his end was close, but he seemed not to, nor open to talk about it. This abruptness is always stark, often inviting a pause for prayer, for blessing and thanksgiving for the lives I am privileged to share, whether short or long.

Another churchwoman, not much older than I, visited me wondering about further, more extensive treatment for her cancer. She asked if the new treatment would provide six more months of a "quality" life. I didn't know. Her friend, visiting from Florida, told me, "I hope she just goes suddenly." There is not much "suddenly" in the world of cancer. This woman also wonders, if she were "cured," what would that mean for her future?

"What would I need to do? What would God expect?" she asked, as if she were bargaining for a longer life. I wondered about the connection. Would a reprieve require payback? She didn't get a chance to find out.

Dad comes to mind when I think about this fear of life as well as death, as if it could be bargained. He is well enough, but confined to a small room alone by choice. Is he clinging to his life, limited as it is? I've always thought death a relief, a release, without fear. But another voice tells me, "you won't feel that way when you're staring it head-on." I suppose so. I've already had to be admitted to the hospital with atrial-fibrillation more than once, and later, more than I can number. Impatient with myself when we have to change our plans, I am relieved the cardiology team can so easily convert my heart back to systolic rhythm. While recovering from a joint replacement, a relatively benign surgery, I've hated not being able to drive, waiting on Ardene for necessities, staying in one place or one position too long. Simply having to ask for help. That's something I certainly need to address. I inherited this from my parents. Had they been able to ask for help sooner, we might have arranged more thoughtfully for their advancing years.

Growing up in a church singing hymns about heaven probably influenced me and a lot of little kids to imagine heaven a better place than earth. But if we're always trying to get there, we don't have enough energy to invest in life here. Death has seemed an end of longing, reaching the goal of full belonging in the realm I left at birth. No doubt that was because I wasn't very confident that I could handle life as I knew it.

In Washington State citizens now have multiple decisions to make about the end of our lives. My father did not want hospice. He thought that meant he was dying, and no doubt, "weak." But he would have prospered with hospice. Now, given terminal illness, we have even more choices about how to end our lives.

As my theology has changed in the last ten years, I dwell less on the death of the man Jesus and more on his life, his courage and willingness to challenge the powers of Rome. He constantly broke cultural rules, ate with prostitutes and tax collectors, healed on the Sabbath, allowed an "unclean" woman to anoint his feet with expensive oil and wipe them with her hair. The stories about his daily experiences encourage me to be more invested in the world God continues to create, calling it good, than trying to be inhumanly perfect to make it into heaven.

I know that people resist death. Will I, also? The life force is fierce and unaccountable. So mine must be. But if I surrender easily enough now, won't it somehow condition my unconscious grasp, loosen it? I don't know.

Poet Jane Kenyon wrote, "One day, it will be otherwise." For all of us, someday it will be otherwise. We won't be getting out of bed on two strong legs. We'll need help. Or we won't be here at all.

Dad feels like walking. So we head down the corridors to each wing of the building, out onto the front porch, and soon back inside because the sun blinds his weak eyes. His hair has begun to drape over his ears. His shirt is buttoned up to his neck as usual, but his cardigan is buttoned just at his hips, with his pockets stuffed with the paper table napkins he uses to dab at his runny nose. Nevertheless, he carries himself with poise and character. When we return to his room, I write questions on the white board. His hearing aides are no longer adequate. Today he has a lot to say and we enjoy an engaging hour. Afterward, Dad walks me to the door and faces me, looking into my eyes.

"We'll make it," he says.

I know, somehow, we will. He's assuring me. Who's caring for whom?

CHAPTER 12

My Father Reaches 100

❦❧

"I searched for God and found only myself.
I searched for myself and found only God."

~Rumi

Sorting through stacks of keepsakes and photographs in my closet on a dreary
October morning, I discover my official black and white portrait as Miss
Everett of 1962. Who'd have thought I'd morph from beauty queen
to pastor? I was a freshman at Everett Junior College when the Junior
Chamber of Commerce called to ask me to compete. Astounded, flat-
tered, I suppose, I agreed, and then thrashed about wondering why. I was
a classical musician: pianist, organist, and soloist. Nothing suitable for
such a contest.

After generous coaching from some of Mom's cronies and a good
deal of rehearsal, I walked on stage at the Everett Civic Auditorium, sat
down at the grand piano and played the stately opening chords of the
familiar Grieg piano concerto. As I modulated into an introduction for
"Show Me!" from *My Fair Lady*, my girlfriend Saundra picked up the
accompaniment on the piano in the orchestra pit. I left the piano bench
and stepped out to sing.

Thrilled to win, I discovered more about community affairs than I
had known. Being a part of Seattle Seafair as a "visiting queen" was a great
adventure beginning with the Torchlight Parade where I rode on a Scott
Paper Company float (decorated in light pink Scott Towels with flowers)
in a light blue organdy gown. In a light mist I was perched with one hand
firmly on a brace and the other waving an over-the-elbow white glove to
crowds lining the sidewalks. We lurched down 2nd Avenue in the chill
night air during Seafair Celebration, *Century 21*: the Seattle World's Fair
(April through October 1962). I was one of over 50 "queens" who stayed
as guests of the Olympic Hotel where one of my two roommates was

Miss Quincy, Washington, who had never been in a building higher than two stories. Every time we returned to our 12th floor room she'd run to our window, throw up the sash, and look down on the passersby on Fourth Avenue. We were chauffeured to Seattle neighborhoods in white convertibles to parades from the International District to Ballard, our white heels saved in plastic bags to protect the leather upholstery. Why so careful then, when we were lined up on a navy pier in two inches of rain water for an hour, waiting for the fleet to arrive? My white pumps did not survive.

By the time I participated in the Miss Washington Pageant later that summer, I was weary of public appearances, tired of primping, smearing Vaseline on my teeth so I could smile for hours slowly waving my arm. Relieved to be finished. My picture was in the Everett Herald numerous times, including at a Kiwanis luncheon while I held a large halibut on a fishing gaff. The headline was, of course, "It's just for the Halibut."

While I was by definition a beauty queen, with the brass plate from the 15" trophy on my desk as I write, the role did not reflect the serious inner me who didn't really know how to "come out" as myself. I didn't have a demonstrative voice as a "queen," anyway. I didn't flaunt the title for long. It's something I mention rarely to break the ice at a party, I've never put it on my resumé, and in the 1980s, I sold my rhinestone tiara at a garage sale.

Dad is well on his way to the century mark. When I paid my weekly visit he was primed to share answers to the very questions I was asking myself.

"I don't think the Carl Ramstad family is close knit," he began. Shocked, I wonder, is he beginning to get it? He had had a long talk with his younger son in a dream, remembering on waking that Lew died in 1996. Dad is finally beginning to recognize—or name?—the family distance that persists among us few survivors. This is *his* family he's talking about!

"I don't remember ever being hugged when I was small. My father wasn't one to express any affection. And Clara"—his stepmother—"was not *mean* (he pauses), but she was certainly cool." When Grandpa Elias moved Joakima and their son, Art, to New Westminster where Carl was born, her parents (Severinson) moved from Bella Coola to support the boys through their mother's tuberculosis. Dad explains the Severinsons lived on the Fraser River in a "house-scow." When the family moved to Everett, the Severinsons followed as far as Stanwood, a town about an hour north. Joakima was gone from the family for at least parts of two years while she was treated at British Columbia's Tranquil Sanitorium near Kamloops. When he was a youngster, there was only his father, a housekeeper, perhaps, his maternal grandparents and his older brother, Art. I hazard a guess that 'Kima was at home only about half of the 6 years of Dad's boyhood. He hardly knew her beyond her absence and her illness.

Overcome at his honesty, I am relieved he can name the neglect. I listened with sadness, empathy and love—thankfully not the fear he once evoked, and reached out to hold his hand.

Although I know some of the family tales, the dates, names, and details are faint. Dave and I have the pictures but not all the back stories, although he's kept up Lew and Mom's geneology research. All of the eldest relatives are gone, and current ones are rarely in touch. Communication is scant among our Norwegian clan. Some years later, when Ardene and I finally make plans to visit Norway, I'd been in conversation online with a distant cousin in her late twenties who teaches in Bergen. We tried to meet. That wasn't possible, so I asked her about the relatives Uncle Art kept in touch with, my grandfather's closest kin who live nearer Andalsnes and the family farm of Ramstadalen. She tells me her parents have no rapport with that branch of their family. What keeps our direct ancestors so isolated from each other? The traumas of poverty and immigration? Recently, however, my brother has taken up Facebook communication with Norway, so I am also receiving news from second and third cousins in Sykkylven near Alesund, and farther away, Andalsnes.

I hear that there are more sociable Norwegians. Obviously we are not among them. "No, Dad," I answer in my head, "the Carl Ramstad family is not close-knit." Are the relationships somehow still being woven? We must all be recovering from the traumas of separation, early death, and great distances from home.

Dad is clearly assessing his past. I am captivated by his trust. Suspecting he would not permit exploring his memory more fully, I change the subject by pulling the pumpkin I'd carved out of a bag and placing it on his television set. (You might wonder why it was I who changed the subject. I know intuitively how to maintain the distance that he/we think(s) keeps us safe.) Both surprised and pleased, he walks me all the way back to the entrance door where we stand together on the porch. I tell him I love him. We hug twice: once for a long, long time—quietly sharing our love. When I get home, he calls me to be sure I know how much he appreciates my visit as well as the pumpkin.

First on Dad's agenda next visit is the Dracaena he's been caring for; it has grown too leggy for his taste. He's given it up and asks me to toss it on my way out. Then, looking up at me, he says,

"You have come a long way." Surprised, I pause and smile at him. Poised to receive the compliment, I wait and he continues, "I'm proud of you." I smile broadly, take in his approval, feeling the warmth of tears in my throat. And then he adds, "It must have cost you a lot of money."

No kidding. How does my achievement cost me money? Did he mean what I had to pay for years of graduate school? Perhaps he's remembering his own necessity to drop out of the UW in the late '20s? I have means he didn't have. He says nothing further about it.

As he stands and walks me to the door, I admire his courage, his will.

Still, I'm irritated that it took Dad until he was 98 to tell me he loves me. But I don't want to create resentment that sabotages everything else. Dad surprises me at every visit with some revelation from his own life that helps me understand him. And others that mystify me. My irritation is childish, I scold. Fortunate that he and I can talk, so many of my blank pages are being filled.

Driving to Seattle in driving rain, I listen to Yo Yo Ma on *Obrigado Brazil*. I wish I were always able to effect such mind control, but I cannot, even when I know I am in a funk. Moods have a way of taking hold, sometimes recognizably, but no more controllable in the sense of tolerance and patience. We are wonderful creatures but our creaturely-ness ensures we are not in control of everything. There's an insightful poem by Rumi describing that if we welcome each mood that arrives by day or night, we might accept it for a time. We are like a guest house where we welcome a new caller every morning. "A joy, a depression, a meanness...." He urges we greet and entertain all of them. The painful feelings may awaken us to something we need to learn. We might thank every emotion for an unexpected gift. He concludes by suggesting feelings are messengers from another world.*

I cling to broken pots; imperfection is a gift. One is incised 'round and 'round with "The Pasture."⌐ I bought it in 1967 in my first year of teaching at Cascade Senior High in South Everett, newly divorced, practically penniless and on a low-cost spring break in the San Juan Islands with friends. Two of us spied the pot at the same time without realizing it. I was so charmed, I picked it up and took it to the cashier unaware of the friend, only to look up to see her gaping at me, as if betrayed. I wasn't sure whether to claim what I had chosen, or give it to her out of politeness. I bought it with a lump in my throat. For once, I refused to defer to someone else.

Later the pot toppled onto the floor and broke into at least 12 pieces. In a long evening of repair, I painstakingly glued them all together. For me the now-leaky pot symbolized both the predicament of its acquisition and its resilience. Now it holds dried flowers or anchors an arrangement.

I glued each shard to the others from the bottom up, holding them fast, waiting for the bonds to firm, while the daughter of a colleague of mine at Garfield High School lay in a coma after a fatal auto accident. With the restoration growing slowly in my hands, I wrote her a poem about brokenness and healing. I knew something about both. Broken things break my heart. They also remind me that wholeness is made up of broken pieces. We grow into ourselves with blemish, error, false step, correction, rerouting, and healing. The Japanese concept *wabi-sabi* honors broken bowls; sometimes enhancing the cracks with gold as they glue them back together, the cracks themselves integral to the whole.‡

Potters may create or keep a flaw in a newly-made pot for the same purpose: there is beauty in imperfection. And with our flaws, how can we continue without forgiveness? Our error lies too often in expecting perfection and condemning ourselves so for being human that we cannot live with our telltale cracks. We all have them.

---

* Jellaludin Rumi, many translations

⌐ Robert Frost, in *North of Boston*, the first collection of his poems published by David Nutt, 1914.

‡ In traditional Japanese aesthetics, wabi-sabi (侘寂) is a world view centered on the acceptance of transience and imperfection. Wikipedia

Scripture makes clear "we have this treasure in clay jars,"* so that the strength that gleams through us is God's and not ours alone. Leonard Cohen sings the same theme in his his delightful "Anthem," celebrating that all we can ever offer is imperfect. Our imperfections allow the light to shine into our darkness.

Ardene and I head to Everett with salt (Dad's request) along with tools to repair his lamp. The socket apparently is shorted out. Having repaired a few lamp sockets in my time, I unscrew it and pull the blackened wires out enough to prepare them to be reattached to the poles. Dad quickly assures me, "I can take it from here, Honey. Just leave it." I hesitate and try to argue. I want to fix it for him.

"Just leave it, Honey, I can do it now," he says with emphasis. I leave it. I don't think the aides are going to give him a knife to strip the wires, but he knows the maintenance man pretty well, and I bet he'll help him out.

"I have lost my enthusiasm," Dad announces only a few days later as I set my purse down and pick up the white board. "Other people have more problems than I," he explains. "They just sit in their wheelchairs, napping." I nod. And perhaps the aides know Dad will dress himself if they wait long enough? A tactic to ensure he gets some exercise? So he takes matters into his own hands, getting himself dressed. But time is weighing heavily. Dad is acutely concerned about how other people see him. He always has been, of course. That was the famous question in our home on Colby: What will people think? How others saw us was the standard measure of approval—and we needed to meet those expectations.

As he moves his left shoulder, he grimaces but says nothing. Arthritis he's never disclosed? Maybe at his age, everyone has it. I suppose there is hardly any cartilage left. He still complains of weakness, not calling it "age," of course, but a flaw. He is not used to feeling less than able to do what he chooses. The podiatrist had trimmed his nails and callouses and suggested Rocky Glen could clear up abscesses on two of his toes. Dad wanted to ignore them. How will this breakdown proceed? Will they simply take this condition in hand without giving him a choice? He wouldn't be happy in pain. I empathize that he doesn't want to leave to

---

* *2nd Cor. 4-7*

see a doctor. Since it is a skilled nursing facility they'll have a solution. I'm fortunate I can leave it to them.

Driving back to Everett I notice seagulls and crows perched equidistant from one another on the tops of light poles and power lines. Some seem to have been spaced by a drill sergeant, someone like Marguerite Snavely, who used to bark orders to the Everett Seagals Drill Team as we practiced for football shows. No one dared be out of step lest her name be announced pitilessly from the PA system high in the stadium control booth. Locked shoulder-to-shoulder, eyes hard-right, we moved our line vigorously between the five-yard markers with five giant steps. It was an accomplishment. There was a rumor that once, on a particularly muddy field, someone lost her shoe entirely to the muck.

We ascribe human motives to animals, and we act like they do. Sitting birds appear to have motive. What marks the spaces between them? Chance? Instinct? Enough room to spread wings to fly? When seagulls are scattered in a field all looking the same direction, they appear to be gathered for a meeting. The arrangement so "human" in a way, it distracts me from my too-serious perspective. From some distance we could be so many seagulls flocking together.

At the end of a fairly short visit I say, "Well, I'll be running along."

Dad says, "It's too bad we don't have more to talk about. We don't have much in common; we're just related." Dismissing our time as if it's only a duty? I try to come up with a retort, then he adds, "Of course if we talked about religion you'd beat me two to one." Well, there's a subtle compliment. I acknowledge it immediately, choosing to ignore the first remark.

Could I be his daughter, the DPOA controlling his steadily dwindling estate, yet somehow still not a person beyond those roles with motive, vision, regret, imperfection, hope, love? I freely choose to support him, to spend time listening. I suspect he's always seen himself as husband, a father with responsibility, rather than a boy whose hopes were dashed when he was very young, longing for something he couldn't name. A man whose elders never listened and who, therefore, never learned how to listen to himself, much less to others. This is generational, clearly, and perhaps truer of immigrants in the great migrations of Northern

Europeans to the U.S., as well as those now coming from the Southern Hemisphere.

An elderly parishioner told me recently that *No one has ever listened to me.* This woman so enjoys talking to anyone who listens that she goes on at length, saying everything that has never had the luxury of speech. The absence of listening is what brings our world to the verge of destruction, writes theologian Beverly Harrison: our deep neglect of "that which is most human and most valuable and the most basic of all the works of love—the work of human communication, of caring and nurturance, of tending the personal bonds of community."* I cannot make up for more than 99 years of anxious, reflexive control of his life—and his family's. But I love the man who is beginning to admit he acts out of love now.

Once, while we were driving to the pharmacy near his home on Fowler, he said anxiously, "I don't need to go by the house." He was afraid I would drive him past what was his home. He controls his feelings by controlling his thoughts and memories. Compartmentalizing. That's a good thing.

"It was a hard time, Dad, that spring," I say now, two years later, as I write key words on the white board. "Mom was so sick, and you were very tired."

He looks right at me and says, "It was hard for you."

"Yes, really hard for me."

By then there were tears in my eyes. Partly memories, partly that we were sharing feelings. As halting and awkward as our exchanges are, we seem to share a deep understanding of the reality of the present and its necessity.

"I'm glad you're happy now, Dad," I continue.

"I'm not happy, Honey. I'm reconciled," he looks directly at me to be sure I get it. I do get it. He has made huge adjustments, an important distinction. Then he repeats "reconciled," quietly, without rancor or cynicism, acknowledging just the right word that captures exactly how he feels. I've not heard such a simple, authentic statement from him in all

---

* from "The Power of Anger in the Work of Love," *Making the Connections.* Carol S. Robb, ed. Beacon Press 1985. p 12

of my life. He has more understanding now, a depth of awareness of my experience, somehow all without my going exhaustively through chapter and verse.

Late one night, before Ardene and I set to chasing what we later learn is a young Norway rat around one of the bedrooms, the phone rings. The evening had been quiet until we noticed Tully scrabbling to climb in her cat door with something in her mouth. She dropped it. Sprung to life, the rodent ran along the baseboard down the hall with Tully behind it, cunningly by one foot. The chase! Once they reached a bedroom I slammed the door behind them. Ardene and I had been catching up with each other on the couch, hand in hand, ear to ear, gratefully cheek to cheek. Then Dad is on the phone to tell me not to come visit him the next day as I planned. Odd. He has never said that things are not as they should be at his nursing home and I ought to come only when "the coast is clear." What's going on??

And right now this wily rat could escape even the duct tape I stuck to the bottom of the door and get loose in the house where he might never be found. (Rats chew right through duct tape, I discovered). I "seal" both the closet and the bedroom doors with more tape after leaving my tabby inside. Tully brought him in in the first place; she can catch him in the night. But an hour later when we check on her she is completely oblivious, napping contentedly on top of the highboy while the two of us plot what to do. Nothing, at that hour, obviously.

After forcing ourselves to sleep, I get up the next morning, pull the tape off the bedroom door and open it gingerly. Tully, glad to see me, meows and bolts for the kitchen, leaving no trophy. Instead there is a tiny hole chewed in the tape at the bottom of the closet door. The critter has escaped the cat. I set three traps with peanut butter, reseal the bedroom door and hope the deed will be done by the time I return. Then I head north to see what is going on with Dad.

I surprise him, still foggy from sleep. The nurse reports he was confused last night and thought he'd missed breakfast. Otherwise, all signs were normal. Normal at age 99 and nine months is not what normal is, however. I sit down beside him on the bed and tell him about the "mouse." He explains he had wakened and tried to dress when it was only

3:00 a.m., clearly remembering telling me not to come. Even though the times weren't in sync, I say, "I know."

"But you came anyway," he observes with some pleasure.

"Yes. Especially because you called. I wanted to see what was going on."

I repeat my mouse tale. He smiles and says, "This is pretty important to you, isn't it?" I think he was amused by the scene, something entirely foreign to his routine, probably a homey memory he hasn't thought of in a long time. Pleased that I came—in spite of the rat—even though he asked me not to, he feels cared for. A landmark. We resort to pest control for the rascal who, trapped in the bedroom, eluded even a pest control specialist for two hours. And then we signed up for bimonthly pest service.

Why don't I just move Dad into our home? I want to feel more in control, present to him. Isolation diminishes the aged. But how could I while I have to work? I have chosen to accept a calling in my "retirement," and have no expertise for caring for the very old. Most of us can't arrange to do this differently. The few friends I know who have broken this trend have just had different sorrows: they could not be there all of the time anyway; they couldn't maintain the support and cordiality they wished. Elderly parents have their own minds about what they will and won't do. We have no more control over how our parents spend their last years than we ever had over their lives in the first place. More responsibility, less control.

I never had the chance to be with Dad day to day without distance, judgment, and perceived rancor—his *and* mine, of course. His, by his role as parent, and mine in self-defense. Now, when I see him once a week, we have more natural conversation than we ever had. Mother had his first place, obviously, and sadly, didn't know how to share him.

We have a long talk today about his feet: nails, hammertoes (he has rigged a way to tape those toes to the others, so they don't rub on the shoe), orthotics (which I also wear), shoes, and socks (not too thick or pulled tightly onto his calf. He cuts the elastic tops off his socks, so they don't bind his calves. They look awful.) He won't accept my having any more say in how he dresses or looks. I hope to God someone will look after my clothing when I am 90. But maybe I won't care, either. He has an appointment with the podiatrist next week and doesn't want to go.

"The doctor *wants* to see you, Dad."

He looks me in the eye and says, "That's what *he* wants." Dad doesn't want to see him. Dad can refuse. I back off.

Needing to shift my mood, Ardene and I drove over the Cascades to indulge in alpine sunlight and dry air. A novel, the PBS program "Nature," or a symphony transport me, but the effect of a foreign landscape is total immersion—refreshing even if it's drenching rain.

The spiritual life takes more than leaning on the everlasting arms. It takes knowing when and on whom to lean as well as standing on one's own two feet. A change in landscape allows us to see ourselves in a new way, contemplating countryside with different shadows. This requires action even if we don't know which action to take. We have learned that *not to decide is to decide.* The only way out of stuckness is to move somewhere—even if we discover later it's wrong. But for fear of this very result, we'd rather not move, thank you very much. *"You've got to move when the Spirit says move."* Maybe you have to move even when you can't hear the Spirit because not to move is not to breathe, not to express what is at work within even when you don't know what it is. There are rhythms on the spiritual path: breathe in life, breathe out blessing.

An SU professor of mine suggested a good definition of sin is holding your breath. It's not that simple, but when you think of a toddler who has said No and means it, she is just as adamant as we are when we cross our arms, say No, and refuse to budge. When a circumstance knocks the wind out of us, we are as good as dead until we take the next breath. In the interim, we fiercely search for how to respond. Or worse—we don't respond at all. I got stuck a number of times in my youth. I knew the "right" answer. But I didn't know how to say it. I couldn't say No, politely. I have learned better ways of saying no now, and I also know myself better so I can anticipate when to begin to decline a request—how to hold back rather than offering an immediate response.

I don't buy anyone's lists of what is *forbidden.* But I do know "right" from "wrong." Everyone ought to have her own list, divined by dead reckoning, experience, teachings, or beliefs. Sin is a loaded word. Columnist David Brooks writes that it is one of those words that has to be reclaimed and modernized. "Sin is a necessary piece of our mental furniture because it reminds us that life is a moral affair." He asserts that sin is communal, like selfishness and thoughtlessness, and errors are individual.*

Dad will turn 100 on July 2. I ask him what he wants for his birthday.

He places both hands on the arms of his chair to brace himself to leap up, and then says loudly, "Get me the hell out of here!" Then laughs. He's joking—although I'll bet he wishes he were somewhere else. He assures me, "I have everything I need, Honey." What a paradox. Many, many seniors placed in nursing homes can't wait to leave, one way or another. Mom packed her things every day for the first month, desperate to return home. But when an aide suggests they might find him one day when his heart has stopped, asking whether he would want to be revived, Dad still answers "Of course! Why wouldn't you?" How on earth am I going to suggest that he begin to consider saying No? If I passively accept all his assertions, how will I ever nudge the conversation toward choices that suit his condition better? I have work to do.

He can't foresee what condition he might waken in and what limitations would result, nor can I. Or perhaps like me he doesn't want to miss anything? Someone will tell him he's at the end of the line and he'll say—what? Lie down and fold his arms over his chest? He's not done. Ardene and I talk about conscious choices in the event of terminal illness, but my parents have had only rudimentary discussions about them as far as I know. My mother's response to the same question two years ago was, "Let me go. I'm tired." She was 14 years younger than he; you'd think it would have been otherwise. But she had had years of pain from arthritis, probably recognized she hadn't long to live, and felt abandoned.

Acting when you don't know what to do, and moving when you don't know where to move, is the paradox of spiritual growth. Roads don't lead directly to destinations you can see or sometimes even imagine. You turn when you expect to stay on center. And remain where hostile forces might move others to safety. That is, if you know for certain what is hostile and what is safe. That is challenging as well.

Walking my father out of his first century is a revelation. Now I know his boyish smile, his eagerness to make a joke, his fussiness. He cannot leave a thing untouched. There is always a partially eaten dark chocolate

---

* David Brooks. *The Road to Character*

on his chest of drawers waiting until after dinner. He eats half at noon and half after dinner. Discipline. I also know his love, hidden until now. Even though I didn't know I was waiting, this was worth waiting for.

When I explain that our finances indicate that Dad will need to go on Medicaid assistance in a few months, he asks me if he'll have to move from his room, and adds, "I don't think I can do it." He grimaces and looks desolate, as if it would be the last straw. I reassure him.

"Dad, when I was small, and I wanted something badly, you would say, 'We'll see…' and never say whether it was going to happen or not."

He laughs. "Grandpa used to say, 'When the time comes…'" He gets it. He tries to comfort me.

Carl Abner Ramstad turns 100 years old today, July 2, 2004. Ardene and I arrange a cake frosted in red, white and blue, with napkins and plates on the table in a nearby conference room, a clutch of red, white and blue balloons at the door. The grandkids come, all four of them, with their partners and a clutch of great grandchildren, so there is the whole fam-damn-ly (even from Georgia) eating and making nice.

Although shy, Dad looks pleased. He smiles for pictures with each group and chats with the grandson who works for Kimberly Clark, the company that bought Scott Paper, his former employer. Then he talks to his grandson-in-law about the car he gave them.

Since he's seen virtually none of them since he moved here, and although they seem to want pictures with him, he mistrusts their presence. He says as much a week later since, of course, he didn't ruffle any feathers at the party. He felt as if he were being trotted out on display. But he does eat two pieces of chocolate cake with fudge filling and takes a third back to his room. I give him a big hug for being on good behavior.

Dad has depleted his resources, including the money from selling their home, qualifying for Medicaid. It was inevitable now that he is living this long, in spite of the fact his resources lasted as long as they did, a tribute to his frugality. I will continue to supply him with Oreos, Lorna Doone cookies, and Hershey's dark chocolates with almonds. Now I pray that Rocky Glen won't need to move him from his single room to what he calls a "duplex." Maybe since he's the respected "old man" of the 70-bed facility (he's the eldest and the healthiest), they won't make him move.

I explain the basics about Medicaid and assure him he can continue to stay where he is. Overwhelmed with gratitude, he takes both my hands and looks me in the eye, "I don't really appreciate enough all that you've done for me," he says. There are tears in his eyes. I am so grateful. I have completely forgotten about the shared legacy I was hoping would be in his will. He has spent it all. His words are enough.

I wonder how his life will end. Whether he thinks about it. Frankly, his ability to close the doors on what was aids his adjustment to what is. What was once too narrow a focus has become a defense against wanting what he cannot have. He strictly limits talk about the past. In a way, he fasts from dwelling on it. He never clamors to see me more often. He doesn't complain about his small room. He doesn't even complain about the food! I hope I can do as well when I am in his position.

When I tell him, I'm pleased he's content, he repeats, "I am not content, Honey, I am reconciled." Reconciliation without rancor. Letting go without visible grief. I can't claim the same gift. I anguish over goals unachieved, standards unmet. I can be a perfectionist, but I pray one who is learning to honor my limitations, accepting what is possible rather than continuing to strive beyond my reach.

Oh, in the past I made colleagues and loved ones—and myself—miserable. There was only one standard: one right way to do everything. Guess who I learned that from! My mom, and the man who describes himself as reconciled to his living arrangements, who is coping with changes in staff and hoping against hope they won't move him to a double room. The seniors I know in other care facilities, assigned to a particular dining table, also struggle to adjust to newcomers, difficult roommates, and new aides. Change never ends. We will never arrive at stability. Living one day at a time is the best way to tolerate unanticipated flux, but it takes—a life time—to learn?

We can learn from one another but only we ourselves can make the adjustments that signal contention, compromise, or contentment. Sometimes only we know the deep tug of dissonance demanding we look at circumstances a new way: with an embrace and a sigh, and not a straight-arm.

Aging forces us to let go of assumptions about agility, memory, strength, independence, and physical adequacy. Humor helps. It oils the cogs that can turn to a different rhythm. Fear enters the picture. Will I lose my independence? I was recently diagnosed with Vasculitis, an auto-immune illness. Since I have been in great health for years I was shocked by the news, but I accept the chemotherapy treatment as an invitation to reflect, rather than an insult demanding redress. It took several months for my doctors to determine the diagnosis because the symptoms were so subtle. But when an incontrovertible sign, lowered kidney function, was discovered, treatment was quickly scheduled. Accepting such a reality feels like giving in. But instead it is the letting go that gives my soul space.

Spending half a day at my doctors' clinic on Seneca Street downtown on Pill Hill near the church, I received biweekly infusions of Cytoxan. These diminished the inflammation and created other symptoms. Progress was being made, however. I told my father about it, and I couldn't tell what he was thinking. He took it seriously but said nothing. But after this he always asked how I was. It took about two months for the disease to go into remission; I was closely monitored for more than the next year.

CHAPTER 13

The Bonus Year

Close to midnight one Saturday in September there are a series of phone calls from Rocky Glen. Dad had fallen, fallen again, and once more. In each case I was told he seemed well enough. And I guessed, he wouldn't *permit* them to call the EMTs. The perpetual question was, how will my father succumb to his age? Is some tangible condition emerging? Or is this what great age is like? Fragility, infection, falls, and serial recovery, each a little lengthier than the one before. Although I am troubled, I make myself go back to sleep by resolving to drive up at 7:30 a.m. I call before setting out at 7 am and am told the EMTs transported him to the ER very early. Before I sigh with relief, they add, he was released and sent back.

This is crazy. His condition worried the medics enough that they took him to the hospital, but the hospital didn't admit him? What in hell is going on? Worst of all, I am booked at a number of command performances (Homecoming Sunday, congregational brunch, the first contemplative labyrinth walk), there is no way I am going anywhere on Sunday but into Seattle. My priorities?! I know, *sigh*. I can't remember now why I thought all those worship events required my personal presence. I regret not going at once.

That next night, Monday, Dad is taken back to the ER and admitted. I am teaching Tuesday at Seattle University and can't extricate myself from that either until early Wednesday morning. So Ardene offers to drive north to the General Hospital campus to see what is happening. Her news isn't good. She talked with the doctors who did not appear concerned. She had to control her anger while explaining to his doctors he read three newspapers and was quite well before his falls. When I finally see him it's obvious Dad isn't connecting. He is in the hallucinatory stage of chemical imbalance. He is sitting up in bed in front of his meal tray, picking up a cup of coffee that isn't there and miming drinking from it. I don't understand a word he utters. He may think he's making sense, but it's gibberish. He doesn't recognize me at the foot of the bed. Agitated and unhappy, he is not at all pleased to be where he is.

Nurses tell me he is not swallowing effectively, a serious condition in the elderly. Although he has no other conditions except susceptibility to infection because of the Foley catheter, his great age may be beginning to make itself known. Dad is released after a five-day stay. But not before a young doctor tells me with stony confidence I ought to sign my father into hospice. I ought "to consider more humane treatment in light of the fact that he will continue to fall and begin to starve if he cannot swallow enough to eat." We had earlier considered and rejected a feeding tube. The doctor persists that eating is dangerous. Aspirating food or drink will cause pneumonia, and that will kill him.

So this is how it goes. Someone who has never met my 100-year-old dad tells his daughter with brutal frankness that he is on the verge of dying and it is up to me to ease him out. At first I feel relieved to know, to be on the cusp of a defined ending. But at the nursing home, ARNP Brenda is furious that the hospital did not consult her or anyone who knows Dad well. "They think because he's 100 years old, he's out of it! They have no reference to his baseline."

When I walk into his room back at home, Dad looks beaten up; his falls have left him bruised and miserable. I find him as I rarely have: in a wheelchair, too weak to stand. For the first time in more than two years, he is in a white and green striped hospital gown, robe and slippers, completely out of sync and understandably unhappy.

And just as I think it couldn't be worse, an aide carries in a dinner tray with three saucers of thick paste. By their color I might have guessed one was tuna, one squash and the last, perhaps, peas? He doesn't even reach for a spoon. He's disgusted. I watch, helpless. Will his condition move him to more realism? Must I orchestrate this? He still is a Yes code; if he stops breathing, he will be resuscitated. He wants to live. That's the last thing he said, believing that without any specific condition like heart failure or cancer, he can't die.

After conversation with Brenda, I learn we *can* change his code status so that if he falls again, or develops another infection which is very likely, they can treat him at Rocky Glen, averting his being transported to the hospital. Urinary infections, his weak link, are where we began this journey. If I sign a waiver for these risk factors, he can resume his usual routine without the nursing home being liable.

"Your dad isn't terminal," Brenda smiles confidently. "Hospice wouldn't take him." He looked terminal. But she is angry no clinician at the hospital could make that assessment while he was hallucinating. No one knew how frequently he walks down the hall to get his meds, or how he follows politics and looks forward to seeing me. I was the one who blew it by not showing up when he fell three times in three days. I am appalled I didn't skip church to be with him. The ER sees a 100-year-old man and makes assumptions even more readily than they did when he was 97 or 99. Dad is a centenarian who defies the norm.

Thank God for compassionate and informed personnel like Brenda. Were it not for her, I would not be able to negotiate Dad's circumstances as well. He gets some of the best care in this facility because he is so courtly and pleasant to be around. It's too long before I can clear the time to return, although I hear regular reports of his slow improvement. When I walk in, Dad looks chastened and fearful.

"How did I fall? Can you tell me how it happened?" He can't remember and doubts what he's been told. He wants my blow-by-blow account. Of course I know only what I was told on the phone, that I did not come when he needed me. He has no uncertainty about his return here, however, to the day and the hour he arrived by cabulance and everything that has happened since. He's back to normal.

It is not many weeks before his food is also approaching normalcy; it's simply cut into palatable pieces for him. At least it's real food and not purée. He still eats on a tray in his room, grateful he chose to do that instead of going to the dining room. The staff dotes on him because he remains one of the few alert gentlemen they have. And even though it takes him a long time to recover from an episode this serious, he's done it before. I wonder how many times he can come back from the dead. NP Brenda describes him as walking along the edge of a cliff. When he falls, it is a long, slow climb back.

It's foolhardy to leave the code as it is. Since he cannot understand anyone well even with his hearing aids, I draft a statement that reasons why he should change the code to do-not-resuscitate, or DNR. He is 100 years old, and finally his honey-blond hair is clearly mixed silver and blond. But it is only as he recovers from these infections that he looks his age. If we agree together to change his code, and he agrees to our waiving the protection of puréed food, then he can resume regular meals and at least appear to be living the life he was not content with, but reconciled to.

Today the courtyard outside his window is bright with sun, but Dad likes to sit with his back to the window with blinds at half-mast. I settle on his bed with the white board. He startles me this warm fall afternoon by saying, "I grew up in a home without love." So clear. So real. An abrupt report of his childhood reveals his distant past, feelings he may have shared with no one. Only he gets to sum up his long, long life.

"Love," he says. "I didn't know how to express it. Your mother asked me once, 'Carl, why don't you just throw your arms around me and tell me you love me?' And I didn't know what to say. I felt guilty."

He disappointed his wife. He wonders why he rarely sees his surviving son but must be figuring that out too. I'm sad. He will not be able to resolve either of these lingering doubts about his competence as a husband and father. Not on this earthly plane. Or maybe he will. Isn't that what his dreams and reveries do?

In my own childhood Mom carried on a monologue while we worked together in the kitchen and walked downtown to shop. I learned to listen without expecting to share in return. She told me what Dad would and wouldn't allow. I sympathized, then took up arms in her defense against my father. We three kids were arrayed against him for different reasons.

Of course he must accept some of the responsibility. It's almost too late. Since that's hard to do alone, he needs a confessor. I'm it. I'm used to therapists and spiritual directors, colleagues in ministry and a loving partner who listens to me parse out my own grammar of life. Dad isn't alone. When I come in with his chocolates, batteries and vanilla wafers, I am the one who invites him to reflect on his remarkable life within a loving embrace. Even forgiveness. Why else would he reach out to me, trying to comfort me? When he's had his say, he looks intently at me and repeats, "Hang in there," and then, "We'll make it." The process is a lonely one, nevertheless. I feel miserable about it; I search for ways to bring him some joy in the midst of his final weeks and months of living. How long will it last?

Later, on the phone, he drawls his elongated pronunciation of my name, "Caa..thyyy?"

"Hi, Dad," I shout, loud enough that he can hear.

"When are you coming up?" It's Thursday, and he's already anticipating my visit.

"Saturday or Monday, I think."

"That's just as well. I'm not a very good host."

Falling short of his own expectations? Perhaps he's finally realizing that his life will indeed end—perhaps in months, not years. I'm beginning to understand how everyday small acts matter more and more when the time is limited. Behaviors and conversation deepen when we know our time is running out. Time is relentless. Things I had long since given up knowing or hearing from my dad surprise me every time I see him.

On a rainy October afternoon traffic prevents me from getting to Dad's till nearly four. Water everywhere obscuring the windshield, distorting my line of sight. I've come with the draft that changes his code, as well as a letter explaining why this is wise. I walk in the door with a folder in my hand, slipping the letter out to hand over. He waves it off.

"Oh, I don't want to read that now while you're here," he says, dismissing it, but not before glancing at the last lines.

"Honey!" He says with passion. "It would be a mercy at my age to let me go!"

That was more than I'd bargained for. I catch my breath, then sit. We talk. He says, "Sometimes I just feel like crying." I wish he were small enough to cradle in my arms. I reach over to squeeze and then hold his arm.

"I know it's hard, Dad." Hanging onto him helps me accept his feelings, and I hope his, mine.

He laughs joylessly. "Hard" is not the half of it. We walk to the day room (where he is now eating with others whose risk of choking is high), him still lifting his walker at every step. He tells me that one of his pet peeves is the applesauce they smother on the medicines he takes on a rigid timetable every day. "Can't *stand* it!" he declares.

Now I can't get him off my mind. I send him cards in the middle of the week. There are no other cards on his corner table, or flowers on his bureau. Does he discard them once he's read them? He calls to thank me. No one knows my father as I do. Oh, the staff, surely; they know him best, bantering back and forth as he walks down the hall. But no one in the family. Certainly some of his good friends knew him well, at least what he would share, but they have stopped visiting. Some are ill themselves, others tire at the prospect of shouting at him or writing on the white board so he can understand them. Always difficult to companion, he's ever more challenging as he visibly ages.

Maybe Mom didn't even know him as I do now. I asked her this morning when she was flying around as I was doing my hair, "Aren't you surprised I'm the one who ended up with Dad?" I didn't catch her answer. How could she ever think isolating him for herself would resolve her neediness? If she had shared more of him with my brothers and me, he might not have become such a fearsome figure to us. He was afraid to let anyone in too close. He had to "parent" his kids, though. With the negligent parenting he had, he was improvising. He must have chosen sternness and absolute answers instead of closeness and encouragement.

I stand to leave. He clings to me and says, "I am perpetually downhearted." I dig deep for a breath and squeeze him tighter, offering us both comfort. We stand there close, breathing together, heart to heart. And then I walk down the hall to the nurses' station to sign the No-code. My acknowledgment Dad is mortal. I am sad, but truthful, and relieved he is freer now to live or die without intervention.

The colors of fall reassure me. I notice not only the deep orange of the neighbor's vine maple, but also my own Japanese maple turning from burgundy to bright red overnight. In the backyard, the graceful maple branches glow with yellow leaves tinged with orange and, against the dark green cedar, appear ablaze. In the kitchen, the incandescence is extraordinary. I am fond of Strauss' *Four Last Songs*: Spring, September, falling asleep, and sunset. All of the songs but "Spring" deal with death and all were written shortly before Strauss himself died. They are suffused with a sense of calm, acceptance, and completeness. My awareness now of how close these seasons are in my father enhances my grief.

Once I would have called these colors death throes, but I have grown. Winter is a time of invisible growth. We see barrenness and dormancy but there is major endeavor underground. Is that the call of eternity that eludes our sight?

My father proudly announces that he is four months past his 100th birthday today. We continue to sit knee-to-knee to talk of current events, memories, what matters, and he continues to step out of the role of arch patriarch to a vulnerable man who knows his limitations.

I've never called him "Dad." He was always "My father," or simply, "Father," the person who assessed people and judged everyone—including himself—mercilessly. "Father won't permit me to drive there." "My father won't let me come to your party because I have to play for the choir." It was always third person. Someone I didn't know. I am delighted to call him Dad.

Since he said he was "perpetually downhearted" two weeks ago, he has had a change of heart. Just last week, he told his caregivers, "I can only give thanks," for his health, his care, and the many graces of his long life. No doubt he has considered what he finally chooses to share with me. In turn, I am learning to see a whole person whom I pitilessly used to divide and diminish, shrinking him to fit my experience. How I regret this. I am doing far more than making amends. As I spend time with him, I hope I am helping him to see the pain of his memories and regrets, and let them go. I am here, listening, loving. I am not only "dutiful daughter," I am companion, confessor, friend. I make him laugh. I laugh with him. We smile a similar shy smile. We hold hands. We face what is to come, together. It is enough.

Fall is a good time for me to harvest the blessings before I dive into the bliss and busy-ness of giving, driven by a market greedy for profit rather than riches. Offer my congregation peace in the midst of the whirlwind of the intangibles of faith and hope. It is a gift to be able to give thanks even in the darkness of valuing things more than human hearts.

The man I call "Dad" tells me stories of his childhood in random vignettes, glistening with truth and heartache. They sum up the openness of a man who trusts me enough to tell me the truth.

"My father wasn't demonstrative," he tells me. "My stepmother was demanding and aloof."

Dad abruptly speaks in Norwegian when he tells about his step-brother falling out of his high chair, bleeding from the mouth: "All his teeth have fallen out!" cried his stepmother, Clara, hysterical. Dad's pitch is perfect. I laugh. He's never spoken to us in his native tongue. Mom used to tell us that when she asked him to say something in Norwegian at a family dinner, expecting an endearment, no doubt, he said, "Please pass the potatoes." Her point was, he wasn't demonstrative then, and he wasn't later. Was he trying to be funny? It suited the occasion, but Mom presented it as a fault.

We kids laughed on cue, little realizing how revealing this was of his discomfort with feelings. And yet his depth has grown, or more correctly, emotion is rising to the surface. The days go by slowly, the nights more slowly. He insists he watches the digital clock flip from minute to minute. *"Literally!"* he emphasizes vehemently. Yet the person on duty who looks in every two hours pronounces him asleep; she's loathe to wake him even for pain medication. His dreams must seem like wakefulness.

He tells me of the time he and his brother, Art, broke an axle while looking for work in Canada (where they were dual citizens) and had to wire home for money. He worked in a cannery in Southeast Alaska with close friends, the Norman Gundersons. But facts are disjointed. His father, brother Art, and he built his and Mom's first home on Alverson Boulevard in Everett. He reminds me he paid for the lot with the $500 the Soundview Pulp Company paid him for his fall from the pulp di-gester. I have pictures of him in jodhpurs with a row of drivers in their chauffeur uniforms in front of their open-topped touring cars at Paradise Inn on Mt. Rainier, shuttling guests from the Sorrento Hotel to Paradise and back. The troop looks so romantic. Reflecting on my illness, I tell him I finally have more spunk now, and he translates that word into Norwegian, too, repeating it back to me.

Is this how wisdom comes? A retrospective relived in the company of a loving child, herself in midlife? In the language he originally knew and suppressed? In his next go-around, when someone asks him to speak his native language, my guess is he won't say, "Pass the potatoes."

I am late leaving. I drive toward home while the half-moon turns gently on its back to nestle in a rising, silvery mist in the west. I would settle in such an eider down myself. Tired, trying to catch up with what I fear I've left undone during my vasculitis and its treatment, I am eager for a sleep that promises to knit the raveled sleeve.

As Christmas approaches, I take Dad cookies and chocolates and hang a wreath on his bulletin board. He seems to have gotten used to my fussing around cleaning the crumbs out of his top drawer and offering to do things he'd rather do himself. When I trimmed the hair over his ears, intolerant of his looking unkempt, he sat patiently until I was finished, then said, "Satisfied *now*?" I should stop fussing.

Ardene and I are on a time-consuming search for new pants that accommodate Dad's girth and height, now a little thicker in the middle and dramatically shorter—he used to be five-foot ten, yet I am taller than he at five-foot six.

Throwing up our hands at Nordstrom and Macy's (new clothes are simply too stiff), we follow the advice of a senior at church who recommends used clothing. Chinos or cords. Three pairs of Dockers. I bring them in, but he doesn't try them on, preferring to wait till he's on his own. That he can still dress himself is remarkable. Each day for three days he tries on one of the three pair of pants, and in time, settles on two of them. This completes his wardrobe once again. Dad is anxious if there aren't several sets of clothes in his closet, all clean and wrinkled from the center's harsh laundry.

"They can do it here, Honey. Give them back to me," he directed, taking the clothes out of my hands. When the facility began laundering every day rather than once a week in caustic soap and hot water, what's left is returned to him the next day at 1:00 or 2:00, hung in his closet as is. They completely ruined the bright red wool cardigan he looked so handsome in. I disagree with his contention that their service is as good as mine. But Dad's insistence hides his true motive: to relieve me of the responsibility. I thank him for that. He is still not a man one argues with.

Once his mind is made up, he will not tolerate petitions to change it. What made this clear to me was our original civil war debating his decision to "send me" to Everett College rather than honor my yearning to move away. I infer why this was so only in our times together at Rocky

Glen. He had a plan. It is what he knew he could do. And he was unable to unstick himself from that resolve to listen to his 18-year-old daughter, who was just as resolved what school she wanted. He didn't discuss or argue with any openness to any other opinion. He simply added evidence and vehemence to his own. In our home, I did not learn to listen and respond, to form evidence and make arguments. I learned simply to accept his decision or give it up. It was no place to learn how to be in the world as a person who knew her mind and could defend herself or share give and take.

In spite of our improving relationship, little by little, and day by day, he's growing more and more ill at ease. His feet continue to bother him in spite of the large, comfortable shoes his podiatrist recommends. He's not sleeping well, and he endlessly laments dressing himself. Some days the complaints outweigh whatever pleasure I can bring.

He is drinking three healthful milkshakes a day with discipline. Three years ago, he was malnourished and recovering from a UTI. He's been so well since then that he hasn't had to worry except to drink enough water, marking each glass on a small spiral pad: one, two, three, four hash marks, and one diagonal. A total of 15 a day. Or even 20. But now, surpassing his obsession with water are these milkshakes the color of Pepto-Bismol.

He's lost 20 pounds in the last six weeks. This is grave and he knows it. "I have trouble swallowing," he admits to me for the first time, and finally concedes that he is "starting to slow down." The end of his life is drawing nearer. As I recognize the truth as well, I can't hide my grief.

"I see your pain," he says. A cliché, but here, as genuine as he is, sitting next to me. When he sees my tears, we both recognize his death approaching. A man who's looked younger than his age all his life still looks as if he's in his late eighties—at 100 years of age. As if he never knew it would come to this, a man whose first impulse was to consult a doctor when the tiniest thing was amiss, he finds his failing body an enormous insult. I don't think he expected it. He never was able to imagine a reality outside of the one he was living.

Not long after he first moved to Rocky Glen, he boasted that his doctor had told him, "You have the body of a man 10 years younger than you." He is proud of that. And I remember the ER doctor who said Dad's heart was better than his own. Now he can't depend on his body. He stops and looks very lovingly at me—rather regally—and then he laughs.

"The nurses tell me I'm handsome. I 'look nifty,' one of them says."

He stands to accompany me to the lobby. We pass several women in wheelchairs scuffing themselves along heels first, others being gently pushed by aides. "This is my daughter," he says in that drawl of his, clearly proud I am walking with him. I am his CEO.

Is Dad bullying me? A friend asks. Demanding more than I can offer?

"For heaven's sake, No." I answer indignantly, "I'm glad I can help. I just do for Dad what I would want to have done for me if I were in his shoes. I treat him the way I'd like to be treated, that's all." People don't get this?

In spite of the fact of my father's age, I am deeply grateful to have this opportunity to sit and listen, to accompany him through the months or weeks he has left. Time passes, one month not much different from the other. It is a rainy spring.

Summer begins just before the Fourth of July. Dad's complaints persist. He is distressed; he struggles to swallow his meals. His 101st birthday looms, but given how he hates attention, I know he's anxious about it. He's not in control of his body any longer, and less and less comfortable with himself. Why would he want a lot of family (whom he rarely sees) all to show up at once?

On this landmark birthday celebration Ardene and I try to keep things low key, but don't succeed. He is not in good spirits, not well, and in no mood for celebrating. One hundred years of age is an attainment, but 101? Not in his case. When we show him our cake he grimaces and turns away. He refuses even one bite for fear he'd choke. We quickly leave; take it down to the nurses' station to share. She and I both have a piece and go back to his room for a long hug. He sits on his bed, saying, "I could cry." I doubt he is *resigned*. Now he is in despair, failing to hold onto hope.

I have been working on a sermon that resists my control, too many ideas, too many quotations, too many words. I keep at it. It's difficult because of Dad. The Scripture passage describes the Promised Land: "a good land, a land with streams and pools of water, with springs flowing in the valleys and in the hills, a land of wheat, barley, vines, fig trees, pomegranates, olive oil, and honey...." (*Deuteronomy* 8:7-10).

God speaks of the bounty of harvest. But every year can't possibly produce a bumper crop. And *harvest* can apply to any experience. Our yield depends upon what we sow as well as our patience, intention, and care of the crop as well as the weather, the soil, water, insects, disease. At life's harvest (if we have the luxury of time) we weigh ourselves too, considering where we've come from and what we have accomplished, or still regret. My father does this and has for some months. When he finally achieved 100 years of age, he looked forward for a while, but then grew disheartened because he felt tired and weak; he seemed to be beginning all over again. He must have imagined—or hoped one morning he would not waken—or all of a sudden, he would blink, and be in a totally new landscape. Instead, this weakness, illness and loss of weight are incapacitating. As his health declines, he knows he will not get better. Death has to figure in his calculus at last. This is his work now.

Do we reap what we sow? Sow the wind, and reap the whirlwind? Not many believe this today, especially reckless hedge fund managers and the prosperity gospel crowd. But the psalmist sings if we sow in tears, we will reap in joy. People of faith do not merely harvest in kind. We sell God short simply to credit bounty to God's favor and want to God's absence, because God has a "preferential option for the poor," Liberation Theologians assert, for those who are unfavored, unlovely, and left out. God's realm operates on a different order from ours. In the parable of the vineyard workers, all workers are paid the same wage whether they started at dawn or at noon. Few of us think this is fair. Where to now? I put my notes aside.

Stepping into the pulpit is a calculated risk, doubtless for all preachers. It's an exercise of trying to get out of our own way. I trust I will have the grace to say what I must, to say what I believe is true, real, hoping that people will hear what they need to hear. Surely, I believe the Mystery of God influences the words I choose, as I pray over the texts, listening for insight. I love to preach and work diligently at preparing. There is no question that I'll learn something new.

"I don't want my obituary to be long," Dad says the next week as I sit down. "I read the ones in the *Herald* and some are just ostentatious, really too much." He is thinking about his death. I listen and nod, but how do I manage this? A number of months ago at his first mention of this, I wrote something and brought it to him to critique. I thought it might be helpful. When I returned the next week, he said, "There are so many errors in there I don't know where to start," shaking his head, discouraged.

Chagrined, I determine to try again, but he didn't say what "all the errors" were. Overwhelmed by the prospect of setting the record straight, Dad was reluctant even to begin. I put it on the bottom of what has become a shorter list. He is beginning to see only loss in his longevity—something none of us looks forward to.

In late July the red, purple and white Impatiens through the wooded corridor that leads to Rocky Glen are glorious. I first saw them in 2002 when I began driving from I-5 west through those trees to visit Mother as she faded into her twilight, surprising me with her haste to leave us all behind.

When I was a kid I used to ride my bicycle to that park, an all-day uphill trek from our home on north Colby. My friends and I packed a lunch. There were no Impatiens then. Just tall, dark fir and cedar, salal, nettles and blackberries, hiding a grotto in the woods near Pigeon creek burbling to the bay. In the summer the Baptist youth group held vespers there by firelight on Sunday nights.

All along that winding road, white and violet flowers flourish in the shade bordering the route I followed to visit Mother and say farewell. Now it's Dad who's at the end of this path. It is the fourth summer I have driven through the stands of fir to visit with my parents.

Resolutely marking down each milkshake he finishes, Dad continues to try to do what he's encouraged to do: take in enough nourishment to keep him strong, his weight stable. He cannot *not* work at it. When will he acquiesce? He won't. Do I expect him to lie down and refuse to get up? To refuse to eat? To not dress fully in the morning in a shirt and Dockers? It's not in him. He knows and does not know. He knows and dares not say.

The impatiens know. They mark my path and also the season, noted by other travelers who emerge from the woods on the hill near the church whose spire rises high in the sky—where his memorial will be held in a few weeks. I celebrate their beauty, blossoming in the darkness, unexpected but welcome accompaniments to the passage of those who come this way. I mark the route from one year to the next, from my mother's death to my father's decline, wondering when the two will meet again. Death is as unexpected as grace.

As I work on the sermon, I remember the fall I planted crocus only to have the squirrels dig up the bulbs. I failed. The following spring, however, some crocus surprised me. There were more than I had hoped. Then Marjorie taught me some techniques for planting the bulbs under little screens so the squirrels couldn't get to them. But I never did it again.

I gave up too soon. Part of what I had planted was hope, hope that something would turn up, something moved by the powers of life in the universe. Any gardener can tell you, you and I put a lot of trust into the ground with our seeds, plants, and bulbs. We also put such trust into people and our dreams. We never know what is going to take, make an impression, pay off, or sprout; whether or how something will thrive if and when it emerges. Gardening is a way we practice life.

How does one day manage to sum up as beautiful, another bland? I never fail to be amazed at the myriad events, nuances, and complications that add and detract from a twenty-four hour slice of life. Weather, people, aches and pains, dread, hope, surprise. I can move from despair to glee in minutes given experiences added up in one column rather than the other. Yet never can I control events.

I tried to call my cat Tully, two hours late for dinner, and finally spotted her padding across the cul de sac toward the front door.

She usually makes a beeline but she veered to her left between lilac and forsythia, hunkering down beneath a small hydrangea. She had cornered a tiny mouse. This had become dinner now. I watched silently as she circled the plant where the rodent sat frozen, hyperalert. Tully reached in a paw and around they both went to the other side. I heard the rustle of leaves and saw a stalk lean to one side. The mouse climbed. Could the stem hold?

Then Tully lost sight of it and walked first one way, then the other, and saw me out of the corner of her eye. She meowed but kept vigil. I tried to find the mouse and couldn't, but I was not about to stop a cat in hot pursuit. Tully spied the mouse again, hydrangea-go-round, but she was tiring. This mouse could hold its own just out of reach. I wondered how long this had already taken and was surprised that the mouse stayed close rather than making a run for it. That must have been even riskier.

Rustling again. Stalk climbing. Tully sighted her prey in the leaves at the top near a still-green blossom, swaying gently with its weight. She thrust in a paw and it fell. She went around to the other side. Could she crawl in underneath? No. So I began to talk to her and she answered. In those seconds the mouse ascended to the bushy leaves once more. Not seeing it, Tully wandered over to me and let me pick her up.

In a flash I was in the house sliding her cat door shut. Safe! I fed her and went back out to see if I could shoo the mouse to his own lair. There he was in the hydrangea, still as a Boehm porcelain, black eyes unblinking, ears perfect shells, alive in the curl of a furrowed green leaf. Such is grace.

At the care conference we determined that Dad should return to drinking only spoon-thick purées, and at the moment, a thickened milk-shake. The staff is not taking chances. They stir a thickener even into water to make it easier to swallow. Were it thinner he could choke or aspirate it. Dad's always wanted the milkshakes warmed anyway. He dis-likes big bites of icy foods—like ice cream. So do I. I lick ice cream; I can never bite a mouthful. His milkshake is melted down so it's not so cold, then rethickened. He tries to spoon that down. The thought of swallow-ing it makes me gag.

"Dad, don't eat this. You don't have to."

"I have to *live!*" he returned fervently. He has lost 10 more pounds. It's impossible to keep his weight stable. Trying so hard in a losing battle, he is making himself sick. He's afraid of the alternative, and of course; few of us "die" before we die, as Rumi recommends.* I try to keep en-couraging him, loving him, but I'm losing my own battle.

Ardene and I have lunch in Everett and visit Dad afterward. He is delighted to see her and extravagantly complimentary. He said, "You look just wonderful!" She beamed. It's good we are both here. His recent de-cline alarms us because we have a long-planned vacation looming, a trip to the Utah and Arizona canyons that we had already postponed last year because of my illness.

---

* According to my friend and colleague Imam Jamal Rahman in Seattle. Interfaith Community Church, and one of the Three Interfaith Amigos.

On the day before Ardene and I leave town, I reluctantly meet with hospice personnel and enroll Dad. He did not want this. But I am signing him up down the hall in a conference room. How else am I going to enlist enough personal support for him while I am gone? Even were I here, I cannot make him comfortable any longer. My helpfulness has ended.

I tell several people how enormously relieved I am to have Dad in hospice, but that is only my own salvation. I don't know whether they will be able to ease his distress or not. Although accepting hospice resolves only his imminent decline, to him it means throwing in the towel, so I don't tell him. He wouldn't allow me to discuss it earlier and frankly, the need then wasn't as great.

Today I hold him, weep with him, and say goodbye, fully aware I may not see him again alive. Our vacation is lined out on his calendar and has been for months; he knows we will be gone these next 10 days. I am not happy. Nor is he. Inevitably there comes a time when each of us must accept the call of our own lives. I cannot live my dad's life for him. Or end it, either. I leave with a heavy heart and a heart-felt embrace. I know, and he knows he has to go on from here by himself.

> *Courage doesn't always roar. Sometimes it is*
> *a quiet voice at the end of the day saying,*
> *I will try again tomorrow.*
>
> ~Mary Anne Radmacher *Op.cit.*

When I go through his last effects late in August, I see that my father's desk calendar is on Monday August 8, 2005. On Tuesday, the 9th, Ardene and I flew to Nevada to join an Elderhostel tour. On Wednesday the nursing staff administered a small dose of morphine to allay his rising anxiety, contrary to the wishes of the hospice staff, who hadn't had time to talk with him. The staff anticipated his death soon. I spoke with hospice last Thursday afternoon—especially about the morphine, hoping Dad would stay alert, fully hoping that if he were dying, he would be with us at least 10 more days. He's surprised all of us with his longevity for so long! Why not just 10 days more?

When I return and visit Rocky Glen, the staff recount to me that that same afternoon, Dad walked fully dressed, walker-in-hand, to his shower. He told his aide and friend, Christie, he was dying.

Christie said, "I love you, Carl," and he responded, "I love you, too."

They hugged. About midnight that night, Dad was up to go the bathroom on his own as usual, distraught about being awake. They settled him down once again. When they looked in on him at 2:00 a.m. on Friday, August 12, he lay in his tidy bed very still, his face calm. No extraordinary measures were ordered. He had begun that new adventure. Five weeks after his 101st birthday, Carl Abner stepped out of his known world.

I meet with the nurses who saw Dad through that night. They tell their stories with tears in their eyes as mine overflow. They cared and doted over him over the three and a half years Rocky Glen was his home: a good place of caring and respect, of enough space for the way he needed to live his life, and not a little joy.

Who would have thought my father's move to a nursing home would become such a gift? The connotations of the place cause most of us to shudder. But Dad's experience was extraordinary. He relinquished the authority he'd wielded. He trusted me. He relaxed into the routine. He was comfortable being left alone, having freedom to do whatever he chose within the constraints of the place. He read his newspapers, news magazines, and the *Wilson Quarterly*, always discovering new ideas to stay current. He watched baseball and laughed—even at himself. He was reconciled, and most importantly, he ceased being my enemy.

Here I discovered his profound shyness, his inability to hold two ideas together, or to imagine another scenario different from the reality he lived, and his great loyalty to my mother. I knew his deep faith, his graciousness to all who helped him each day, and his appreciation for my own regular appearances at his side, listening, responding, asking questions, and—truthfully?—getting acquainted.

His pastor once said of him, "I have never known such a Lutheran conscience." A left-handed compliment. His staunch Lutheranism committed him to what he thought right, and eclipsed his ability to be flexible with his wife and kids. It was admirable, yet too rigid. Maybe that's all the compliment any of us gets: an admiring onlooker, envious of the iron will, the constitution, and the sense of humor that gets any of us from 1904 to 2005, or from 1942 to 2043, when I will reach his age. My dad will rest in peace; he would have nothing less.

A friend asks me to recount the final days of my father's life. And as I do, full of remorse that I wasn't there, she breaks in with confidence, taking my arm: "You had to leave, so the angels could come and take him!"

As I finish the preparation for my sermon, I write, "Harvest is participation in mystery on a scale we can manage—the practice of birth, nurture, and fruition in miniature, an experience kinder to our psyche than our own lives can be. Somehow, by walking one way, and then another, we discern a better way, turning again and again to walk with purpose and resolve to true up the direction we take. This turning again to follow the path we know is right for us, is called *metanoia* in Christian terms, a change of heart, even repentance. But it can simply be remedying something that made us feel out of balance, out of tune with ourselves, selves we continue to seek all of our lives. Every now and then we feel resurrected, born anew, refreshed with a new perspective. The new bearing probably is not due to our own navigation, and it may not last forever. But the posture has allowed the mystery of God to come alongside to help us walk in loving, forgiving ways.

"My father told a good friend," I went on in the sermon, "that he was disappointed that he had not expressed enough love in his life. This friend wrote on the white board, 'There is still time,' and he answered, 'No. It's too late.' "And then I describe, as I had done several times in sermons in the last few years, how close he and I had become." He and I walked a day at a time across the biggest distance of our lives. He became, in my presence, a whole person, a man with faults and great expectations. How he must have wished he had more time to express his loves. How I hope he had found the words to forgive himself for anything that diminished his life of loyalty, commitment, responsibility (too much for him at times), a love of music and art, and a generous heart, to say 'Well done, good and faithful servant.'"

We didn't learn of his passing until our tour bus returned from the North Rim of the Grand Canyon to the Kaibab Plateau where cell phones were once again in range. I could barely hear through the static on my phone as the bus rumbled along toward Bryce Canyon. I listened to the message three times to be sure I had heard it all, holding my breath each time. Simple, it was, "Your father, Carl, passed away at 2:00 a.m. on Friday morning."

Sick at heart that I had missed Dad's send-off in Everett, at dinner that night Ardene and I ordered champagne and offered a toast for Dad's 101 years of life, especially for the last three years that he and I had shared so deeply. Our traveling companions lifted their glasses with us.

I picked up his clothing and books, left-over Oreos and chocolates, hearing aid batteries and nail scissors and threw myself into washing, ironing, hanging and folding all his clothes, saving a number of his shirts for myself. His wonderfully classy navy blue suspenders are still in my closet as well as a navy blazer and several ties. One day I will find some gracious gentleman who would appreciate them.

On the night my father died (unbeknownst to Ardene and me) we experienced a colossal electrical storm at the lodge at the North Rim. Struck with awe, we watched and listened to the splendiferous booming, splashing of heavy rain against the tall windows, brilliance of lightning streaking across the dark abyss. Stunning. Many people stood outside just under the dripping eaves, enjoying the power of nature.

Perhaps it was the fury of Dad's liberated energy returning to the cosmos, his letting go, as it were, of the world he knew and loved in his way for 101 years.

A week after our return home from Arizona, after I filed a number of papers and felt as if I understood where I was and what yet needed to be done, I worked a little more on my sermon. I now knew a thing or two about harvest. I had been harvesting my investments in a relationship with my father for the last three years. All the years before this I had invested in explanation—argument, sometimes—exhortation, kindness, respect, helpfulness, and yes, love, to Dad by treating him and Mom with respect and care. In the three short years after Mother was gone I expressed love, support, gentleness, helpfulness and respect to my father in ways he could interpret only for himself alone. I returned the respect fully, as I never had.

Using Dad's Bible, I included the Scripture he first recited to me from memory, the Scripture he trusted:

The fig tree has no buds,
the vines bear no harvest,
the olive oil yield fail,
the fields produce no yield,
the sheep vanish from the fold,
and there are no cattle in the stalls.
But I will rejoice in Yhwh,
I will exult in God my savior.
My Sovereign Yhwh is my strength!
God makes my feet as agile as a deer's,
and teaches me to walk on my high places.

~Habbakuk 3:17-18

It was not anger in his silence. He simply had no words. He gave us everything he knew how to give. I will not question that. Harvest. The acceptance of what is and thanksgiving for the labor of its attaining. We can't heal ourselves. We offer ourselves to God for our healing by yielding and letting God be our God, listening for the Spirit who is always present, often when we are unaware of her. I felt steady, clear, relieved, and grateful for all that had emerged. Suddenly I was flooded with a sense of well-being I hadn't felt in years.

I was euphoric. Images of people I care for moved into and out of my awareness, and not only that. I felt a sense of wellness, competence, worthiness, ability to cope—giftedness. Chosenness. Blessedness. My eyes flowed with tears of joy and sadness, fully alive, aware and grateful for the gifts of these years when my dad and I became family. *Family.*

I expect to sense Dad flying around now as Mother did, but I am not sure he is as eager to set out as she was. I am very sure he is free of his anxiety and his need to get it right. There is plenty of time now between his death and the memorial service for me to prepare myself to make my official farewell. I feel bereft as well as complete and grateful.

I learned to love my enemy.

At the graveside, one of Dad's good friends walks toward me with his remains to place in the ground, cautioning, "It's heavy." Indeed it is, suitably weighted with a life that took so many years to understand. I hold my father carefully, kneeling on the ground to place him securely at rest.

Think of the happy reunions in heaven! Elias, Joakima, June, Arthur, Kittie, Lew, even Chuck, Mom's oldest brother, and his cigars! Of course. Why not cigars? Dad always shared one with him when we celebrated the holidays at their home.

Loss is loss, whether it comes soon or late. Our illusion of connectedness fades when even one person crosses over. We rage against the givens and then we rage at the emptiness and the constant challenges of peopling our own constellation of family—all on a relentless journey to its natural end.

It's a typical Saturday in September, a month after Dad's death. I no longer leave home about 10:30 and visit him from 11:00 until noon and after. Those hours that spanned more than four years saw us become adult partners regardless of our 38-year age difference. We held our dependence on Scripture in common, our love of worship, music, and the zeal to do things right. Perhaps even his shyness and our introversion is held in common. I know far more about these things than I ever did.

I don't know about death. I'd like to think, even imagine, that there are reunions with those who have gone ahead of us, but perhaps there is only deep peace that makes reunions redundant. I'd like to think that at the moment of death I will have complete understanding of myself, my loved ones, and my world, but perhaps, as in life, in "post-life" birth and death aren't instantaneous, but gradual. Scripture tells us we will be resurrected in whole bodily form. And our pets, animals in general, all of creation will be included in the great ingathering at the end of time. What a lovely thought. Scripture comforts us with as many images as it frightens us with. I read Scripture with the Spirit's guidance, an inner inquiry as well as trust and knowing. I read it in community, and where I worship and study. I have gradual and progressive understandings of the stories, histories, and characters in Scripture as I visit and revisit them in my reading, and work them out myself or hear them in sermons. Some truths will not be revealed in our time. Now we see indistinctly, as in an antique mirror; one day, we will see face to face. One day I will know even as I am known. Until I cross that threshold, I see only glimpses of what is possible in this life. These brief signs are all I need to live in faith and keep learning to love.

ACKNOWLEDGMENTS

I am indebted to a cloud of witnesses—dear friends, colleagues, consultants, and mentors who have encouraged this project from the very first sketches I wrote in e-reflections titled *Spirit Stones* in the early 2000s, principally the congregation of Seattle First Baptist Church. As I grew into a weekly writing/e-publishing habit, Rita Bresnahan encouraged me over coffee as we shared our experience and our writing. Lynne Baab, on seeing nearly a ream and a half of text, urged me to keep writing, but start organizing. Gretchen Gundrum offers a steadying hand in everything I attempt. Ann Keppler often speaks encouragement. Friend Brent Bouldin, who saw in my reflections the beginnings of something greater, encouraged me to consult my first editor, Trent Duffy, and then Meg Blackstone, author, editor and publisher, who helped me rearrange vignettes, add and remove characters, polish sentences, and deepen my own understanding. I am indebted to both these wise editors for their expert skill and moral support. I invited close friends and allies Dee Munday, Ann Nicholson, Pastor Don Mackenzie, his colleague Jared Keiling, peers Diane Hansen and Suzanne Seaton to read the drafts and respond with what worked and didn't, smiling at anecdotes and nodding at truths—all of which kept me going and rid me of most—but not all—of my doubt. And certainly not least, "Catherine of the South," M. Catherine Smith, who at the end labored tirelessly with the niceties that make text readable.

I ask forgiveness for lapses of memory, unkindness, or slight to any of the people and relatives I name, including my family. Some names are changed.

A writer all my life, from early journals and school writers' clubs to high school and college literary magazines, I have published articles in the *Seattle Times* and with several faith organizations. There is an excerpt of this work in *Personal Safety Nets*, by Dr. John W. Gibson and Judy Pigott, titled "Rest in Peace." Classic Publishing, 2007, Seattle, 2007. p. 181. And another in Northwest *PrimeTime*, titled "An Apparent Treachery," November 2015.

My loving companion, Ardene, has entertained and cared for my parents, lived with the manuscript, and borne my writing temperament. Her constancy, love and confidence in me are gifts.

PERMISSIONS

Unless otherwise noted, all excerpts from Scripture are taken from the following:

Priests for Equality. 2007. *The Inclusive Bible: The First Egalitarian Translation*. Lanham, Maryland: A Sheed and Ward Book. A Division of Rowman & Littlefield. Used with Permission.

‡ ‡ ‡

The Author wishes to thank the following publishers for permission to reprint excerpts from the work of authors cited in this book. They include:

THE PERMISSIONS COMPANY:

Jane Kenyon. Excerpt from "Otherwise" from *Collected Poems*. Copyright © 2005 by the Estate of Jane Kenyon, Reprinted with the permission of The Permissions Company Inc. on behalf of Graywolf Press, Minneapolis, Minnesota, www.graywolfpress.org.

Kathleen Dean Moore, excerpts from *The Pine Island Paradox: Making Connections in a Disconnected World*. Copyright © 2004 by Kathleen Dean Moore. Reprinted with the permission of The Permissions Company, Inc. on behalf of Milkweed Editions, www. milkweed.org.

Rainer Maria Rilke. "Gott spricht zu jedem.../God speaks to each of us...,"and "Geh bis Deiner ehnsucht Rand/Go to the Limits of your Longing" from *Rilke's Book of Hours: Love Poems to God* by Rainer Maria Rilke, translated by Anita Barrows and Joanna Macy, translation copyright © 1996 by Anita Barrows and Joanna

ABOUT THE AUTHOR

CATHERINE FRANSSON began writing *Spirit Stones* in 2000, when ordained to the ministry at Seattle First Baptist Church. As staff pastor she also served as adjunct faculty teaching Pastoral Counseling Skills with colleague Dr. Gretchen Gundrum at the School of Theology and Ministry at Seattle University. An experienced counselor and spiritual leader, Cathy brings to her current spiritual direction practice her lifelong faith and commitment to empower others. She has master's degree in English (1972) and Educational Psychology (1977) from the University of Washington, and a Master of Divinity (1999) from Seattle University. She lives with her partner Ardene Adams and their affable cat, Sugar, in Edmonds Washington. This is her first book.

Catherine Fransson blogs at www.SpiritStones.net.

CPSIA information can be obtained
at www.ICGtesting.com
Printed in the USA
FSHW021940170919
62126FS